THE MEN WHO MADE HOLLYWOOD

Also by Michael Freedland

Jolson
Irving Berlin
James Cagney
Fred Astaire
Sophie, the Story of Sophie Tucker
Jerome Kern
The Two Lives of Errol Flynn
Gregory Peck
Maurice Chevalier
Peter O'Toole
The Warner Brothers
Se Let's Hear the Applause, the Story of the Jewish Entertainer
Katharine Hepburn
The Goldwyn Touch
The Secret Life of Danny Kaye
Dustin
Leonard Bernstein
Kenneth Williams
Sean Connery
André Previn
Music Man
Bob Hope
Bring Crosby
All the Way: A Biography of Frank Sinatra
Michael Caine
Doris Day
Some Like It Cool: The Charmed Life of Jack Lemmon
Lisa with a 'Z': The Traumas and Triumphs of Liza Minnelli
Witch-Hunt in Hollywood *(published by JR Books)*

THE MEN WHO MADE HOLLYWOOD

THE LIVES OF THE GREAT MOVIE MOGULS

MICHAEL FREEDLAND

First published in Great Britain in 2009 by
JR Books, 10 Greenland Street, London NW1 0ND
www.jrbooks.com

A catalogue record for this book is available from the British Library.

ISBN 978-1-906217-63-1

1 3 5 7 9 10 8 6 4 2

Printed in Great Britain by Clays Ltd, St Ives plc

CONTENTS

For my children, Fiona, Robin, Dani, Dave, Sarah and Jonathan, who seem to understand everything perfectly, and my grandchildren, Beth, Ellie, Ben, Jamie, Jacob and Sam, for whom the great adventure is still ahead.

ACKNOWLEDGEMENTS

This is a book that I have wanted to write for years. When I finally did so, I think it gave me more fun than has any other project, also for years.

It couldn't have happened without a great deal of help over those years from people for whom Hollywood is just a place in which to work – and to live. Alas, many of them are no longer with us, but equally the names of many will live on as part of the history of Hollywood I have tried to create here. Try these names for size – there are so many more where they came from, but for various reasons they liked to remain, like me, observers of the scene and not – officially – participants:

Fred Astaire, Betsy Blair, Mira Broder, George Burns, Lillian Burns, James Cagney, Sammy Cahn, Frank Capra, Saul Chaplin, Cyd Charisse, Dane Clark, Joan Cohn, John Cohn, Betty Comden, Jack Cummings, Bruce Curtis, Bette Davis, Dmitri Tiomkin, Julius Epstein, Irving Fein, Nina Foch, Glenn Ford, Betty Garrett, Larry Gelbart, Sam Goldwyn Jr, Johnny Green, Barbara Hale, Paul Henreid, Gloria Henry, Bob Hope, Marsha Hunt, George Jessel, Gene Kelly, Evelyn Keyes, Michael Kidd, Stanley Kramer, Erle Jolson Krasner, Evelyn Lane, Jesse Lasky Jr, Jack Lemmon, Jesse Lasky Jr, Joan Leslie, A. C. Lyles, Stephen Longstreet, Jean Louis, Lorna Luft, Sid Luft, Rouben Mamoulian, Walter Matthau, Virginia Mayo, Pat O'Brien, Bill Orr, Gregory Peck, Jerome Pickman, André Previn, Dick Quine, George Raft, Raphaelson, Edward G. Robinson, Ginger Rogers, Hal Rosenbluth, Lester W. Roth, Virginia Schiff, Sidney Skolsky, Walter Scharf, Melville Shavelson, Milton Sperling, Robert Stack, Dennis Sykes, Joni Taps, Dan Taradash, King Vidor, Hal Wallis, Raoul Walsh, Jack Warner Jr, Linda White, Cornel Wilde, Billy Wilder, Fred Zinnemann.

1

THE MOGULS

Just a few yards down Laurel Canyon, close to its junction with Sunset Boulevard, is a street sign. No different from many others in that huge conurbation called Los Angeles. But its significance is immense.

Unlike virtually every other designation in what has so often been called a group of cities searching for a centre, it immediately sums up an image that is more true than could be possibly imagined by the casual driver humping his gas guzzler up the steep, winding hill. The name of the street is Mount Olympus.

Did the man who gave that road its name think about its significance? Was it a joke? Or was it just a name that he thought would add nicely to the collection already assembled for that place which few people had ever heard of – Hollywood?

If the gods really dwelt on the original Mount Olympus in ancient Greece, they could only marvel at what would be happening in that area which these days is so often dubbed Tinseltown. That wasn't the name much used by those gods living in this quarter of California in the early years of the 20th century. But to millions of people around the world, gods these were, whatever they called their home district. Up Mount Olympus to its summit high in the Hollywood Hills, those gods would sometimes gather and look down on normal mortals. And not just *on* them. From the hills, the observant among them could see the homes of the men who sometimes regarded their employees as mere puppets; dolls who for fabulous sums of money could be bought – and sometimes sold – and made to dance to tunes manipulated by pieces of paper known as contracts. To some, this was a kind of modern slavery. To others – in fact, for most – it was a wonderful opportunity to earn vast sums of money, occasionally without ever doing a day's work.

The people who paid that money and who initiated what the ingrates – always the successful ones – called their slavery were the ones who worked those invisible strings. Years later, the actress Ida Lupino would tell me how she and Errol Flynn, for so long the idol of anyone who believed that swords had to be fenced and swashes buckled, would throw stones from the top of the hill on to the house of their employer Jack L.Warner. For those in the business, that was no more than he and the other people who ran the Hollywood studios deserved. They were not mere men, any more than the people they called stars were ordinary gods. They were the group called, collectively, The Moguls.

They were moguls as much as they themselves were super gods controlling those other idols who ventured to the top of the Hollywood Hills. In India, mughals were the princes, the men whose word could not be countermanded, men with riches beyond avarice, occasionally men of culture, always people who ruled their own fiefdoms as though there was no world outside. The principal difference was that the studios that they ran could never be said to have come to them as of divine right. On the other hand, they ruled them with the secure knowledge that they had given birth to it all. Jack Warner, Louis B. Mayer, Sam Goldwyn, Harry Cohn and Adolph Zukor and Jesse Lasky created studio empires, the likes of which will never be seen again.

The epitome of Jewish immigrants, often working their way up from poor background, they were extraordinary entrepreneurs. They didn't hide their Jewishness – as if they could – but they hoped it wouldn't matter. They smothered themselves in enough Americana to produce a daily Fourth of July parade, all of their own making.

They mostly married Jewish wives and had Jewish children. With a few exceptions, they later divorced those Jewish wives, married gentiles and then had gentile children. Perhaps on an occasional High Holy Day or for a wedding or funeral, they might enter a synagogue or a temple that was very different from the ones in their birth city or, more likely, *shtetl*, but they showed no interest in Jewish affairs.

The only exemption that he and the other moguls would make to their rule about participating in anything they construed to be Jewish was, on occasion, to help raise money for the State of Israel. (That is, apart from joining the virtually all-Jewish Hillcrest Country Club, established because the other clubs in Los Angeles wouldn't have them. By doing so, they had their revenge: they struck oil in the club's grounds.)

To have failed to attend the various fund-raising functions on behalf of the state would have looked churlish. So they went – en bloc. At one of these, an appeal was made on behalf of the country, then in a parlous state, with five enemy countries ready to pounce over their borders once more. Sam Goldwyn was the first to make a commitment. 'Five hundred dollars,' he announced. Louis B. Mayer was the next to stand up with the pledge of a donation. 'One thousand dollars,' he announced proudly. Then Jack L. Warner, boss of Warner Bros. entered the picture. 'Two thousand dollars,' he announced and smiled into his champagne. Goldwyn couldn't stand it. He jumped up again and bid against himself. 'Five thousand dollars,' he announced.

The most dedicated Zionist was Harry Warner, the head of the Warner Bros. clan. 'My uncle wouldn't allow anyone say anything bad about Israel,' Jack Warner Jr told me.

Harry's brothers, like most of the other moguls, were more ambivalent. They supported the state, just as they very occasionally supported other Jewish causes – quietly, and providing nothing they did could be thought of as compromising their love for the United States of America, the country which they metaphorically had proved did have streets paved with gold (those in Beverly Hills, that is). It was why they wrapped themselves in the Stars and Stripes and showed a kind of patriotism so strong that it was almost unique to immigrants, to what they firmly believed was the Promised Land.

They didn't want to make Jewish movies. Films based on stories about rabbis became pictures about Irish priests. What seemed like the archetype Jewish story, *All My Sons*, starring Edward G. Robinson, featured an Italian family – which conveniently *was* the way Arthur Miller wrote it in his original Broadway play and which suited Universal International perfectly. (The ambivalence of show business generally at the time was probably the reason Miller substituted Catholic for Jew and why he never actually said that Willy Loman, the central character in his *Death of a Salesman*, was Jewish, even though it was difficult to imagine his being anything but.)

They had the power of the captain of a ship at sea. And all the responsibilities. If they failed, their studio failed. And like the crew of a ship, if the officers – the producers and the stars, the non-commissioned officers – the more lowly employees like scenery painters, make-up artists and secretaries, and the ratings – the cleaners, the porters, the electricians, didn't shape up, they were out, ready to scrub decks elsewhere.

Each studio had its own personality. Rouben Mamoulian, one of the most respected directors who worked for most of the moguls, told me that he preferred to use a similar military metaphor. Shortly before his death, he said that directors liked to think they were generals in charge of an army. 'In an army, the general's word is law,' he said. 'You can't argue with it. In Hollywood, the generals were always being overruled. At MGM, there was almost a slogan: "We don't make films. We remake films." The film would be made. The producer would go on vacation and come back – and tell the director to re-shoot whole sections of films.

'The moguls were mostly uneducated. But they all loved films. They all had an ambition to make money. You have to make money or you don't do anything. The point was to make money out of something that is fine and quality, rather than something cheap and forgotten.'

The studio system that the moguls created enabled talents to shine that might otherwise have been hidden.

The studio heads were derided as despots, yet that very despotism ensured the success of their products. They were gamblers – and not just at the poker table. Every time they approved a screenplay – and the final word was always theirs – they were doing so with fingers crossed that their hunches would come off. Every time they signed a new player, they did so with the knowledge that a sizeable amount of their fortune could be at stake.

They held screen tests for new artists who had not necessarily gone through the procedure of the casting couch. If they liked what they saw, they not only offered the aspiring player a chance in a film – perhaps just a walk-on experiment – but also a seven-year contract. Stars like Bette Davis, James Cagney and Olivia de Havilland would go to court to complain that their deals resembled the slavery about which they constantly complained – seven years was the longest period that the law of California would allow an employee to be indentured – but for every one of these important stars, there was a hopeful who would never appear on a screen, yet went to the studio every week to pick up the kind of pay packet they could never dream of receiving as a shop girl or an accounts clerk. The fact that they failed had simply to be written off, put down to experience and cast on to the studio's debit column. A star, on the other hand, could find him or herself farmed out to another organisation for an outrageously large fee, of which they sometimes – although not always – saw little or nothing.

Yes, the founding fathers were indeed despots, yet in some ways, they were benevolent ones. Certainly, they were out to protect their investments, which in turn, protected the lives of their stars, even if the performers didn't always appreciate the fact. Certainly the way that stars were paraded, as if at a cattle show – at the mercy of a publicity department who chose husbands and wives as frequently as their bosses selected roles for their actors – was outrageous.

Only once did a couple (and, to their everlasting shame, only a couple) of the studio heads waver from what they took to be the norm – the unwritten law that said they should speak with one voice – just so long as it didn't affect their box office returns. That was during the era of what has come to be known as McCarthyism. Samuel Goldwyn stood out against the mass capitulation of the studio bosses to the House Un-American Activities Committee (otherwise known by the acronym of HUAC). Louis B. Mayer refused to give evidence to the committee, but for his own reasons. The other moguls issued a declaration affirming their total support for the witch-hunts that actually predated those of the junior senator from Wisconsin, Joe McCarthy. They were scared out of their celluloid-coated wits and surrendered lock, stock and camera to the search for reds under their beds. Had they stood firm and declared they would never fire anyone for their political beliefs, HUAC would have died in ignominy long before the 12 years it took to kill it – and, at the same time kill people in their industry and destroy so many of their careers.

Sam Goldwyn made sure people understood he hated what the committee was doing. One of the names he singled out for support was that of his former United Artists 'partner' Charlie Chaplin, who was not officially a HUAC victim, but who had his British passport made non grata by the head of the FBI, J. Edgar Hoover. Chaplin was, said Sam, 'the greatest comedian and artist who has come along in my lifetime. I have known him for nearly forty years and I sincerely hope that what I've read [that Chaplin was working against the American government] will not be proven a fact. We need him in our business as we need every artist that is greatest.'

It is fair to say that, collectively, politics was probably the only thing outside of their own businesses that interested the moguls – well, almost the only thing; affairs with women to whom they were not married, apart, that is. But political contacts brought prestige – and, more so, influence. They loved inviting political figures to their studios – and sometimes not just American politicians. Jack Warner, as we shall see, was thrilled (disastrously so) to welcome Mme Chang Kai-Shek. Louis B. Mayer smiled widely when Winston Churchill came to his studio for a lunch on a sound stage, and in whose honour he brought out the entire MGM symphony orchestra to play during lunch.

Most of the moguls were on the right of the political spectrum, even though, like many Jews, they started out as Democrats. (Harry Warner briefly switched at the time of the 1932 election and, in a rare moment of family unity, his brother Jack did too, and became head of the Roosevelt for President organisation in Hollywood.) Louis B. Mayer became Chairman of the Republican Party of California. Sam Goldwyn also switched from the Democrats to the Republicans. He and President Eisenhower were close buddies at one time – dating from when they met in London during the war. Sam said he wanted to make a movie about 'Ike's' life, but the president didn't (possibly worried that the affair he had had with his wartime driver Kay Summersby might become public knowledge 20 years before the story did break.)

Everything about the moguls bespoke – a highly appropriate word – power and authority. As Milton Sperling, the producer son-in-law of Harry Warner, told me about one of his father-in-law's rivals: 'Sam Goldwyn was always very imposing. Impeccably dressed. Tall, thin, and with piercing eyes. Eyes that indicated a threat. I would never have wanted to work for him. He was murderous; he was a killer. He drove people to distraction. But he was an artist. He was a bespoke filmmaker. The others, Mayer, the Warners, Cohn, were mass manufacturers.'

The conversations around their dinner tables was movie talk, their 'tame' guests, producers particularly in favour, directors who were currently being seen to do a good job (when that job was thought to be not quite so satisfactory, the invitations would cease) or stars who were currently making them another fortune. Those absent would inevitably be other studio heads. Inviting a rival mogul, on the other hand, was virtually an invitation to industrial espionage.

They didn't engage much in sports – unless it was on the proverbial casting couch. The old story about the starlet's introduction to that distinctive piece of furniture (usually in a room behind a secret door at the back of the mogul's private office) has, with a few embellishments, a considerable amount of truth to it – the comely girl with all the right measurements in all the right places is asked if she would like a 'place in pictures'. Once she says she does and performs the necessary recruitment rite on the couch, she has to answer another question: 'Now would you like to try for the Academy Award?' Not a few household (to say nothing of bedroom) names achieved their universal fame from such introductions.

They liked to be seen at race meetings, because that was proof of their social standing. Sam Goldwyn always had problems with that, although he tried: once he recalled, 'My horse was in the lead, coming down the homestretch when the caddy had to fall off.'

There were, naturally enough, other activities that could be classified as sport. Jack Warner played tennis, because it had useful social associations. Sam Goldwyn tried his arm at croquet after deciding that golf was a waste of time. But then Goldwyn had an advantage over most of the other studio bosses: on the whole, his employees liked, rather than feared, him. The other moguls ruled with a balance sheet bound in iron.

Goldwyn was also regarded as the man of taste. He mangled the English language with a fluency that Richard Brinsley Sheridan, who created Mrs Malaprop in *The Rivals*, would have envied. But he had an artistic integrity not shared by the other studio bosses. He also had a temper that distinctly *was* shared by his competitors. A temper and a determination not to be outfoxed. To allow that to happen would, in each of their eyes, be more of a help to the other studio bosses than to the employees, accountants, agents or anyone else they had chosen as their current targets. You rarely argued with a mogul and if you did, your life was, metaphorically, in your own hands.

The moguls decided the fate of the movies themselves just as they judged the future of their actors. They saw all the rushes – the cuts of a day's work – and pronounced which should stay in a film and which should go, frequently to the chagrin of the director. They went to the sneak previews of movies at out-of-town theatres, studied the cards filled in by audiences who had no idea which film they had come to see – sometimes they looked at the charts of the electronic wiring to which patrons were linked, as if subject to a lie detector – and decided whether or not to take any notice of them.

When a film failed, they put the blame on their producer or director – if not on the star or the writer who gave him or her the lines to recite. If it succeeded, they were there to bask in the glory of an Academy Award.

Occasionally, they basked in the success of their families. But not always. David O. Selznick's temporary ascendancy at MGM – corresponding with his marriage to Louis B. Mayer's daughter Irene – before going it alone was greeted by snide comments of the 'son-in-law also rises'. And Sam Goldwyn welcomed – after a time – his son Sammy Junior's arrival as a producer at his studio. (Sam Jr, as he was to be known in later years, said that he remembered from early childhood his father being surrounded by piles of scripts. That, along with frequent visits to the film sets prepared him for a life in movies.) As we shall see, Harry Warner paid tribute to the god Nepotism. Jack Warner once said that Carl Laemmle, of Universal, saw it as his mission in life 'to make the world safe for nephews'.

Jack Warner Jr, son of Warner Bros.'s ebullient producer-in-charge, was given a production appointment at his father's studio and for a time was a senior executive at Warners' British studio. But then, one day, he drove into the Burbank enclave of the head office as usual, only to have the barrier come down in front of his car – and then be handed a parcel. It was the contents of his desk. His father had fired him – without having the decency to tell him first or to offer any other form of consultation. It was not an unusual situation.

The relationship between brothers was even more fraught than that between fathers and offspring. The Warner brothers were a united clan only as far as what has come to be known as the bottom line was concerned. Harry Warner, the eldest of the four brothers, regarded himself as the guardian of the family's fortune and, simultaneously, of their morals. Which explains why on one occasion he was seen to be chasing a naked Jack through the main studio lot with a crowbar in his hand – screaming, 'I'll get you, you son-of-a-bitch, you see if I don't.' The fact that they were both sons of the same mother (whom neither of them would have thought to call a bitch) had little to do with it. Harry had discovered that Jack was in bed with a studio employee and that was just too much for family decency for him.

The other brothers were never surprised at the way Jack behaved. He had more chutzpah than all his other siblings combined – which he had had all his life, or at least since their father bought their sister Rose a piano and Jack found that he loved performing, singing along with her. From that time on, he himself was 'on'.

Jack had a sense of humour and a determination that the studio bearing his name should produce quality products. Harry looked upon things differently. As he told one studio executive, 'I don't want it good; I want it Tuesday.' It was he, and not as is usually thought, Goldwyn, who declared: 'We should leave messages to Western Union.'

The Warners, like MGM and Columbia Pictures, operated their business departments (or, rather, had their business departments operated for them) from New York, which became known as the home offices – although places quite less like home would be difficult to imagine. As far as Columbia was concerned, that 3,000 miles between home office and studio was enough to enforce an unbreachable divide between the two brothers, Jack and Harry Cohn. Harry Cohn was the iron dictator of Columbia, loved by some but hated by others, who ran the studio as if he were Mussolini in Rome; his brother Jack, sitting more modestly in the New York office, controlled the purse strings. As Sam Goldwyn once said: 'In this business it's dog eat dog – and nobody's going to eat me.'

Harry Cohn certainly didn't want to waste money (unless it was on girls), and looked at every employee taken on to the books and into every scene shot by one of his cameras as a potential knife in his back. But to his brother Jack, he was nothing less than a profligate and the fights between them have become part of Hollywood folklore. If they quarrelled as brothers in the New York tenement in which they grew up, it was as nothing compared with what electrified the wires between the office in downtown Manhattan and the studio on Hollywood's Vine Street.

Yet these arguments were still seen as family affairs, a suggestion doubtless engendered by the relationship not just of brothers, but of brothers-in-law. As we shall see, the nepotism that reigned in the studios was invariably a certain recipe for discord.

But it was all worth it. They gave a great deal of pleasure to the masses – not least to those who were privy to the fights and other shenanigans that were Hollywood bread and butter.

2

SAM GOLDWYN

Shmuel Gelbfisz was the man who really did make Hollywood. And, likewise, Hollywood made him. He was a man of dreams – and, similarly, the dreams made him just as they made America itself. But as in all dreams, they are now sometimes remembered slightly differently from the reality of what actually happened. That was no more than should be expected of a man who, when a publicist described a film as the 'world's greatest-ever entertainment', responded: 'That's what I like – facts; not exaggeration.'

Which is why he liked to say that he was 11 years old when he left Warsaw and began a long, treacherous journey on foot all the way to Germany (swimming a river in the process). That story was true, except that he wasn't born in the Polish capital precisely on 27 August 1882. There were no birth certificates to confirm the details, but it was likely he was born four years before that, which means that he was 15 when he went on his trek.

Neither his widowed mother Hannah Gelbfisz, nor his siblings – two brothers, Benjamin and Berel and three sisters, Nettie, Mania and Sally – in Warsaw were totally surprised that he decided to leave their world after his father Aaron, who had run a poorly-stocked second-hand shop, died. Shmuel had been particularly close to his father and even more so to his paternal grandparents, with whom he frequently stayed. Warsaw was not only the capital of Russia's Polish province, it was also the city (before the huge influx into New York) with the world's largest Jewish population. When Shmuel was living there, 300,000 Jews were said to be in residence. There had been Jews in Poland for 800 years but, even as a child, Shmuel didn't want to be one of them (it was a wise thought; virtually all of Poland's three million Jews were massacred in the Holocaust). At the time, many of the city's doctors and lawyers were Jewish and most of the bankers, businessmen and small traders were too.

Warsaw, on the fringe of the Pale of Settlement to which Jews were confined in order not to sully the streets of Moscow or St Petersberg (unless they were deemed to be particularly useful to the authorities), also had its share of hard-working tailors, craftsmen and people who were scraping a living at whatever work they could find. It had to be work that would allow them to go to synagogue twice a day and pay for enough kosher food for their family's table.

The Gelbfiszes were not among the very poor of Jewish Warsaw. Aaron's shop had never done well, but it was a business and Hannah, in addition to cooking food for her family and cleaning their small apartment, was a moneylender – she had an acute enough brain to know how to borrow money herself and then make a profit on the interest she earned. The family spoke Yiddish among themselves and Polish when necessary among their customers. But that was rarely the case and so they knew very little of the language.

Shmuel worked as an office boy and took other odd jobs, but it was never sufficient. He decided he had had enough of his life at home and would try his luck elsewhere. However, there was no 'elsewhere' in Poland for a Jewish kid from Warsaw. Not a Jewish kid with plans.

His mother wasn't too pleased the day that he packed his belongings in an old bag and began the long journey that he determined would take him out of the country. He decided that England, where he had relatives, was the place to go, even if he did have to walk his way there.

He made it to London but couldn't find any work in the capital and slept nights in Hyde Park. He thought there would be a home for him in Birmingham where his mother's sister Dora Salberg lived with her husband Isaac, but it wasn't one of those places where Jews settled en masse. Apart from London, the main centres of Jewish life were in Manchester and Leeds. There were a couple of streets where Jews lived and there was also a synagogue, both of which had tempted his relatives.

His uncle Isaac found him a job working for a blacksmith – not making horseshoes but irons like grates and pokers for fireplaces. Shmuel wasn't a born blacksmith. Had he had a chance to design his own irons and sell them in a novel way, he might have been more satisfied. But he still wanted more. He moved on to Liverpool. The English city hadn't yet earned itself a reputation for producing international entertainers. Even if it had, Shmuel had no intention of settling there. For him, it was just a way station. On the way to America. He had heard about the pavements made of gold. They were the ones he determined should be under his own feet.

America

Schmuel had saved enough money to get a steerage ticket to New York – which was the obvious place for him to settle. It was, after all, the centre of the '*goldene medina*', the golden land, where not just those sidewalks glistened. So did everything else he had heard about: the buildings were framed in gold; the women – ah, the women! – wore brooches and bracelets of the precious metal as casually as those in Warsaw had worn headscarves. He would get there and he would do well there. Could anything else be possible? But he would do it with a different identity. Either while still on the ship or on arrival, he was given a new name. The official charged with such things couldn't get his pen around 'Gelbfisz' when recording his entry into the New World and wrote down, instead, the name 'Goldfish'. The man could, of course, have been having a joke at Shmuel's expense, but that we shall never know. He changed the name Shmuel too – to Samuel.

New York, he told his family, was where the ship would take him once he had passed through Ellis Island, a mere stopover on the journey into Manhattan. It was within the boundaries of the city – or, at least, the Port of New York – while not being part of it. The theory advanced by the writer A. Scott Berg is that the youngster born Shmuel Gelbfisz never actually went through Ellis Island at all, but had taken a ship to Canada, and then walked over the border into the States. But there are no records to confirm that fact – or theory – any more than there are any details of a birth certificate.

Ellis Island could have been a lot more precarious a proposition for Sam. Every hour of every day, some hapless prospective immigrant was turned away from this promised land, the promise unfulfilled – because, perhaps, his eyes showed signs of glaucoma or his back was crippled or maybe there was clear evidence of tuberculosis.

None of that worried Shmuel, who had to get used to calling himself Samuel and before long, Sam. He was a healthy lad with never a day's illness behind him. The question was: what was he going to do with his life? How was he going to make a living? And a living not just for himself, but also for his mother and his siblings back in *der heim*. He knew full well that Mrs Gelbfisz would never follow him to America, although his brothers and one sister would do so. No, Hannah was not about to become an American. This was plainly a heathen land, certainly not one for a pious Jewish woman who had to observe the Sabbath, keep the dietary laws and fast on Yom Kippur, even though her son assured her he wasn't going to leave all the old ways behind. Such promises were being made by three million other people as the 19th century turned into the 20th. Sam was certain that his mother would stay in Poland, though he wasn't so sure about his brothers and sisters. There was a regular mail service to Poland and he'd send them all the cash that he could, along with his regular letters. It was a promise to himself that he kept.

He made inquiries and, for no apparent reason, found a train that would take him to upstate, New York, to a place called Gloversville. It was one of just a few towns in America with industries big enough to give a name to its environs. Once having gone to Gloversville, he was determined to make good there. A glove factory advertised for labour and he was taken on – with the promise of an apprenticeship. If it was hard work that a glove firm wanted, he was the one who was going to demonstrate he could do it. Gloversville fitted him . . . like a glove.

He was now 16. He did every dirty job on the shop floor, but spent his evenings studying at night school, the Gloversville Business College. He worked at English lessons as hard as he had gathering skins for the more senior workers. It would be essential, he decided, for the businessman he now intended to become – even though the spoken language would prove often enough to be beyond his ken. He got to the factory at 6.30am every day, long before anyone else crossed its threshold, and left later than any of his colleagues. For that, he earned $3 a week. Soon, he was promoted to becoming a glove cutter. He was told that there was no better way of understanding the business and it proved to be perfectly true. But he didn't want to be a glove cutter for long, any more than he wanted to be someone else's employee for long. At 18, he made the big decision. He was going into business on his own – as a glove salesman. A self-employed glove salesman. Within months, he had the reputation of being the best salesman in town. Firms were clamouring to have him represent their companies. Within a year, he was making more money than anyone could imagine. He was the most successful glove salesman in the United States.

It was a good time to be in the glove business. Virtually every woman, from shop girls, to actresses (and even ladies of the night), to society women and dowagers, wore gloves: short white gloves to go to work or for a stroll in the park on a Sunday afternoon, long elegant gloves to go with the long elegant dresses worn by society women in the evening. He supervised not only the products made by firms in Gloversville, but he also began importing gloves from France. Like everything else, when it came to women's clothing, Paris was the place where, seemingly, only the best would do. And that was the way Sam Goldfish wanted things to be. He knew that if he were going to make real money, he had to offer what other salesmen did not have on their books. He wanted gloves that would be bought up, not just by the dozen, but also, perhaps, by the hundreds of dozens by the most fashionable stores on New York's Fifth Avenue.

He bought items made of the finest silks and the smoothest kid, designed by the most outstanding practitioners of the art of glove making, and created by the best cutters and seamstresses in the business. That desire and search for quality would remain with him for the rest of his life.

Goldfish was doing well enough to need the services of an accountant, a man who would spend hours going through the intricacies of the American financial world and explaining them to this young immigrant who absorbed figures with somewhat greater alacrity than he did the English language.

Frequently, they turned to the American tax system and, in particular, the way they administered their requirements for import duty. As they poured over the current books and balance sheet, Sam asked in his high voice – very high for a vibrant male such as himself – to explain one particular set of figures. 'That, Mr Goldfish,' said the accountant, 'is the amount of money you have been paying in import duty.'

'Import duty, you say?'

'Yes, import duty. You see, for every pair of gloves that you import, you have to pay twenty per cent in duty.'

'Say that again . . .'

'For every pair of gloves that you import, you have to pay twenty per cent in duty.'

Goldfish pondered that information for a few days and then ordered not just one consignment of gloves from the French capital, but two – to be delivered to two American ports. To New Orleans went right-handed gloves and to New York, left-handed gloves. He had a team of girls ready to match up the two – and not a cent had to be paid in import duty. Not quite. American law dictated that 'unwanted' items such as single gloves had to be auctioned. Not surprisingly, he was the only purchaser. He got the whole lot for $10.

Although he was undoubtedly the most successful glove salesman in Gloversville, and by virtue of that the most successful man selling the garments in America, he was getting bored with the glove business. Yes, it made him money, but even for him, life had to have more to offer. And the business didn't seem to be growing, despite the fortune he had already earned. He spent most of his daylight hours thinking about gloves and how to improve the income they gave him, but he wanted still more than cash. And that accountant made an important point to him: government tariff policy meant that business was getting harder and the profits less.

Entrepreneur

It was about this time that he met a woman named Blanche Lasky. Blanche was a friend of the girl with whom he had fallen desperately in love: Bessie Ginsberg. But Bessie had someone else she loved, a vaudeville comedy musician called Jesse Lasky, whom Sam met while he was working in that cradle of American show business, the Borscht Belt resorts in the New York State Catskills Mountains. Jesse worked with his sister, Blanche. Possibly to get Sam off her back, Bessie introduced Sam to Blanche. Whether they actually fell in love is a matter for speculation – she probably loved him more than he loved her – but they married and she gave him a daughter they named Ruth. It wasn't long, however, before Blanche would complain that he didn't spend enough time with the two of them. The truth was that he always had something else to occupy his mind. And if it wasn't gloves that took his time – along with his accountant – it was probably poker.

Unusually, in a relationship like theirs, Sam was spending a lot of time with his brother-in-law, Jesse, who was also a man of ambition. He was a successful entrepreneur like Sam, but gloves weren't part of his life. He had something far more exciting to think about. In addition to having worked on the vaudeville stage, he had tried his hand at being a theatrical producer. Now he was in the motion-picture business, which intrigued his brother-in-law. Sam really wasn't sure what the motion-picture business was, let alone what constituted a motion picture.

Lasky owned a series of nickelodeons, which were, in some cases, rather like 21st century launderettes – only instead of washers, there were banks of machines with leather-trimmed viewers (Sam probably could have made another fortune selling those trims), down which customers could see what the butler saw, while excitedly turning a handle.

But Lasky was no more content with the nickelodeon business than Sam was with gloves and wanted to branch out as others had done. Only, he wanted to do it bigger and better than anyone else had done, which is why Sam provided such a ready audience for his plans. He was going to *make* films. His idea was not just to turn out a two or three-reel picture of indifferent quality, he wanted to tell a story that would fascinate audiences who would sit in a real theatre, watching a movie on a big screen – much as they would if they were watching a live production. Sam wanted to hear more. On a trip to New York, he had strayed into a theatre on Herald Square and seen his first films – badly flickering shorts. So Lasky's idea inspired him. Here was a chance to put into what was not yet known as the movie business, the standards he had adopted producing and selling gloves. He would introduce quality to the screen. If Lasky thought that his brother-in-law was taking over his own ideas, he didn't complain. Sam had a lot of ingenuity – and a lot of money. As for Jesse Lasky himself, he had a story to film – and an actor who would star in it, even though that, too, was a term for the future.

Lasky had done his research. He knew that there was nothing that attracted people to watch the primitive movies then on offer more than Westerns. With Sam's help, he was prepared to take the risk of making another one. With Sam, that connoisseur of glove perfection, at his side, it was going to shout that one word his brother-in-law talked so much about, 'quality'.

Their film was going to be called *The Squaw Man*, based on a story by Edward Milton Royle, about a British officer who goes to the Wild West. It was all set to be no *Great Train Robbery*, which had excited audiences with the audacity of a moustachioed man in a cowboy outfit pointing a gun, seemingly, at the audience. The age of the gimmick was already over. These producers were going to make a play – only one that could be projected on to screens. And on to screens all over the country, and perhaps the rest of the world besides. Which was precisely why they had a real actor to play the lead. What they had now was a STAR. His name was Dustin Farnum – one that would, a couple of generations later, be adopted by a certain Mr and Mrs Hoffman, for their baby son born in Los

Angeles in 1937. Farnum, born in 1874, had been working on the stage since he was 15. He was now 38.

Lasky and Goldfish bought a camera and hired a camera team to go with it. And they also planned something that had rarely been attempted before. They were going to film *The Squaw Man* on location (another new term). Plainly, Sam Goldfish would never be satisfied with a movie that looked as though it had been shot within the plywood boards of a studio set – unless it couldn't be helped.

The pair were taking no chances. They knew where they were going to make the picture. People had told them that the ideal spot would be in Flagstaff, Arizona, a place that they were sure would have just the right Western atmosphere they needed for their 'play', even though it had a reputation for a shaky climate – and the weather was vital in those days, long before anyone had thought of using *klieg lights* (intense carbon arc lamps). But the man who had gone to such lengths with selecting the right skins and silks would never accept the word of well-wishers, even if they really were the experts on American Western geography. His brother-in-law agreed that they had to do what later filmmakers would call a 'recke', a reconnaisance expedition. Both were too busy to contemplate doing the trip themselves. They had businesses to run. But they knew two men whom they could trust to understand what films needed. Both would, before long, make their own impact in the movie business. One was Oscar Apfel, who had already tried his hand at directing movies. The other was a man who became a virtual household name whenever films – particularly films involving spectacle – were discussed. He had already adopted a style for his name that he was convinced would resonate with, not just the general public, but also professional filmmakers: Cecil B. DeMille.

The men boarded at the Pennsylvania Central station in New York, accompanied by Dustin Farnum and his dresser. Two days later, the train drew up at the Arizona station – in the midst of a snowstorm – to be greeted by a group of what were then called Red Indians. They looked at each other, took hold of their suitcases and opened the door of the train, but before it steamed off they took their seats once again. They had decided to go to the end of the line. When they finally got off the train, they looked at the bright sunlight above, the palm trees close to the station and, dusty and tired, took a horse and carriage to an hotel.

The next day, they sent a telegram to New York: 'FLAGSTAFF NO GOOD FOR OUR PURPOSE. HAVE PROCEEDED TO CALIFORNIA. WANT AUTHORITY TO RENT BARN IN PLACE CALLED HOLLYWOOD.'

They added the cost of the barn: '75 DOLLARS A MONTH'.

'It's called Hollywood,' Sam might well have repeated, as he read it. Not even Mr Goldfish could predict how important that telegram was. He replied: 'AUTHORISE YOU TO RENT BARN ON MONTH-TO-MONTH BASIS. DON'T MAKE ANY LONG COMMITMENT.'

The film team got to work. As we have seen, it was not the first movie to be made. Neither was it the first to be shot in California. As far back as 1907, a man called William Selig had made a moving picture in Santa Monica, which was regarded as Los Angeles-by-the-Sea. There were dozens of small outfits shooting small films and packing up their small cameras once they had finished showing films to small audiences. But as far as Sam Goldfish was concerned, those facts were hardly significant. The pictures that had been shot there were no more like his idea of a real movie than the hand coverings sold from a pushcart on New York's Lower East Side could be called gloves. They were short subjects with no real stories, shot by fly-by-night organisations who neither stayed for any length of time in California, nor had the money to do so – even if they had wanted to.

The results confirmed how lucky Farnum, Apfel and DeMille had been in getting on that train in Flagstaff. The bright, occasionally almost blinding, light of California, combined with the equipment they were using, provided a degree of perfect photography never seen in what the team were now calling the movies. They made their film – and told *The New York Times* and the other metropolitan papers about it. The press were almost as excited about the development as the filmmakers themselves – even if the Manhattan journalists did allow themselves to worry about the loss of jobs on the East Coast that might result from the Hollywood discovery. But still, there weren't that many movies being made. Most people had never heard of them, let alone seen a picture flashed on to a screen. The Goldfish-Lasky film was directed by DeMille – with Apfel looking over his shoulder– the first of 70 in a career that spanned almost half a century. More significant for the history of the movie business, this was the first ever feature-length film shot in Hollywood.

The Squaw Man was an immediate hit as it played all over America in February 1914, first in New York, then in every town in the country. There weren't any real cinemas – or motion-picture theatres, as the brothers-in-law now learned to call them. But in vaudeville and burlesque houses, church halls and even funeral parlours (anywhere, in fact, where seats were either already there or could be laid down and a screen put up), crowds – spurred on by their local newspapers – were mesmerised by what they saw. The film was not only a sensation in America; in Europe, too, it scored an immediate hit (another term that was hardly yet in general use).

The company followed this success with a Lasky brainwave. *Brewster's Millions,* about a man who discovers he has been left $8 million – on condition that he spends $1 million of it first – had been a big hit on the London stage. He bought the film rights for $5,000. In perpetuity. It became the second production of the partnership. It was also their second big hit.

Goldfish realised that the titles they used in lieu of spoken dialogue could be translated into dozens of other languages without affecting the success of the picture. There was to be a big change: the company was now registered as the Jesse L. Lasky Feature Play Company, capitalised at $15,000, a company that made 21 films in its first year. Lasky was president (after all, if this had been a baseball team, he would have said he owned the ball), Goldfish was treasurer and sales manager and Cecil B. DeMille, not yet a name to conjure with, was to serve as a director.

It was in 1915 that a relationship all three men had with another movie entrepreneur was formalised. Adolph Zukor, a small, wiry man, had his own company, Famous Players. Both he and Lasky believed that there was no point in two men with similar ideas working in opposition, so the two organisations merged. Sam, by now recognised as knowing more about business than the other partners, wasn't so sure. But he was made chairman of the board – although it was clear the arrangement wouldn't last. Zukor didn't like Sam – and nor, it would soon become evident, did any of his other competitors. Zukor saw trouble from the beginning. 'Sam is like a Jersey cow that gives the finest milk,' he said at the time, 'but before you can take the bucket away he has kicked it over.' By that, he presumably meant that Goldfish would agree to certain projects and then, when most of the work had been done, would have second thoughts. He did a lot of second thinking. And always would.

The business got going and all concerned seemed to be very serious about it. Cecil B. DeMille was taking his responsibilities very conscientiously indeed. Sam saw the rushes of one of his earliest movies and complained that the lighting the director had chosen for a certain effect cut out half the face of his actors. 'I can't sell pictures that show only half the hero's face,' he ranted. 'I'll have to charge half price for them.' Lasky worried about that. But DeMille had an answer: 'Tell him it's Rembrandt lighting,'

'Good,' said Sam, 'I'll charge them double.'

It was developments like this that persuaded Sam to make one of his many revolutionary decisions. Before long, he was renting his films, not selling them outright to movie theatres. The profits were astronomically larger.

This was to be a Goldfish swimming in a very comfortable environment – until (in a situation quite familiar to other brothers-in-law) he and Lasky decided to do without each other's company and expertise. It was music to Zukor's ears. The rows between the three – but mainly between Adolph and Jesse on one side and Sam on the other – got ever hotter. The main fight was over who was boss. Each thought they were in charge. Sam thought he was more boss than the others were. He hadn't given up the glove business to work for someone else, had he? He was certain he had not.

But he wasn't leaving his partners just yet. He was far too clever for that. There were plans he needed to gel before he went out into the big, wide movie world all on his own. Sam was remaining as chairman of the board for the time being. But no one was in any doubt that he had his plans.

Now, the words on the movie posters and the beginning of each movie, which he had astonished friends by accepting, 'Jesse L. Lasky presents', were rankling more than ever. At the slightest thing, his temper flared. One man said that he had fights even with people who agreed with him. Sam explained that by saying that he had learned that the only things worth having were the ones that he had to fight for. So he said a final goodbye. He signed an agreement whereby he had nothing to do with the firm that became known as Famous Players-Lasky (a title he would never have accepted) for a consideration of $900,000. Then he did something for which, before long, he would be famous. With the help of a man whose command of English was considerably better than was his own, he issued a statement – always, he decided, the best way to get publicity; far better to give papers a news story than to depend on PR blurbs. In this, he said: 'I have contemplated retiring from the active management of Famous Players-Lasky Corporation for some time.'

He was doing so now, he said in the announcement, 'in order to mature certain personal plans which are of great importance to me, which I could not mature if I continued as one of the executives of the company.' No one needed to doubt they were Goldfish's true reasons, even if the words had been put into his mouth by one of the various people he was employing as a 'ghost'.

Sam Goes it Alone

Whether Sam's split from Lasky and Zukor was the principal reason for his marriage to Blanche breaking up is difficult to assess after nearly 100 years. Whatever the reason, the Goldfishes were not exactly the perfect example of a marriage made in heaven and, although he was a remarkable provider, neither his wife nor his young daughter could remember the words 'I love you' coming from his lips. If it wasn't work (which it was very often) or poker, it was other women. As a wealthy man who had already shown he could run a motion picture company – whatever that was – he had no difficulty in finding nubile girls willing to give their all – and more – to him. If the offer so often made 20 years later, 'I can get you a job in pictures', was never actually on his lips, it was fairly certain to have been made in other words capable of conveying precisely the same meaning.

But those words would not have been his principal interest in those days. Having split up from the Jesse Lasky partnership – and the Lasky-Zukor partnership doing a little too well for Sam's liking – Goldfish set about making his own movies the way he wanted to make them.

Now, he was going to put a Goldfish stamp on the film business – practising all that he had preached as a glove salesman. Plainly, despite all his old problems, Sam was still a good business bet – which was why he had an offer from George M. Cohan, the actor-singer-dancer-producer who had just written a march for the coming Great War, called *Over There*, a tune that fitted in well with all his other patriotic ditties like *Yankee Doodle Dandy* and *You're a Grand Old Flag*.

Cohan would say that Sam was the one who did the approaching – only to decide then against taking another partner. Neither could he come to a deal with Cohan to make screen adaptations of his big, blockbusting shows.

He was going it alone and, with that aim in mind, he hired the best actors he could find to be filmed by the best cameramen who would turn the handles of the best cameras, choose the best locations for the films he was going to make and had the best designers put together the sets that had to be confined to the studio. As with all filmmakers at the time, the scenes came together in large rooms with no roofs – how else could they take advantage of the bright sunlight? The clothes were made by tailors and couturiers who could never have imagined they would have such marvellous opportunities to demonstrate their skills. It goes without saying that only the finest cloths would be used. If someone asked Sam why he bothered to go to such extremes for the manufacture of outfits that would only be seen sometimes for a few minutes on a flickering screen – and in black and white, at that – he would have replied that he himself knew they were the best and that was all that counted.

It was a similar philosophy to the one that was being adopted by Florenz Ziegfeld Jr, the man who revelled in his reputation as the king of Broadway impresarios. His *Ziegfeld Follies* boasted the most beautiful girls on a live stage, wearing the most beautiful costumes. That being not far from the truth, it was hardly surprising that he had the idea that he and Sam should put both their heads and their bank accounts together. Goldfish was not totally immune to the idea, except that the notion of a partnership with anyone, following his experiences with Lasky, wasn't exactly a temptation.

But Ziegfeld was persistent – and invited him to dinner at the restaurant on the roof of the Follies' home, the New Amsterdam Theater, where people sat in glass-walled booths – 'perfect for a goldfish,' joked the great Ziggy's partner, George Buck, 'behind glass.' Sam didn't share his sense of humour and decided that a partnership with the man from Broadway would probably produce more problems than achievements.

In any case, he had plans and wouldn't want anyone else to share them. Or to let other people interfere with his ideas. Nevertheless, when he thought about it, he recognised that he needed money – something that Ziegfeld, who was continually on the brink of bankruptcy, could not give him. What was more, in a climate not that different from one 80 years later, there was always the talk of mergers between businesses that had success and talent on the one hand and others which had enough money to guarantee even more success.

Which was how Edgar Selwyn, his brother Archibald, and the playwright Margaret Mayo came to call on Sam with a proposition. The Selwyns, who were highly successful theatrical producers, wanted to get into the movie business. But they needed the expertise of someone who knew that business from start to finish. Sam fitted that criterion perfectly.

The Birth of Goldwyn Pictures

After weeks of talks – and the inevitable arguments – the Selwyns came to an agreement with Sam late in 1918. It was an appropriate time. The Germans had signed an armistice with the Allies and Sam's conditions for the partnership might have resembled in his mind the terms of the ending of the First World War.

Sam and Selwyn would go into business together, although Sam would have the last word. They would set up a new business centre. The only thing left to decide was the name of their enterprise. Clearly, it wouldn't satisfy the partners to have Sam's name alone on the notepaper of their new business. So the Selwyns suggested, why not have *both* their names? 'Goldfish and Selwyn present . . .' didn't sound right. But what if they 'invented' a new name? A name that combined their two names, a name that used syllables from them both? A name with the first syllable of one and the second from the other? They agreed. The new organisation would be named 'Goldwyn'. Sam liked that so much that he set about changing his own surname. It wouldn't be long before this Goldfish would have been thrown out of the bowl and cast into history along with Gelbfisz. The proud movie mogul would forever after be known as Sam Goldwyn. Of course, the wags would have their day with that name just as they had with his earlier nomenclature. One man said, 'He got the syllables round the wrong way. He should have called himself "Selfish".' But that was one thing that could never be said about Sam Goldwyn. Selfish he wasn't – as he continued to lavish money on his staff, the clothes they wore and the sets in which they performed. Which was no more than ought to be expected of an outfit which billed itself as 'Goldwyn Pictures' and then added: 'Brains write them. Brains direct them. Brains are responsible for their wonderful perfection.'

There was an immediate policy statement. The new company would go for quality. It would all be built on 'the strong foundation of intelligence and refinement' said advertisements published in the *Saturday Evening Post.*

Sam had taken on new actors and actresses like Mae Marsh and Maxine Elliott (a stage performer whom he hired on the basis of pictures he had seen and on her reputation for having the most perfect breasts on Broadway and the curviest hips, to say nothing of her beautiful face. When he saw the results of her first film scenes, he had to reluctantly conclude that the bust had fallen, the hips were rounder than he had been told and her face would have benefited from the administrations of a better make-up artist than was the available). There were also the leading actresses, Jane Cowl and Madge Kennedy. Strangely, he also brought in the famous opera singer, Mary Garden, who made two films for Sam, both appalling disasters. Hardly surprising when you import an opera star to make a silent film.

The first Goldwyn films did exceptionally well, particularly *Laughing Bill Hyde*, starring Will Rogers. Then there was *Thirty a Week*, starring Tallulah Bankhead. His partner Margaret Mayo's play *Polly of the Circus* was also a big success.

He was to go on a world tour, looking for new talent – and inevitably that search was also directed at possible bed-mates. He had been told that in Hungary there was a plethora of untapped resources – actors and actresses who were completely unknown in America. What was more, it would be a chance to see his mother and his siblings on the way. But, by all accounts, once he had kissed Mrs Gelbfisz, enjoyed her kosher cooking and found that his brothers and sisters, the ones who had not yet made the journey across the Atlantic themselves, were alive and well – if a little too anxious to show how much they loved their rich and famous brother – he was only too ready to get away again and continue his journey to Budapest and its environs.

In fact, he made only one discovery that he thought was worth putting on a ship bound for New York and then on the train journey to California. After seeing pictures of Vilma Banky it took days to arrange the meeting; Miss Banky was always too busy and too anxious to play hard-to-get until the very last moment. But if he never signed another actress in his life, he knew that his journey had been worthwhile. She was more beautiful than any woman he had seen on the screen before; a beautiful face, aided by superb bone structure and a figure that he was convinced was magnificent even without the aid of the corsets she probably wore.

Vilma (whom he persisted in calling Banky Vilma, the way her name would appear in Hungarian, a language which always used the surname first) couldn't speak a word of English, but what did that matter? She was persuaded to make the trip to America. Not only was this a marvellous opportunity for her to see the New World, but for the New World to see her. Very few ambitious actresses – and she was as ambitious as they came – would turn down that opportunity. Particularly for the kind of salary that Goldwyn was offering. He knew she would get all the publicity he needed without being able to speak a word of the language.

Vilma looked good, but he thought she could appear even better. As good perhaps as his other big discovery Mabel Normand, with whom Sam fell desperately in love, although that was to be just one of his ambitious, but thwarted, attempts at forming a romantic liaison.

Another actress complained about being chased around Sam's squeaky-clean desk, at the end of which the only thing the mogul could raise was a severe cough. He ended up showing the girl the door, complaining that he had never been so insulted in his life.

He never felt that way about Vilma Banky, although from his first meeting with her, he knew the young woman's value to his company. But there was something lacking. Her country might be the home of great operetta and even greater food but a man with his pulse on public taste like Samuel Goldwyn knew that its fashions were not exactly the kind that would make American women drool. What was more, without that added ingredient, he might find it difficult to get the kind of magazine publicity he had in mind. So, he decided to make a stopover on the journey back to the United States – in France. In Paris, he arranged for his new discovery to visit the great couture houses and be fitted for the kind of dresses she would need to excite not just the magazine and newspaper writers, but their readers, too.

The rest, he believed, would follow. The journalists, who had all been primed by Sam's publicity department (he had been one of the first to realise that stories about his films and the actors playing in them was an essential part of his sales campaigns), were on hand at the docks to welcome employer and employee as they stepped off their Hamburg-America ship. On the journey, Sam had tried to teach her a few English words, which she used over and over again to the delight of the newsmen and women. Goldwyn had told her to say nothing more than 'lamb chop and pineapple' when she was asked questions by reporters. The prospect of Sam Goldwyn, who was already earning a reputation for himself as one of the principal executioners of the English language, schooling anyone in his adopted tongue was the delighted subject of studio commissary conversation for months to come. That publicity department, incidentally, was proving to be as inventive and as resourceful as Sam was himself. At the head of the operation, he had installed a young man called Howard Dietz. Dietz would before long decide that songwriting would be more in his line, with the result that he produced such gems as *Something to Remember You By*, *Dancing in the Dark* and *That's Entertainment* with his partner Arthur Schwartz.

But what he produced for Sam was to be equally seminal. Gazing out of his New York office window at the bronze lions standing guard outside the public library on Fifth Avenue, he thought that a lion would be the perfect trademark for his boss, the 'lion' of motion pictures (another story was that he took it from the logo on the magazine of his alma mater, Columbia University). He made it look like a royal coat of arms – inspired perhaps by the British Royal Family's, which had both a unicorn and a rampant lion guarding the insignia of the Order of the Garter. Dietz had a lion – which at the beginning of his pictures would move and appear to roar – as the centrepiece of Goldwyn's arms, surrounded by a coil of film, which then straddled the foot of the crest to give it depth and perspective. He also gave it a slogan above the animal's head, 'Ars Gratia Artis', 'Art for Art's Sake'. It would prove to be one of the world's most recognised symbols, and undoubtedly the most famous of all Hollywood trademarks.

It was a great publicity gimmick. Sam always searched for publicity stunts – even though they might have no direct connection with any film he was making. Just so long as they featured his name – and spelt it right – and didn't involve lawyers, he was happy.

A generation later, in 1952, he addressed a dinner of Hollywood publicists. 'Tonight, I feel the way I imagine a college professor must feel when he attends a meeting of his old students and finds they have been doing very well ever since they left the peace and quiet of the campus to shift [sic] for themselves. I am sure all of you – particularly those who have worked with me – will agree that this is a very apt comparison, for what words could better describe the day-by-day relations at Goldwyn College between my publicists and myself than "peace" and "quiet"?' If ever was a tongue more firmly placed in a cheek?

One of the most effective members of his PR department's alumni was Pete Smith. It was he who suggested that Goldwyn issue a statement in which he said he had 13 favourite actors. He would then list them all – all, that is, except the one in the 13th position. That would, he was advised, have every leading actor in Hollywood not on the original list trying to convince his or her employers and friends (and enemies) that he or she was number thirteen.

It had precisely the desired result. As did the campaign for Vilma Banky. She was an immediate hit in her first Goldwyn movie, *The Dark Angel*, and Sam took advantage of the fact.

When *The Dark Angel* was released, *The New York Times* confirmed that view. She was, said their writer, 'a young person of rare beauty who might be American or English, with soft fair hair, a slightly retroussé nose and lovely blue eyes which have the suggestion of a slant. Her acting is sincere and earnest and her tears seem very real. She is so exquisite that one is not in the least surprised that she is never forgotten by Hilary Trent (Ronald Colman) when, as a blinded war hero, he settles down to dictating boys' stories.'

The question about her being either English or American was a reasonable one to ask. No one heard her in the silent pictures he was making and whatever she might say to others on the set would be drowned out by the full orchestra Sam brought on to provide the most soothing mood for his most important stars.

He rightly thought that all the publicity she was getting would endear her to the public. He also knew that nothing would do it more than a wedding. So he did what the moguls always did. He arranged a marriage for her – to the actor Rod La Rocque – and paid for the celebrations, described at the time as one of the most extravagant Hollywood parties of all time. It worked a treat. There was no doubt she was the most popular female star in Hollywood.

PR men all over the world would appreciate some of the things that Sam got up to – like the time he wrote to the pope. Sam decided he hated bobbed hair (or at least his publicity people decided it for him). He wrote a letter to the Vatican, suggesting that the current incumbent of the throne of St Peter support him in what he decided was an assault against indecency. His Holiness thought otherwise and refused to cooperate.

Meanwhile, Sam wanted to cause as much of a stir with a male actor as he had with Vilma and Ronald Colman was an obvious asset to him. There would be no language problems with this master of English. But Sam always had to have something to complain about – a condition without which he was seemingly incapable of living. Colman didn't like all the roles he was given and he decidedly did not like the money he was getting for them. There would be a whole series of rows between the two men. While the actor complained constantly, Goldwyn would shout and scream and insist that his star honour his agreement. Then, just as demonstrably, he would placate him with a few soothing words and a fatherly hand on his shoulder.

Colman, of course, knew how important he was to his boss. Not only did he speak his native language more perfectly than almost anyone else in Hollywood, he did so with a voice so mellifluous it was positively wasted in silent pictures. If the 'talkies' were created merely to find a movie voice for Ronald Colman, it would have been reason enough to invent them – but that cataclysmic event for the film industry was still ahead.

On the other hand, the Englishman was handsome enough without his voice to be nothing less than a Hollywood sensation. It wouldn't be long before Sam realised the value of the investment into which he had entered when he signed Colman to his seven-year contract.

His films, like most of Goldwyn's productions, augmented by Selwyn's money, were doing exceedingly well and there were plenty in the business who watched what he did with admiration – and not a little envy.

Two people who fitted into that category were his wife and his daughter, Ruth. Husband and wife were permanently estranged now and a divorce was inevitable. A settlement was agreed by which Blanche received $2,600 a year alimony and another $5,200 a year as compensation for all she had lost by no longer being Mrs Goldwyn. The figures were phenomenal for the time.

Sam and his daughter would keep in touch with each other only rarely and then strictly by correspondence – which usually meant that he was complaining to Ruth for not doing things right in his eyes or not showing sufficient respect to her 'loving Father'. But the truth of the matter was that Goldwyn's lack of attention to his family was mirrored in exact reverse by the reverence he showed for his business. He continued to attract the best stars who made what he liked to think were the best movies.

He had bought a new lot for $50,000 in Culver City, which he boasted was no strain on his organisation. As he wrote: 'The Goldwyn Company stands as solid as the Rock of Gibraltar in the eyes of the public, as well as in the banks. We have today $5,000,000 in cash in the banks, which is more than any company in the world has laying in the banks and that balance puts us in a position where we have a credit of [a] like amount. In other words, if we needed $10,000,000 cash tomorrow, we could get it.'

That sort of statement made his competitors only more anxious to put his enterprise under their metaphorical microscopes. He feigned no interest in their attentions. And then, quite suddenly, and to the amazement of both the industry and the trade press, he and the Selwyns accepted a takeover bid. It came from the Loews group – who, in addition to owning the biggest chain of motion-picture theatres in America, also ran Metro Pictures.

They made an offer which even a man with $5 million in the bank, could not refuse. Sam would remain chairman, which satisfied both sides for a time. But before long, his fellow directors were doing all they could to ease him out – although 'ease' was never an appropriate word where Goldwyn was concerned. Life was made impossible for him. So impossible that he made himself a promise: never again to be a member of a partnership. As he said on more than one occasion, 'I discovered I was spending more time trying to explain to them what I was doing than in making pictures.' The company made a similar decision and he was out.

In typical Goldwyn form, he would later say (with some truth) 'I was always an independent, even when I had partners.'

Metro-Goldwyn-Mayer

The new company became the Metro-Goldwyn company (Sam's name was too valuable to lose, even if he himself could be discarded). The company would soon add the name Mayer to its title, which couldn't concern Sam. He now had no financial interest in the organisation and the feud that would eventually develop between him and Louis B. Mayer hadn't yet got into its stride.

He had sold his business, his studio – and his lion, which was now known in the business as Leo. But he had not lost his stars like Banky and Colman, who remained his own.

What really startled Wall Street and other watchers of the Hollywood business scene was how willingly Sam had seemed to surrender his own name. How was it, they wondered, that someone who had always been seen as such an astute businessman could so willingly give up his prime asset? In truth, Goldwyn himself wondered about that. But, as far as he was concerned, he wasn't giving the name away. He was merely lending it. His enemies and competitors chortled at that. But not his lawyer, who managed to persuade a judge in a landmark case, to agree that a slight change of words would end forever any suggestion of anonymity.

Now, to the utter amazement of Loews, he was told he could, after all, use his own name in business. It was quite simply given back to him by the aptly named Judge Learned Hand. The words, 'Samuel Goldwyn presents . . .' were declared to be all his own. But in a decision that would have satisfied King Solomon, the judge ruled that Sam would not be allowed to use his name on a film's credits (delight all round from the Goldwyn Pictures Corporation, in other words MGM, in an effort to emphasise their rights to Sam's name) unless, Judge Hand added, he followed the credit with the words, 'Not connected with the Goldwyn Pictures Corporation'.

Not that Sam would have wanted it any other way. Being able to print 'Samuel Goldwyn Presents', added an additional proprietary factor to his films, which delighted him. As always in his career, he was doing things his own way. It wasn't just a matter of quality, although, of course, it was that. More, it was to put his own individual stamp on the movies he was going to make which would be created in the United Artists studio and distributed by First National.

He made a picture that he decided would set the tone for everything that followed. It would be a quality unique to Goldwyn productions. *Potash and Perlmutter* seemed to be totally out of character for the Goldwyn of the time. It was a Jewish comedy, as ethnic as a box of matzos or a plate of gefilte fish. But it was a *good* film that people wanted to see. His second 'Goldwyn' picture couldn't have been more different: *The Eternal City* was a love story which he intended to sell more for its setting than for the fact that it featured the beautiful Barbara La Marr and the always impressive Lionel Barrymore. The scenes emphasised the most exciting views of Rome ever seen on a screen and boasted 20,000 people in crowd episodes. It even caught moments featuring Benito Mussolini and King Victor Emmanuel. This was not a good idea as far as the Italian Government and the Fascist Establishment were concerned. Once they heard about it, they dispatched the local *carabinieri* to confiscate the film. But the Goldwyn outfit outsmarted them and beat a hasty retreat with the film and all their other equipment smuggled in their luggage.

Not only did Sam have Ronald Colman on his own private books – the most handsome man in movies, said Mr Goldwyn – but he also had another star he was creating in what he took – and hoped other people would take – as his own image. Not that Sam looked anything like the tall, gangling man whom he assumed women would regard as the new Valentino. But Gary Cooper was so handsome, Sam felt certain that every time he appeared on screen, the sound of females swooning would be a regular occurrence. And he wasn't wrong. The swoons went with the sound of cents over the box-office counters.

Cooper was a big hit with the public – and, therefore with Sam, too. Although when, at the end of 'Coop's' career, he gave a dinner for him, he said in his speech: 'I have known Gary Cooper for over thirty years, since he made that famous film for me . . . what was the name of that film?'

He should have known that, for Cooper starred in, most notably, *The Adventures of Marco Polo, The Westerner* (which Sam declared to be 'better than *Gone With the Wind*, but not as long') and *Pride of the Yankees*, about the famous baseball player Lou Gehrig, whose name was given to a disease – the muscle-wasting affliction that killed him, just as it would David Niven 40 years later.

It was a part made in heaven for Cooper, who not only had never played baseball in his life, but was also right-handed while Gehrig was famously left-handed. The problem was saved by reversing the film (and the number on Gehrig's uniform), to give the impression that the star's orientation was the same as the eponymous player's. Sam thought it turned out to be a great tribute to a man he considered to be a great American by a great actor.

By the time Cooper arrived on the movie scene, Sam was more than merely established as *part* of Hollywood. To some people, he *was* Hollywood. He made decisions and took risks that few others would have attempted. In 1924, his link with United Artists provided him with both studio facilities and a distribution deal – giving the outfit founded by Mary Pickford, her then husband Douglas Fairbanks, Charlie Chaplin and the pioneer director D.W. Griffith 25 per cent of the Goldwyn gross business. He was not part of their United Artists *partnership*, but if people thought he was, he was not going to correct them. And in 1927, Sam did become a director of the company.

The Talkies

Sam was still constantly travelling, looking for new talent and when he went to Europe, he would always try to find opportunities to be with his mother and siblings. They were on the move, too. Sally had gone to live in England while his brothers Berel (now called Bernard) and Benjamin (who as Ben Fish now worked for Sam), and sister Nettie joined him in America. His other sister, Mania, stayed in Poland. They all got together again in Berlin, as a sort of halfway house for their meeting at the fashionable Adlon Hotel (all paid for by Sam, of course).

He used the visit as an opportunity to tell them about the progress his business was making. But finding new talent was top of his agenda.

Where his potential new stars came from and how they spoke mattered not at all. Sam didn't give a hoot for their voices. Why on earth should he bother? As long as they looked good, it wouldn't matter in the least. That was until the coming of the revolution.

On 6 October 1927, the cinema screen learned to talk. With the release of Warner Bros.' *The Jazz Singer*, the silent movie was consigned to the scrap heap. Sam was affected along with all the other moguls. For a time, he continued to waiver. But then, when it was obvious that all his competitors were wiring their studios for sound, he couldn't afford to be left out.

It was goodbye to Vilma Banky and the other actors and actresses who had come over from Europe and could say no more than 'Hello' in an impossible accent. Well, almost. He could still be tempted by a woman whose bust and hips beguiled him more than the way they spoke.

One of them was a lady called Anna Sten, who had made a number of films in both Russian and German. She was Ukrainian (which was part of Russia at the time) and arrived with a figure that took the best manufacturers of foundation garments in America to reshape. But Sam still thought she was sexy. To ensure that she looked good and felt good, he not only gave her an English language coach, but also a masseuse – and dancing and singing coaches. She was, he said, going to be a Big Hit. She wasn't.

Ms Sten, who had been billed as the new Vilma Banky, failed at almost everything she did for Sam. In 1934, he made *Nana*, the Zola classic about a courtesan, with her. He then realised her accent was so thick nobody within shouting distance could understand it. When Sam saw the film, he scrapped the entire production at a cost of $411,000. Laughing at Ms Sten was one thing, having people laugh at *him* – and the foolish investment which they saw that he had made – was another.

The movie was remade – with Ms Sten having to recite again and again each and every syllable (and there were now not many of those). It did no good. The film opened to excoriating reviews.

But Ronald Colman was plainly not just in his element, but proving to be as superb an investment for Goldwyn as Anna Sten was a disaster. His perfect command of the language and his dulcet tones stunned people in his own country. As for his biggest audience, the Americans, they were amazed. Most had never heard an English accent before. Certainly, they had never heard anything like Ronald Colman before – and many of them thought that all Englishmen sounded just like he did.

Colman knew the value he represented to Sam Goldwyn. Once again, and with the added asset of his voice as a bonus, he was demanding more money and better conditions. Sam merely told him that he had a contract, which should be honoured by both sides in every respect. It would come up for discussion over and over again.

Sam was having no noticeable problems with Gary Cooper. 'Coop' might have seemed best cast when he had merely to keep his biceps seen and his voice quiet – and if he could get away with just 'yep' and 'nope', that was OK with the audiences. And now there was another actor who promised he could be a great star. At least, that was what David Niven promised about himself. Sam wasn't so sure. He liked the idea of another English voice on his roster, but was not so sure that Niven was really star material. Somewhat reluctantly, he took advice he didn't want and put the Englishman under contract, but didn't allow him to do more than small parts in small movies. There was, however, an uncredited role in *Barbary Coast* in 1935 (he played a cockney sailor thrown out of a bar in that film, which starred Edward G. Robinson, Miriam Hopkins and Joel McCrea) and a small part in *Splendor* in the same year. Ask Sam why he couldn't be sure that Niven would be up to standard, and the answer was always to quote that one word which remained his mantra: 'It's the Quality, stupid.' He didn't think that Niven, despite all his elegant front, appeared to be a 'quality' actor.

There were, however, always films and stars that he thought matched his criteria. There was, for instance, the film of Tolstoy's novel, *Resurrection,* called *We Live Again,* co-starring Fredric March with – despite everything – Anna Sten. Rouben Mamoulian was persuaded against his better judgement to direct. He turned what could have been a disaster into a quality movie. As for Anna Sten, she was never given another Goldwyn star part, although she continued to make films until 1964, nine years before her death.

But 'Coop'? Sam decided he would only be worth employing in Westerns. So he left Sam's organisation, ready to pick up his glory years with Warner Bros. and beyond. Before long, Goldwyn regretted that decision and invited the actor back – at, it was calculated, 60 times the price of his original $60 a week contract. Certainly, Gary Cooper wasn't the most articulate of actors, but he was the exception that proved the rule when the talkies came.

Meanwhile, Sam had adopted another star – one who showed that the name Goldwyn could stand high for quality comedy and musicals no less than it did for romantic dramas and historical epics. And once more the comparison with Florenz Ziegfeld was particularly apt. He signed a contract with Eddie Cantor, currently the biggest star of the *Follies*.

It was arranged that Ziegfeld would get a cut from the filmed version of Cantor's Broadway hit *Whoopee*. The resultant 1930 picture would be Goldwyn's first talkie. Generously (although he had little alternative), he also gave Ziegfeld a say in how it was to be made. Ziegfeld thought it should be filmed at the Astoria studios in New York. Sam, always determined to have his own way – which meant full control – wasn't going to agree to that. As he told the Broadway producer: 'Ziggy, the facilities are so good in Hollywood. For instance, you have that Indian scene. We can get our Indians right from the reservoir.'

The film did just as well as Sam thought a movie featuring a big Broadway star should do. He followed it with another Cantor winner, *The Kid from Spain*, which was most notable for the debut of another Broadway figure, Busby Berkeley. It was his first film work.

The success of that and *Whoopee* was mirrored by an even more triumphant Cantor triumph, *Palmy Days*, about shady fortune-tellers. Plainly, Eddie was Goldwyn's golden boy. When Cantor starred in *Roman Scandals* for him, he was the happiest man in Hollywood. This story about a young man (Cantor) who dreams he is in ancient Rome became the most successful comedy of 1933.

Cantor was considered to be Al Jolson's main rival and in the 1930s, when Jolson's star seemed to be fading, he was bigger than ever. *Banjo Eyes* was the title of another Cantor-Goldwyn movie and one look at the star confirmed that the title also applied to Cantor himself. He would dance, moving his eyes in rhythm with the music, clapping his hands at the same time. Like Jolson, he was happy in blackface. Unlike Jolson, he usually wore a straw hat. He rolled his eyes at the girls who always accompanied him and, for their part, they always laughed in the right places – as did the people who had paid to see his films in record numbers.

Cantor was the father of five daughters and was, by all contemporary reports, a perfect husband – a title that Sam Goldwyn would have dearly loved to have for himself. He was now married to a woman with whom – he told everyone who would listen – he had fallen madly in love. She was much younger than he – and of a different religion. He met Frances Howard at a housewarming party and she appeared to answer all his needs: she was young and she was an actress, currently playing a girl about town in the Broadway play, *The Best People*. She was also 21, pretty and the kind of woman he could take to the various occasions when a film magnate needed to be able to show off. From the moment of that first meeting, at which he cut into a foxtrot to dance with her, he was as sure that she was for him as he had once been that he was going to make a fortune out of Vilma Banky.

They had a son, whom they called 'Sammy' – a demonstration that Sam's Jewish days were behind him since Ashkenazi Jews do not name their offspring after living people. Other demonstrations would follow – like his agreement that Sammy would be brought up as a good Catholic.

Sam's mother had died by then. She would never have approved the match. It had been clear when Sam visited her in Europe that their two worlds were growing further and further apart, although he did his best to speak to her lovingly – in Yiddish.

Even Frances learned to speak that language. Or at least, to use it when she thought the occasion demanded, which was generally when they were fighting. She only needed one (Yiddish) word to make her point. '*Shveig*, Shmuel,' she would call – 'Be quiet.'

Goldwynisms

There were any number of Goldwyn employees who would have wished that Sam kept quiet more often. The truth was that he would have been happier at times if he were taken a lot more seriously. He was becoming the butt of Hollywood jokes. Eventually, he would see the value of those gags, but for a time they were somewhat embarrassing.

Sometimes, they were just examples of his search for perfection. That search was the reason why it so often seemed that money was no object. One film idea, his team advised, was 'too caustic'. 'To hell with the cost,' said Sam. 'If it's a sound story, we'll make a film of it.'

That was never a bad philosophy. When in 1938, he produced *The Goldwyn Follies* – Sam's Hollywood version of what Mr Ziegfeld was doing on Broadway – his cast was strong enough to have had people lining up for months outside the New Amsterdam Theater to see a live show. There was Vera Zorina, the Ritz Brothers and Adolphe Menjou. But to really underline just how perfect this was going to be, he commissioned the music for the movie from the Gershwins – George and Ira. They had never been better. The score included *Love Walked In* and *Love is Here to Stay*, the very last songs that George was to write. He died while the *Follies* was on the floor of Sam's studio on Formosa Avenue.

The film was a big success, despite Goldwyn's continuing search for perfection. In one scene in the movie, the Goldwyn Girls, his contribution to the cause of American womanhood, were supposed to dance around a fountain of peppermint ice cream. He had been told that the only thing that could look like ice cream was . . . ice cream. So he went down on to the set to see how it was all turning out. He liked what he saw – until he put his finger into the spouting stream. 'Stop,' he called. 'This isn't peppermint ice cream. It's pistachio.'

All credit to him, Sam was the first to admit that he made mistakes – like turning down the chance of making *The Wizard of Oz*.

He also made mistakes over actors that he later regretted. He thought that Clark Gable would never make it because of the size of his ears. He didn't even think that Greta Garbo had much to offer. How could she amount to anything, a woman who, when invited to dine at the home of the most famous producer in Hollywood (which is how Sam saw himself), spends the whole evening in the kitchen talking to his Swedish cook?

Sam himself spent whole nights thinking about movie ideas. Like the time he rang up one of his writers with a query. It was 2.30 in the morning and if the man had things other than sleep on his mind as he lay in bed, talking to Sam Goldwyn about a script problem which could be dealt with six or seven hours later, certainly wasn't one of them.

'Sam,' said the writer, 'do you know what time it is?'

'Just a minute,' Goldwyn responded – and tapped his sleeping wife on her back. 'Frances,' he whispered, 'Bob wants to know what time it is.' 'Bob' was Robert Sherwood, who would later write one of Sam's most successful movies, *The Best Years of Our Lives*.

It would be a pity if Samuel Goldwyn was to be known only for the funny things he did or said but as the writer Melville Shavelson put it to me: 'He was a shark in a sea of whales.' Yet, because he respected his writers, those wordsmiths respected him. 'He always thought he was speaking for America – which was perhaps unfortunate because he didn't speak very well and that was why he tried to avoid public appearances where possible.'

He wanted to know all the details he could find out about his films. Like the time there was a story conference going on and the subject at hand was the name of a leading character. He was going to be called 'Bob'. 'No, no, no,' said Sam. 'Every Tom, Dick and Harry is called Bob.'

Such statements became known as Goldwynisms. They have entered the movie culture to such an extent that the word has come to replace 'malapropism' in the modern lexicon.

With statements like this it is hardly surprising: 'Do you expect me to put my head in a moose?' On the other hand, he was a firm believer in the mantra: 'You've got to take the bull between your teeth.' Especially when things looked bad. That is when he would say he was 'standing on an abscess'.

He declined to consider writing an autobiography. 'I can't do that,' he declared. 'Not until long after I'm dead.'

He also, much more memorably, declared: 'An oral contract isn't worth the paper it's written on.' Or even better, 'Anyone who goes to a psychiatrist should have his head examined.' Then he complained about members of his staff giving him as much trouble as was received by 'Mussolini in Utopia'.

What is probably the best known Goldwynism of them all has been copied by countless jokers over the years: 'Include me out.' The son of another mogul, Jack Warner Jr told me he was present on the occasion when Sam made that seminal statement. 'It was at a meeting of producers – the Hays Office or, as it was officially known, the Motion Picture Producers and Distributors of America – and he got into a row with my father. He said: "The Warner Brothers are just pissing in the wind. So include me out."'

That one went hand in hand with 'I'll answer you in two words – impossible.' Yes, they appear to be Sam's words, although it is true that a gaggle of writers say they were encouraged by Goldwyn's publicity department to invent new Goldwynisms. One of those who did so was Melville Shavelson. 'I made up, "Everything he says, you can take with a dose of salts".'

What he seems to have said himself was 'the publicity for this picture is sweeping the country like wildflowers' – which demonstrated a certain satisfaction with the way his PR people did their work.

It would be a shame, though, to think of those people as merely part of a publicity machine. There would be far less to talk about were it not for those phrases, which have certainly gone down in history. For, as Sam also said, 'We've all passed a lot of water since those days.'

The water must have flowed down the cheeks of a British stately home owner during World War Two, when Sam went to London to advise General Eisenhower on the use of film in wartime.

They went round the house's stately gardens. Sam admired the roaming animals, loved the flowers, but was a little put out by the object standing in the middle of a lawn. 'What's that?' he asked the peer.

'That, Mr Goldwyn,' his host replied, 'is a sundial.'

'And what does it do?' Sam pressed.

The man wondered about explaining such an everyday object as a sundial, but he tried his best.

'You see, Mr Goldwyn,' he said, 'when the sun moves, it casts a shadow and as it does, you tell the time.'

'My goodness,' said Goldwyn. 'Whatever will they think of next!'

What Sam thought of next was always the new film he had in the works. But this time, he was also anxious to enhance the relationship between Britain and his own adopted country. 'To those in Great Britain who argue against the importation of Hollywood talent,' he warned, 'I would say, you are short-sighted. They don't take jobs; they make jobs. The sooner we forget the idea of British stars or American stars, the better we will be. I don't like this idea of Britain and America. I resent it. I think after this war, we should live together.'

Winston Churchill loved to hear that and immediately rushed off a telegram to President Roosevelt.

In another speech at Balliol College, Oxford, he nailed his colours even more firmly to the US-GB mast. 'For years,' he declared, 'I've been known for saying, "include me out", but today I'm giving it up for ever. From now on, let me say, "Oxford and Balliol include me in." Understanding alone can save our world from future wars. Only information and learning can create that necessary understanding. The newspapers, films and radio of Great Britain and the United States of America have done an outstanding job in giving our free peoples truthful information. Germany burned the books and, as a result, she herself is now burning.'

On his behalf, a ghostwriter wrote an article for *The New York Times Magazine* called 'The Future Challenge of the Movies', in which he stressed what he considered to be the picture-makers' responsibilities. 'There will be a better place,' he wrote, 'if the soldiers who come back understand the European viewpoint as well as the American.'

When the war in Europe ended, the moguls were shown around the death camps by Eisenhower, who chose that occasion to thank the film industry for all it had 'contributed to our successful war effort'.

'Morale,' he said, 'is as important on the fighting front as it is back home and wherever people have worked for our victory. The films for which you gentlemen have been responsible have been of more help than you can possibly imagine. Your contributions to the production of training films were also a major factor in rapidly turning our peacetime citizens into skilled soldiers, sailors and airmen able to successfully meet and conquer Hitler's forces. The film medium has preserved the great events in our struggle for freedom just now concluded – and by seeing them again on the screen in the future, perhaps we may learn from the past and never again have to experience the great tragedy of war. I hope you profit from the too-brief time you will be here with us. I have issued orders you are to see whatever you wish.'

The Boss

Goldwyn gave plenty of orders to his staff – particularly his directors. William Wyler wasn't too keen about that. Merle Oberon recalled Goldwyn's reaction to his employee's disobedience, as he saw it. 'He said, "I'm going to make him eat apple pie."'

Going to see where things happen was always part of a film industry's boss brief; to see the sites of where the action was. In peacetime, that was going to be as important for Sam as it had been for him and his competitors in war. Michael Kidd, who choreographed *Guys and Dolls*, which, as we shall see, was one of Goldwyn's most successful movies – if a flawed product – told me about going on location with Sam.

It was all part of Sam's search for perfection. The Frank Loesser-scored musical was based on Damon Runyon's Broadway characters, not the actors who worked along the 'Great White Way', but the gamblers and other inhabitants who made their living by activities not necessarily approved of by the dolls who ran the Save-A-Soul Mission, the ones who wore uniforms suspiciously like those of the Salvation Army.

Sam wanted to see what Broadway and those characters were really like. During their hike past the theatres and unsavoury shops and pushcarts, Sam said he felt hungry. 'Michael,' he said, 'you know what I fancy? Jewish food. Is there anywhere round here that I could get a good Jewish meal?'

Kidd suggested Lindy's, an establishment much favoured by the citizens of Broadway, to quote Runyan (who in his stories dubbed it 'Mindy's' for fear of giving free advertising to the providers of the cheesecake which would feature so much in his stories, to say nothing of in the coming movie).

'Can I get a good Jewish meal there?' Goldwyn pressed, and then added for good measure: 'You know, at heart I'm very much a Jew.' And as he talked, he was positively salivating. He talked about his mother's cooking in Warsaw – *der heim* [that home] – and revealed all the Jewish dishes he craved constantly and were certainly not on Frances's menus, which she handed to their cook.

He loved, he said, gefilte fish. And then there was chicken soup – particularly with kneidlach and kreplach.

As the two men walked into Lindy's, the scene was set. The head waiter recognised Sam immediately. 'Ah, Mr Goldwyn,' he said. 'Welcome to Lindy's.' There was no doubt that the mogul was going to be well treated in this restaurant. There would be no fear of Sam asking what the fly was doing in his soup and the waiter replying: 'At first glance, I'd say the backstroke'. (That joke featured on Lindy's tablemats.)

Sam loved the scene. As he looked at the fawning waiter, he asked: 'What's the special today?'

'Irish stew,' cut in the maitre d'.

'Good,' said Sam. 'I'll have it.'

The truth was that when he decided what he wanted, there was nothing that was going to deflect him from what he had determined to do.

Like many people with certain characteristics that made people laugh, he enjoyed meeting others with similar idiosyncrasies. Like the Russian-born composer Dmitri Tiomkin who spoke with all the enthusiasm – and joy – of a tsarist officer being served a particularly tasty bowl of borscht. He reported: 'I was engaged at Goldwyn studio and finally they told me I must meet Sam Goldwyn. Can you imagine my great joy and excitement to meet this great man? So I put [sic] my best suit, went to office and saw Mr Goldwyn.'

'How is your accommodation?' Goldwyn asked him.

'Fine, Mr Goldwyn,' he answered.

'Tell me, and how is secretary?'

'Fine, Mr Goldwyn, fine.'

Goldwyn then bowed at him and he bowed at Goldwyn and left. The next day, he was invited again into the Presence. Again, 'How do you feel? How was the accommodation? How is office? How is secretary?' Again, bows and again Tiomkin left. A third time he was asked and for a third time he answered the call. Was he now going to ask him to do some extra work on a movie? Was the composer of *High Noon* going to be asked how a Russian-born composer could write for Westerns? He dared to ask a Goldwyn executive the question that was beginning to worry him. 'I am sure he heard me to speak and wonders how I can do it. Why you say he is a tough? He is charming man.' The executive told him to relax. As Tiomkin told it, the man said: 'No, he just like to hear you to speak English.'

Frances wasn't all that keen on the way Sam himself spoke English. But she liked him to think he was boss – especially when she made decisions which she convinced him were his own plans. Others frequently suffered from the Sam-Frances relationship, not least of all the couple's son, Sammy. He was sent to the Black-Foxe Military Institute. Frances thought that was just what people in the social stratum she believed was theirs should do. Sam himself believed it was proof that he had arrived as an American. The one person they never consulted was Sammy himself, who hated the place. He probably also hated the fact that he was taken to the academy each day by his father's chauffeur driving the family Rolls Royce. Sam explained the reason for that: the Lindbergh baby had just been kidnapped and murdered and he was taking no chances with his own son.

Sam didn't often argue with Frances, however. He thought she was beautiful – and particularly loved the look of her hands. 'Yes,' he told another producer, 'they are so beautiful, I'm going to have a bust made of them.'

He always wanted to have what he fancied – in films every bit as much as in food. In 1935, he agreed with William Wyler that Lillian Hellman's new play *The Children's Hour* would make a good film. The only trouble was that those guardians of Hollywood morality, the Hays Office, said that they needed a new title and the little matter of a new story. It was set in a girls' school and involved a love affair between two women. That had to go.

'You can't make this picture,' he was advised. 'It's about lesbians.'

'All right,' said Sam, 'we'll make them Ukrainians.' He was quite serious. And so was the resultant picture starring Merle Oberon, Miriam Hopkins and Joel McCrea, which ended up as being the tale of the two women loving the same man.

Solving that problem was no more than what Harold Macmillan, the British Prime Minister of the late 1950s and early 1960s would describe as a 'little local difficulty'. There were others that Sam Goldwyn regarded as a lot more serious.

He once rang Louis B. Mayer, a man with whom he was on anything but friendly terms. 'You and I are in terrible trouble,' he told him. 'What's the matter?' asked Mayer convinced that some calamity was about to hit the movie industry, since Sam frequently had an 'in' on new developments before his competitors had heard anything. For Sam to share his problems was remarkable. 'It's a serious problem,' said Goldwyn. 'You've got Clark Gable and I want him.'

The really big success of the Sam Goldwyn Company had been the 1945 movie, *The Best Years of Our Lives* – a title that took a great deal of time to see the light of day. But it was a brilliant success and probably would have been so, no matter what they called it. Had it been made by Warner Bros., it would have surprised nobody. It was straight out of contemporary America, dealing with the kind of problems that homes all over the country were to experience.

There had been literally dozens of movies about the war, but this one directed by Goldwyn's still most prestigious director, William Wyler – a man with whom Sam was still constantly in legal battles – dealt with a problem that the Army itself had been considering as a top priority: what happens when the troops come home?

It was straight up the then 44-year-old director's street. He might well have been suffering from worries about the future himself. He had gone into an Army Air Force uniform, as a lieutenant colonel, making films for servicemen, and had travelled on the floor of a bomber to make the documentary *Memphis Belle*. The Flying Fortress was on its 25th and last bombing mission over Germany, which Wyler filmed the only way he knew how – by actually flying with the plane's crew. The aircraft was so noisy and the only way the director (who held the camera, too) could do his work was by lying on the floor, where the noise was loudest of all. He got his film – and became profoundly deaf as a result. It didn't stop him working on commercial pictures after that, however. And *The Best Years of Our Lives* would serve as his crowning glory – even though Sam would want to take all the credit for himself.

The writer Dan Taradash, who would later write the screenplay for Columbia's epic, *From Here To Eternity*, had already been deputed by the forces' film division, working under the control of a certain Major Ronald Reagan, to make movies for the troops, stressing that things might not be as wonderful as they think when the men finally get out of uniform. There would be difficult moments with wives who had lived independent lives in the past four years (which is putting it politely in certain cases). There could be children they had never seen before, some of them not their own. *The Best Years of Our Lives*, based on a novel in verse by MacKinlay Kantor, called *Glory For Me*, with a screenplay by Robert Sherwood, told the story through the lives of a group of returning soldiers from the same town, who fly home in the same aircraft. Fredric March played the middle-aged bank manager who returns to what seemingly was the perfect rose-cottage home, with the perfect rose-complexioned wife. She was played by Myrna Loy, who was probably wearing the perfect rose-patterned pinafore when she wasn't on screen. Teresa Wright, as their daughter, completed the picture of wholesome Americanism. So all was lovely in their household. In fact, March discovers, too lovely. They seem to have managed their lives perfectly well without him. That was a revelation he had not expected.

Dana Andrews played the former soda jerk who had married the girl played by Virginia Mayo, who proves to be not quite the example of perfect womanhood the Andrews character had imagined. Mayo was a Goldwyn Girl, who thought she never needed drama lessons. Sam believed otherwise. 'Goldwyn always seemed to be interested in making me a star,' she told me shortly before her death. 'It was his perception of me and why, he told me, he was going to keep sending me off to dramatic coaches. He was constantly on my neck. He'd ring me and say, "I want you to come in. I've got a new coach for you." It was a bee in his bonnet and once he had one of those bees it was difficult to get it to go away. I was a very eager student and didn't need all that. But he would say, "Look, you were very good in that." He gave me the same coach who had been teaching Ingrid Bergman, so I guess that was a compliment.'

There was also a cameo role, as a bartender, by Hoagy Carmichael, whom Sam insisted on calling 'Hugo Carmichael'.

But the real surprise of the picture was Howard Russell, who played Homer, the sailor – a sailor with two hooks instead of hands, which he had lost in battle. His story was about how his family, who had never seen him with such catastrophic wounds, had to learn to adapt to his strange affliction. He wasn't an actor, but a real sailor who really had lost both hands. His performance was so outstanding that he won two Oscars for his role. It was the only time this had happened, two Academy Awards for the same role in the same picture. One was for best supporting actor, the other 'for bringing hope and courage to his fellow veterans through his appearance in *The Best Years of Our Lives*'. Altogether there were eight statuettes for the movie – more than any other in Sam's career.

Goldwyn would have liked to take every one of those bronze figures for himself. As Wyler said, 'That son of a bitch. He would have liked the credits to read, "Sam Goldwyn presents Sam Goldwyn in a picture called Sam Goldwyn, produced by Sam Goldwyn, directed by Sam Goldwyn, written by Sam Goldwyn."' Dana Andrews said he thought that producer and director had had a row over billing. 'He was so upset, he sent everybody home for the day.' But Sam tried to use his charm with Wyler, if not always in the most charming way. He once introduced him to a visitor to the studio: 'He's a son of a bitch, isn't he? But he's my son of a bitch.'

The director Henry Koster gave this explanation about the way Goldwyn thought: 'He always wanted the best. He wanted the best writer, so it had to be Robert Sherwood. He wanted the best director, which is why he used William Wyler. He wanted the best actors, so it was Cary Grant, David Niven and Loretta Young [who later appeared in another Goldwyn film, *The Bishop's Wife*]. If he could get someone better, he would fire the one he had and start all over again.'

Dana Andrews put it simply: 'He was the most indefatigable man who would never settle for second best.'

Even without that much kudos Goldwyn was like a puppy with two tails wagging simultaneously when he attended the 1946 Academy Award presentation at the massive Shrine Auditorium in Los Angeles. No matter how much money his films had taken, Oscars for best movie had always eluded him. Bob Hope who had failed to get Awards for his work in specific pictures (although there were to be two special Oscars for him) described the night of the ceremony as 'Passover in my house' – which would have been too Jewish for Sam. For him, in 1946, it was pure Christmas.

Sam was ecstatic. The critical acclaim *The Best Years of Our Lives* received was more important than the money it took at the box office. As Sam said, only half seriously, 'I don't care if it doesn't take a nickel – just so long as it is seen by every man, woman and child in America.'

He went on an interview spree to publicise the film, in addition to one of the biggest press campaigns to come out of Hollywood. Possibly with the thought in mind that they had had something in common, Goldwyn was booked on to the Bob Hope radio show. He was told that Hope would ask him, 'How's business Sam?' and he would reply, 'Bob we're having the best year of our lives.' Which wouldn't have needed any of Hope's famous ad-libbing qualities. However, he had a quip all ready – on the lines of, 'to coin a film title'. But Sam was having too good a time to worry about a script. He answered the question in his own way: 'Bob, things have never been better.' Collapse of free publicity opportunity.

And also collapse of Willy Wyler's relationship with Sam Goldwyn, with whom he had one of his by now celebrated rows. These had begun when Wyler made the archetype movie about life on the seamy side of New York, *Dead End*, which featured the Dead End Kids, led by Leo Gorcey, who always wore a flat cap back to front, and whose group eventually became known as the Bowery Boys. It also starred Sylvia Sidney, who would not have been Sam's choice for a film lead (she was Jewish and, as always, he worried about the problems Jewish actors might bring in parts of America where the kind was unknown). But she had done incredibly well six years earlier in *Street Scene*, another film that demonstrated just how seamy the seamy side of New York could be. So he accepted the idea of casting her. It was a good move. She was a superb actress, who used all her talents in the role.

'We had nine murders in that film,' said Rouben Mamoulian, the director, 'yet I didn't show even one of them. It was not necessary. Even the gangsters liked it. Afterwards, a man came up to me in a restaurant and said, "My brother loved the film." I said thank you, but I didn't know who the hell he was. Then I was told. He was the brother of Al Capone.' Such was the power of a Goldwyn film – and a Goldwyn director.

But, in production, Sam was confused. He had visited the set and was appalled by what he saw. The scene he happened on was centred on the slums of Manhattan – complete with a terrible mess of broken bottles, garbage and assorted rubbish. 'It's so dirty,' Goldwyn exclaimed: 'Clean it up.' He could not be persuaded that this was entirely appropriate for the 'dead end' of humanity being featured in the movie, so cleaned up it was – at least slightly.

The rows Wyler experienced were suffered by most of the people working for Sam. Almost everyone really did have those confrontations, it seems, although Goldwyn preferred to ignore the effect they might have on his reputation in the film capital. Melville Shavelson told me about the movie party when Goldwyn was delighting at how popular he thought he was. The writer Don Hartman was at that party and Sam put his arms around him. 'Don, I know you're suing me, but don't. There's no reason for us not to be friends. No one else ever sues me.'

'What do you mean, Sam?' Hartman asked him. 'Look. There's Billy Wilder over there – and he's suing you. And Theresa Wright, she's suing you. And see Ben Hecht, everybody knows he's suing you.'

Goldwyn was unfazed. 'OK,' he said. 'Present company excepted.'

Mind you, according to Shavelson, anyone choosing to sue Goldwyn was usually on to a safe thing. As he told me: 'Of course, we were always having rows over scripts and it was usually a pretty good bet to sue him – because he wouldn't go to court. So I was always resigning and he was always bringing me back.'

What Sam didn't like doing was firing people, Shavelson also told me. 'There was one director he had imported from England, whom he thought wasn't doing as well as he could. So he called him in to fire him. He looked him up and down and said: "That's a beautiful suit you're wearing. And those shoes, they're wonderful. I always admire people who are well-dressed. Goodbye." He never said a word about firing the man.'

He tried to find solace in the law about the law. As he pointed out: 'There is, you know, a statue of limitation.'

George Choderov was not included in that suing list – although he might easily have been. The reason he was excused calling in the lawyers was that he decided to 'include himself out' from a Goldwyn project. Chodorov's friend, Irving Fein, told me about the meeting between writer and mogul. Goldwyn asked him to act as a script doctor for a film called *Woman Chases Man*, directed by John Blystone. 'George said, "Sam. There's nothing you can do with this turkey," and refused to have anything to do with it. The film was made and it was terrible. Years later, they were talking about another picture and someone suggested that George should be brought in. "What?" said Sam. "Choderov was associated with one of my worst flops."'

Sam wasn't alone in having problems with a certain other star named Bette Davis. She and Warner Bros. were in a constant state of war. Sam didn't have enough to do with her to share in that particular conflict. But when she starred in another of Sam's big hits, the 1943 film, *The Little Foxes*, she was trouble all the way.

The picture received some of the most ecstatic press reviews of any of Sam's productions. In *The New York Times*, Bosley Crowther – or 'Crowtherley Bos' as Sam used to call him – described it as a movie that 'leaps to the front as the most bitingly-sinister picture of the year and as one of the most cruelly realistic character studies yet shown on the screen.'

The picture was directed by Wyler, who constantly complained about Goldwyn's interference. Another of the reasons for his unhappiness could have been Sam's insistence on calling the movie 'The Three Little

Foxes', which was almost as bad as turning *Wuthering Heights*, his 1939 Merle Oberon-Laurence Olivier triumph, into 'Withering Heights' (*Black Narcissus* to him was 'Black Neurosis').

Sam fell in love with Oberon, although there is no proof that he took her to his bed. And that was what he liked about her – she was no easy touch. As he once said: 'For this part, I want a lady, somebody's that's couth.'

His misuse of movie titles extended to those of stage shows. *West Side Story* was always 'West End Avenue'. He once said that he thought *Hello Dolly* should never have been produced. The film, he said, was indecent because it dealt with drugs. After a rather protracted discussion, Sam revealed that he was thinking not about *Hello Dolly* but *The Valley of the Dolls*. 'Yes, that's what I said,' he maintained, once more showing that in his eyes he could never be wrong, 'The Valley of the Hello Dollies.'

Sam held back on nothing while making *The Little Foxes* – including denying respect to those who thought they most deserved it. The director and the stars fought with him in a metaphorical boxing match in which Goldwyn determined he would never be the one to hit the canvas. But it would never be a question of money. The film was set on the Yorkshire moors. He wouldn't film it there, but he did the next best thing. A second unit was sent to Britain, but for the main scenes he contented himself with importing heather and other vegetation to the studio on Formosa Avenue.

Wuthering Heights was Wyler's work, too, and he felt considerably withered by the experience, even though he earned an Oscar nomination for the project (he didn't win; neither did the movie itself). A newspaperman once began an interview with Goldwyn by saying, 'When William Wyler made *Wuthering Heights*—' The producer interrupted by saying: 'I made *Withering Heights*. Wyler just directed it.'

As a demonstration of precisely how Goldwyn felt about his director, Wyler was not invited to the film's world premiere. People acclaimed the movie as a Very Important Picture. Mrs Eleanor Roosevelt did come to the premiere. Her son James had been appointed a vice-president of Goldwyn's operation – no one doubted it was more for the prestige of having the president's son on the roll than for any work he could do.

Sam took all the credit he thought was due. And always said it was his favourite picture. To him, it had both 'warmth and charmth'.

Why he couldn't be more generous remains today one of the most puzzling of all the unusual Goldwyn eccentricities. But then you just had to take him, as he might have said, though actually didn't, with a dose of salts.

Wyler told his biographer, Axel Madsen, 'With Goldwyn, I was always the hero. But much later, I was sometimes the bum. Then, after the preview, the hero. Then if the picture was a failure, I was the bum again.'

David Niven played what he considered to be the lowly role of Edgar in *Wuthering Heights* and at first refused to play it because it was such 'a terrible part'. But Goldwyn won after some syrupy words and a dose of suspension – both of which were calculated to get the actor back into the fold. That was Sam's usual way. So was his insistence on happy endings for all his movies, even at the cost of anything but a happy ending for his relationships. Which was why he insisted that *Wuthering Heights* should end with the two leading characters, Cathy (Oberon) and Heathcliff (Olivier) meeting up in heaven. 'I don't want the film to end with two corpses,' Goldwyn explained.

It seemed as if his relationship with Wyler, while continuing to be something of a roller-coaster ride, would go on for as long as they both lived. Wyler himself would say: 'I guess he believed I'd never leave him. He had a sort of father complex.' A father who believed he was spoiling his children.

'The trouble with these directors,' he said once, 'is that they always bite the hand that lays the golden egg.'

True, there are some fathers who never stop telling their sons what they have done for them. This father, the epitome of the perfectionist, complained to Wyler about the time he took to make his pictures – and criticised the amount of film he used up in that time.

But the moment did come when they parted – and neither was sorry to end the relationship.

It could be argued – which, of course, was Sam's favourite occupation – that employing Wyler and people like him was his greatest quality. He knew, and always knew, that he could be only as good as the people who worked for him; the ones who put his films on the screen. Wyler and Mamoulian were directors in classes of their own.

Sinclair Lewis was undoubtedly one of Sam's favourite writers, although whether Sam actually sat down to read any of his books is debatable. But he did know about his novel, *Arrowsmith*, about a doctor who cared more for his patients and medical science than he did for money.

The film of that book starred Ronald Colman. Choosing John Ford to direct was a more daunting prospect. Ford told the star's daughter, Juliet Benita Colman (for her memoir, *Ronald Colman: A Very Private Person*): 'When you work with Sam there are always problems if you allow them to worry you. He would come on to the set after I started work and I would sit down and order tea or something. He'd say: "Why aren't you shooting?" And I'd say: "Well, if I came into your office while you were working and watched *you* work, you'd be very much annoyed. This is my office and I am working here and I am not going to be rude and work while you, the president of a company, are here. Very bad manners!" He couldn't understand that, so we'd wait until he'd left, then we would resume shooting.'

Actually, Sam probably realised it completely. He may not have admitted it, but he usually believed due deference should be paid when it was due – and especially when that deference was due to himself.

In fact, he always liked people to think that his directors were unimportant. After all, it might give rise to their thinking less of what he himself did. As we have seen, William Wyler constantly suffered from that syndrome. Billy Wilder was another director who Sam thought the public did need not to know much about. As a writer, he would always be useful – but not too many people needed to know that either. There was the celebrated occasion when Wilder and his partner Charles Brackett were brought in by Goldwyn to 'doctor' a script with which Sam had been experiencing problems. The movie was *The Bishop's Wife*, starring Cary Grant, a picture scheduled to be a Royal Film Performance. The British film industry was not exactly delighted that the honour was going to Hollywood and not to a local product. Goldwyn couldn't understand what they were worried about. Granted it was made in America and the eponymous female star was Loretta Young, but David Niven who played the bishop was as British as Sam believed they came and Cary Grant had been born in Bristol.

But that wasn't all that there was to worry about. Niven didn't want to play the bishop. He fancied Grant's role as a mysterious angel instead. Once that was sorted out – with Sam winning, of course – he had to deal with the script and the 'script doctors'. He offered them $25,000 for the chore, which was remarkable for Sam who always maintained that he wouldn't 'sign a blanket cheque'.

The two writers spent a whole weekend going through the script and, by all accounts, were thoroughly enjoying themselves. When they delivered their work, Sam turned to the question of the money he owed them. Wilder was in a good mood. Before Sam could complete his sentence, the writer burst in. 'We've had so much fun with this,' he said, 'we have decided not to charge you anything.'

Sam needed no time to think about his response. 'Yes,' he said, 'I came to the same conclusion.'

Of course, as far as the public was concerned, it was the stars who made the biggest impact. Farley Granger and Lucille Ball had their first chances with Goldwyn, though there were others whom he would have liked to forget. Anna Sten headed that list. But when he smiled in the 1940s, it was Cooper, Colman, Niven and Banky who, along with Eddie Cantor, came to mind.

He also had a great deal of respect for Bob Hope, who seemed to epitomise all that was good in American humour. When Melville Shavelson, who had been one of Hope's first writers, succeeded in getting the comedian for the film he had just written, *The Princess and the Pirate*, Goldwyn was ecstatic. 'As always,' Shavelson told me, 'Sam went into every detail. He wanted to approve all the costumes. When [the actor] Walter Slezak, dressed in all his finery, came in to see Goldwyn, Sam looked him over and said, "Great! You look very periodical."'

He liked 'periodical' films. But within limits. As he once told a writer: 'Let's bring it up-to-date with some snappy nineteenth-century dialogue.'

On the other hand, getting him to make films like *The Princess and the Pirate* was never easy. Shavelson said: 'He really wanted to make very special films, but he also made comedy films – because he wanted to make money.'

The Princess and the Pirate was the second of two films that Hope made for Goldwyn. The first was *They Got Me Covered.* Sam was more sure than Bob about how he himself was covered. Sam made an announcement about the contract between the two at a film premiere. Bob later told me: 'I thought that was wonderful. We'd done a deal and I didn't know about it.' But Hope wouldn't let Sam get away with it. While the audience at the premiere were thundering their applause, Hope interrupted the producer with the historic words, 'Wait, Sam. We haven't done a deal yet. What I suggest is that we lie down right now and talk money.' Which is exactly what they did. They lay down on the stage and did a deal for $125,000 – for Hope.

It was a serious business. As Sam noted: 'Our comedies are not to be laughed at.' The trouble was getting to the point where both he and his writers as well as the directors and stars were ready to start filming.

Shavelson remembers: 'You'd talk to him about a project he dreamed up and say, "What do you want?" The answer would usually be "I don't know." All Sam did know was that he wanted it good and if it wasn't he'd tell you.' But the frustrating thing was that there was always a string of writers on every one of his projects. 'That was terrible because you never knew where you were with him. There were plenty of writers who because of this took his money and didn't do anything for it. They didn't respect his intelligence as much as he respected theirs – and there is no doubt that he respected writers more than did any of the other Hollywood bosses. '

There were always others – celebrities in their own world – who would help Sam maintain his definition of quality. Which was why he wasn't satisfied just to employ, on contract, the people he believed to be the best fashion designers in New York. There always had to be an additional factor: they had to be the best, yes, but also worthy of a bit of publicity for the Goldwyn outfit. With that thought in mind, he brought Coco Chanel from Paris to Hollywood – not to design for a specific film, but to advise on film fashions. And, he stressed, she would give the entire United Artists organisation the benefit of her advice. 'She will reorganise the dressmaking department of United Artists Studios and endeavour to anticipate fashions by six months to solve the eternal problem of keeping gowns up to date.'

That actually was a real problem: no art form so demonstrated the sweeping changes of fashion as the movies. Gowns and hats really were frequently out of date by the time films came out. What was actually in Sam's mind was having a chance of sneaking an advantage over his competitors. If he was paying Mme Chanel a huge amount of money – which he was, although he never disclosed how much – she would surely feel that she was in his debt in other ways – and the one way of repaying that debt would be by letting him in on a few secrets of the world of haute couture. If Parisian pigs could fly, that is. She no more gave him that lead on the future of the fashion industry than he would have revealed any secrets of the Goldwyn operation.

Partnerships Don't Work

The Goldwyn-United Artists arrangement remained in force until Sam bought all their assets in 1935. The company, nevertheless, continued to distribute his films.

And then, once the Hollywood community had digested the news, quite suddenly and unexpectedly, Goldwyn announced a deal with the only British movie mogul, Alexander Korda, to take even more control – by buying up all the UA shares owned by Mary Pickford, Douglas Fairbanks and Charlie Chaplin (the director of *Birth of a Nation*, D.W. Griffith was now out of the picture completely). It would cost him $10 million. The President of UA, Dr Amedeo Peter Giannini who, as head of the Bank of America, had helped Sam in his early days, confirmed the sale was going ahead.

But going ahead meant going nowhere. Seven months of publicity and plans for Sam once more being the undisputed head of a major studio (after years of proclaiming his happiness as an 'independent') led to an announcement that it was all off. Not because Sam was against having partners once more, it was claimed, but because they both said the UA directors were demanding a say in what the new outfit would be producing. However, before long, it became obvious that disagreements between Goldwyn and Korda were the real reason for the deal collapsing – which surprised nobody.

It turned out that Sam started bad-mouthing his erstwhile partner at a dinner given for the Prudential Assurance Company, which was helping with the finance for the merger – while Korda sat next to him, totally stunned.

'He started saying that Korda's pictures weren't worth a damn in America – right in front of the guy who was backing him and in Korda's presence, too,' David Rose, Goldwyn's business adviser, remembers. 'Korda got mad, turned the whole table of food over and broke that up. We were actually getting the papers drawn up. It took three days with lawyers to get the two together again.'

The story then was that Sam was going to be the head of a new UA-RKO empire – which would net Goldwyn $18 million. But then Sam thought about it again – it meant partners once more – although in 1940, Sam did a deal for his pictures to be distributed through RKO. For a time, however, it seemed as though he was going to be in partnership with yet another company – International Pictures. He would share his studio facilities with them – for posterity. But they only made three films on the Goldwyn lot, because they complained that they were continually being obstructed. They couldn't get their trucks on to the complex. They were unable to move sets. Sound equipment was remaining stationary because the way through was blocked by Goldwyn's own vehicles. Sam called a meeting of his executives in which he introduced all the International bosses. He apologised for the problems (itself a unique event) and promised that, in future, everything would be done on a 50-50 basis.

When his 'guests' left, he told his board: 'Everything I told you, I meant. I want this to be 50-50, like I said. But I want you to see that I get the best of it.'

That was another reason why partnerships wouldn't work for Sam, although he kept trying them. He revelled in the title of the only independent producer to have his own studio. He wanted the best out of everything that he touched. He was, like all his fellow producers, a believer in the American dream and an enemy of anything that he thought could turn it into a nightmare. For that reason, he frequently talked about how much he hated what he believed was going on in Russia and Communism in general. A writer came to him with an idea that he thought would give him a chance to demonstrate how bad the Russians were. 'I want to make a film about the Russian Secret Police,' he announced, 'the GOP.' [The GOP, the Grand Old Party, is an alternative name for the Republican Party.] What Sam meant was the KGB. During the war, he had joined other producers in making a film in praise of the Soviet Union. President Roosevelt had rung them all to ask them to do that. Warners made *Mission to Moscow* and MGM came up with *Song of Russia*. Sam's contribution should have had everything going for it. *The North Star* was about a Russian village facing the 1941 Nazi invasion and the cruelty of the occupation that followed. It starred Anne Baxter, Farley Granger, Dana Andrews and Erich von Stroheim, was written by Lillian Hellman and directed by Lewis Milestone, who had literally created a milestone with his World War I opus, *All Quiet on the Western Front*. But it wasn't quiet on the *North Star* front. The film was virtually laughed out of the critics' columns if not out of court. Lillian Hellman threatened to sue Sam for destroying her original book; the reviewers said it was terrible and Goldwyn himself decided he didn't want to talk about it. Helping Russia was a patriotic gesture on behalf of an ally. It didn't mean that he felt anything but distaste for the country's Communist regime.

But his hatred of Russia didn't mean he had a hatred of individual communists. Much more, he was concerned about those who sought – and for the most part succeeded – in operating a blacklist against people suspected of being communists in the film industry.

The success of any movie producer can be measured by his triumphs, not simply at the box office, but also by the way he ran his studio. He wasn't going to allow anyone to tell him how to make films – or who to employ. Which was why he stood out when most of the other moguls caved in to Congressman J. Parnell Thomas's House Un-American Activities Committee, HUAC. He refused to go along with what became known as the Waldorf Declaration – in which film producers meeting in conclave at the Waldorf Astoria Hotel in New York declared that they wouldn't employ anyone they believed to be Communists.

While the 'Declaration' was being released to the press, Sam made a statement of his own: 'As an American, I have been astounded and outraged at the manner in which the committee has permitted our industry to be vilified by gossip, innuendo and hearsay. I had hoped that a committee of Congress would be sufficiently aware of the traditions and background of American democracy so that it would not permit itself to be used as a sounding board for a smear campaign intended to destroy public confidence in the integrity of an industry which so many of us have spent the best years of our lives building up.' (The reference to Sam's film might or might not have been purely coincidental, but it brought additional attention to what he was saying – through the pen of George Slaff, his lawyer, who ghosted it for him.)

'The most un-American activity,' he went on, 'which I have observed in connection with the hearings has been the activity of the committee itself. The purpose of these hearings seems to have been to try to dictate and control what goes on the screens of America. I resent and abhor censorship of thought. I assure you that as long as I live, no one will ever be able to dictate what I put on the screen so long as I continue to honour and obey the laws of our country.' They were brave words, which Sam deeply intended to keep, but a metaphorical line of writers standing outside his door looking for work could only be a drop in the Pacific Ocean. And he also had to be careful. The blacklist didn't only cover the people who producers were employing, but also the theatres that were showing their films. When Goldwyn met President Harry S. Truman, he told him that there had never been any Communism in any of his films and nor would there be any, but he wasn't going to allow any committee to tell him how to run his affairs. Had Sam decided to employ people he knew to be blacklisted, none of his movies would ever have been shown. He was still brave to have made his statement, a courage none of the others demonstrated in quite the same way.

But, then, Sam always let people know that he was unique – which is why he ran his business in a unique way. No other mogul used his own money to finance his operations, but Goldwyn did. No other mogul was quite so concerned with the way he ran his own house but Sam's, off Coldwater Canyon, was one of the most luxurious residences in Beverly Hills. He was also concerned about the way he dressed. He went to the studio wearing a suit that seemed to have been sprayed on him, it fitted so perfectly. It would also land him in trouble.

Sam didn't want to disturb the line of the suit and he never carried cash. For the same reason that he didn't want to spoil his appearance, he was careful to take exercise. He did a lot of walking and was always equipped for it with a good pair of shoes. He employed a chauffeur to drive him around in his Rolls-Royce, but only for part of the journey, and would walk some of the way back from the studio. One balmy sunny day, as usual, he ordered his driver to stop on the way, so that he could continue the trail on foot. It was on this trip that he passed a grocery store. Outside was a box of shiny red apples. Without thinking, he took one and started eating it. The proprietor of the store, however, thought that this late middle-aged man was stealing one of his apples. 'That'll be ten cents,' he told him. Not an easy thing to be heard by a man who dealt in millions of dollars – and never carried money in his immaculately sewn pockets. It took some persuading that the apparent thief was Samuel Goldwyn, film producer. The money followed the following day – with an invitation to Sam's next movie premiere.

Strolls were part of his business life, too. As Melville Shavelson said: 'If you wanted to talk to Sam, you had to walk with him. We had to take constitutionals to get anything talked through.'

But they did talk a lot in his private office – which he occasionally, only occasionally, looked over with the same careful eye he used on film sets. In those days before electronic storage, he was appalled by the amount of paperwork piling up in the room. 'We have to get rid of all this,' he ordered his secretary. 'But make a copy first.'

When he was in that office, he wanted nothing to disturb his train of thought – which was why, once, he grew furious at the sound of fire-engine sirens getting louder and louder. 'Ring the fire station and tell them to keep the noise down,' he shouted to the same hapless secretary.

As the musician Johnny Green, who witnessed the scene, told me, it was a moment to cherish. 'You can't go a half hour without hearing sirens so close to Santa Monica Boulevard,' he said. 'So no one took much notice of these, except that they got closer. Sirens do get closer and then they go away. Only, this time, they didn't go away. Before long, one realised that they were so close, they were almost in Goldwyn's office.

And for good reason. Now you could see bellowing black smoke covering the windows, cutting out the light and even it seemed, coming through the Venetian blind.

'At that point, someone shouted, "Sam, the fire's here. It's coming from the sound stage below." His studio's burning down. Sam opens up the Venetian blind, opens the window and gives a holler to the people running below. "Go back to your desk. I do not pay you to run." The studio was burning down, but all he could think of was that they weren't at their desks.'

Before he could get an answer, he saw a fireman at the window – the fire had reached an adjoining room.

Yes, it was easy to laugh at Sam Goldwyn, but it was just as easy to find reasons to praise him. In 1950, *Daily Variety* voted him the best movie producer in America. Meanwhile, the *Saturday Review* described him as Hollywood's 'loyal opposition', a term they borrowed from the British parliament. But he was not happy for their reasoning in granting him that title. The magazine said there should be greater care taken about the kind of films exported and that Washington should take a hand. Sam thought that government should mind its own business.

'A distorted picture of American life might well be any one aspect of it taken alone,' he declared. 'Our way of life cannot be portrayed if one shows only sweetness and light, as if one would present America only as a haven for gangsters. This is America. We have all types here!'

And all types included a man who could still make flops as well as hits. *The Edge of Doom* in 1950 was a title that seemed dangerously close to the truth. The film was shot and Goldwyn hated it. He brought in Charles Brackett and Ben Hecht to try to effect some kind of magic recovery from that doom. The two men, after all, had once been dubbed 'geniuses' by Sam. But even they had to give up. Goldwyn was furious: 'This is a simple story about a boy who wants a fine funeral for his mother, so he kills a priest,' he said. Melville Shavelson remembered that conversation: 'Sam thought about what he had just said and then added: "Let's not spend another cent."'

Danny Kaye

When Al Jolson died in 1950, a critic wondered who would be the next claimant to his throne as the World's Greatest Entertainer. He then added: 'I can think of only one name – Danny Kaye.'

Kaye was the singer, dancer, comedian who had wowed audiences all over the world. For two weeks, outside the London Palladium, ticket hunters had queued three deep and twice around the block in the hope of getting seats for what all the papers had described as a sensation.

The King and Queen came to a performance at the recommendation of their daughter, Princess Margaret, who was in the third row of the stalls every night. Kaye was the big star of the era – and, arguably, it was Sam Goldwyn who had made him so. Not that he was unknown before Sam entered the picture. The Brooklyn-born performer had started as a 'toomler', the mainstay of the Catskill Mountains Borscht Belt nursery of budding entertainers. His job was to 'start a tumult' – or, in the parlance of the Yiddish-speaking hotel owners – 'get toomling' when the weather was so bad that customers were ready to check out. He caught them on the hop, singing songs, some of which had been composed by his wife, Sylvia Fine, daughter of his neighbourhood dentist.

Kaye's big break came when he was discovered by the proprietor of the Martinique nightclub in New York, who gave him a job. He was a thrilling success. So much so, that he was featured with Gertrude Lawrence in the Kurt Weil show *Lady in the Dark*, with some hilarious moments, trying to prevent the big star upstaging him. In the middle of his big scene, he had noticed that Ms Lawrence was capturing the audience's attention fiddling with a scarf, while sitting on a swing. So when she had her main number, he was in the background playfully making faces. It was the best part of the evening.

His wartime Broadway show, *Let's Face It*, about the problems of a young soldier, was an instant hit and made into a film – although with Bob Hope in the starring role.

It was Sam who gave Danny Kaye his own start in movies – and his first international audience. 'The thing about Sam,' he once said, 'was that he was an incredibly proud and resourceful man, a loner in an age of Warner Bros., MGM and RKO. I think he took more chances with more people than anyone I ever knew.'

It could be said that Mrs Kaye took a few chances with him, too. Indeed, Danny called himself a 'wife-made man; she has a wonderful head on my shoulders'. He had good reason to say that, since she wrote almost all his early songs, and the numbers that allowed him to twist his tongue with the same dexterity with which he made his hands dance. Much of what she produced were works of genius. Numbers like *Anatole of Paris* and *Pavlova* were unique both in their style and the way Danny sang them.

In 1944, when World War II was on the way to being won, Sam bought the script for a film called *Up in Arms*, a picture with several similarities to *Let's Face It*. It was another army story – about a hypochondriac recruit. Having Danny, an unknown outside of New York, in the starring role was going to be a risk.

Frances Goldwyn, who more and more was acting as Sam's adviser – whether he liked it or not – raised another objection, which might have said more about her than about Danny. She said he had too big a nose. In other words – which she used, too – he seemed too Jewish. To be truthful, Sam worried about that himself. It wasn't that young Jewish boys weren't being drafted. They certainly were and a lot of them were being killed. Some were hypochondriacs, too. But in the world outside of New York or Los Angeles, would the country people, who also paid ten cents to buy a cinema ticket, like him?

Sam raised the question of Danny's nose. Perhaps he ought to have it changed? Kaye said that perhaps he ought not. So Goldwyn, who fancied Danny as the new Eddie Cantor – the days of Banjo Eyes as a film star were plainly over, the mogul decided, even though he still had a hit radio programme – agreed to leave it alone. He wanted a new face and he was convinced Danny's was the one he needed. But that face, he had to accept, was not really right. Then he had a brainwave: Danny's red hair didn't look good in Technicolor. How about making him blond? Danny said he had no objections, and, as a result, audiences all over the world were talking about the blond kid with a big nose. He was a sensation and there were among those people who saw him in the film some who would swear they had never laughed so much watching a movie.

Again, it was Sylvia who helped him along the way. For Danny, she recreated a superb 'scat' number that had wowed them in *Let's Face It*, 'Melody in 4-F' – 4-F meant medically unfit to be admitted into the forces and the one in which the Kaye character believed he should be classified. So in three minutes in that number, she describes how he was actually enlisted, followed by all the humiliations this sick fellow had to experience with his medical examinations before being declared A-1 and fit for duty.

There was also the performance, which for a time became virtually his signature routine, 'Manic Depressive Pictures Present', also known as 'The Lobby Number', in which he stood on the staircase of a super picture theatre and parodied the then regular situation of people going into a cinema for a continuous performance halfway through the main feature. 'This is a picture that begins in the middle for the benefit of the people who came in . . . in the middle.'

Sam followed *Up in Arms* with the much better *Wonder Man*, in which Danny played identical twins – one a cabaret entertainer (the opportunity for more Sylvia written routines); the other a brilliant bookworm, so clever that he was able to write with both hands simultaneously. The link between the two brothers was the murder of a nightclub entertainer and the presence of his brother bringing confusion to the killers (the chance for Danny to get involved in grand opera – passing messages to the DA sitting in a box, via his own 'libretto' to an aria, 'Me Scaredo, Me Fraido'). At his side during much of the film was Virginia Mayo, who before long found herself his regular screen mate. She was with him in his next Goldwyn film, *The Secret Life of Walter Mitty*, which was by far his best movie. This was based on the James Thurber story of the same name – about a fantasist who imagined himself as a surgeon (which Danny liked to do in real life), an RAF air ace, a sea captain and an orchestra conductor (which in reality he 'played' at being, too).

The film featured Danny's famous number, 'Anatole of Paris', written by Sylvia, as well as 'The Little Fiddle', which gave him a great opportunity for using an accent that, seemingly, only he could master – which was his gift.

Danny was supposedly the only man who could make Sam laugh. On one occasion they spoke on the telephone. Danny was in Manhattan, Sam in Beverly Hills. 'I'm making the fish face now, Sam,' he told him. Goldwyn fell out of his chair, laughing. 'Sam had instinctively good taste,' Kaye once told me. 'He had immense courage. He'd walk on the set and ask: "Is this what I saw on paper?" He would be told, "More or less," to which he replied: "This is not how I wanted it. Would you please take it down and start again?"'

Eve Arden was one of the female stars of an earlier Kaye film, the 1946 *The Kid from Brooklyn* and saw that Goldwyn perfectionism at first hand: 'I had selected one of my own hats,' she recalled for my BBC radio programme. 'This hat was a creation and just right for the part. I came in the next morning and the hat was missing. I said, "Where is my beautiful hat?" and they said, "Mr Goldwyn has sent down another hat which Mrs Goldwyn had selected."

'I then sent back a note and said, "I positively will not wear that hat –

Mrs Goldwyn's face is not going to be on that screen in that hat and mine is." I never heard another thing about it.'

The Kid from Brooklyn was a title made to measure for Danny, even if the story wasn't. This was the film that Goldwyn had seen as the perfect demonstration of Kaye being the new Cantor. It was difficult to imagine Danny as a boxer, no less than Cantor's *The Kid from Spain* had featured anyone's idea of a bullfighter. However, since it was followed by *The Secret Life of Walter Mitty*, in 1947, *The Kid from Brooklyn* was easy to forget. A *Song is Born* in 1948 left a more unfortunate taste. It wasn't nearly as successful as *Mitty* and not anywhere as good. It was, in fact, a virtual carbon copy of Goldwyn's film *Ball of Fire*, made just seven years earlier, which had been written by Billy Wilder and Charles Brackett.

They had nothing to do with the second movie, perhaps as a result of meeting Sam on the set of the original production. He told them then, 'Listen boys, I will not make any publicity for any French wine, any French aperitif, what do you call it?' And then went on to demonstrate what he meant. 'It says here,' he said, looking at the script, '"After dinner how about a little Debussy?"' Wilder explained: 'He had confused Debussy with Dubonnet.'

Ball of Fire had starred Barbara Stanwyck as a showgirl who, in order to escape from a gang of crooks (where have we heard that before?), is given a home in their mansion by a group of professors involved in a mammoth work on the English language. She was a welcome guest – how else would they be able to get the low-down on what was hip? The most notable academic was played by Gary Cooper. It was all very reminiscent of the Snow White story.

A *Song is Born* was more than just reminiscent of *Ball of Fire*. This time, it was Virginia Mayo who was on hand to educate the professors, who now were writing an encyclopaedia of music – and it included Benny Goodman in his only acting role. She took them to all the nightclubs and jazz joints they could take – which was surprisingly many. Now, Danny was in the old Cooper role and probably should never have gone near it. Not only was the story totally interchangeable with the earlier Goldwyn film, it looked it (even though, unlike the original, the second picture was in Technicolor.) The professors seemed to be wearing the same tweeds, the house looked as if it hadn't even been redecorated.

It was after the completion of that film, the movie executive Jerome Pickman told me, that Danny went to see Sam to discuss the picture.

'Oh, Danny,' Goldwyn replied, 'it's doing wonderfully. It's the best picture I ever made.'

Danny responded with doubts. 'Sam,' he said, 'I was at the preview.'

Goldwyn wouldn't let him continue. 'Don't worry, Danny,' he said. 'We can fix it.'

Kaye came back to Goldwyn's lot after a couple of excursions, to Warner Bros. and Twentieth Century Fox, to make a movie that Sam had been planning for 20 years – the story of Hans Christian Andersen. A number of leads had been suggested over that time, other scripts had been submitted, considered and then turned down. Then, in 1952, Goldwyn offered the part of the Danish storyteller to Danny – much to the distaste of both the Danish ambassador and much of the Danish population, who saw their national treasure as a near god-like figure. For them, this was close to blasphemy.

It was Sam who defused the issue – admittedly, not a usual situation in which he would be involved. (People were beginning to ask what he was doing for aggravation.) The film would actually be called *Hans Christian Andersen*, but he made sure that the publicity for the movie –and a disclaimer in the opening credits – would stress that this was not a biography of Andersen, but a story based on Andersen's stories, a tale written by one of America's leading playwrights, Moss Hart: 'Once upon a time, there lived in Denmark a great storyteller named Hans Christian Andersen. This is not the story of his life, but a fairy tale about this great spinner of fairy tales.'

The film cost Sam $4 million, a huge amount for 1952. When it was completed, the Danish government were more than satisfied. They issued a statement in which they said the only problem that the people of Copenhagen or other parts of Andersen's homeland would have to deal with would be how to accommodate all the tourists who would flood into the country. They were proved right in spades.

Hans Christian Andersen featured the longest ballet interlude ever to be included in a film musical. Walter Scharf, the musical director, told me: 'Sam asked me what the longest-ever ballet in films had been. I checked and told him it was the one in *An American in Paris*. He said that this one had to be longer. So "The Mermaid Ballet" was made longer for the sake of the statistics.'

Originally, the principal ballerina was going to be Moira Shearer, who had become famous in her starring role in the movie *The Red Shoes*. She found Goldwyn too intimidating for his own good. Ms Shearer – wife of the British television personality, Ludovic Kennedy – told him she was pregnant and couldn't go on with the filming. It was up to Scharf to break the news to his boss, who became apoplectic. Before long, he had a replacement in the French prima ballerina Zizi Jeanmaire, who managed well enough.

As for Danny, this was not his usual cup of tea at all – but his songs, written by Frank Loesser, like 'Wonderful Copenhagen' and 'I'm Hans Christian Andersen' itself became huge hits. Most of them were based on an Andersen story, like 'The Ugly Duckling', 'Thumbelina' and 'Inchworm'. But it was 'The King's New Clothes' that best demonstrated how an Andersen story could be transplanted on to sheet music and, more importantly, on to shellac records spinning at 78 rpm, or the much newer vinyl 45s. Even today, it is regarded as a standard.

The film did better than any that Danny Kaye had ever experienced. The critics weren't so sure. *The New Yorker* hated the fact that the sets didn't look like anyone's idea of Denmark, but 'a German principality, a sort of community that the Shuberts [Broadway producers] used to construct when Romberg was lining out his songs. With the Shuberts of course, it was *Alt Wien* [Old Vienna] but, what the hell, Denmark's on the same continent.'

Danny Kaye saw his responsibility as backing Sam Goldwyn. 'I am playing the role as straight as I can. After reading the script, I couldn't see any of my particular brand of comedy. I have as much respect for Hans Christian Andersen as the Danes and as much warmth in my heart for his writing as the millions of kids who have enjoyed his stories.'

Guys and Dolls

Meanwhile, Loesser had another project to excite Sam Goldwyn's taste buds – the score of *Guys and Dolls*, which, as we have seen, Sam didn't quite understand and wanted to know more about, hence the walk down Broadway with Michael Kidd. And it wasn't just food that featured in their conversation. He went through the tunes in the original show, analysing them all. The one that stumped him, however, was the chorus number by the girls in the nightclub where Adelaide, one of the two female leads, worked – *A Bushel and a Peck*. He pumped Michael Kidd for explanations. 'What is a bushel?' The choreographer tried to explain that it was an agricultural weight. 'And what does peck mean? Who's pecking who?' Again, Kidd explained it was a term used in farming. Whether Sam was satisfied with these explanations is not immediately apparent – except that the number, which had been a big hit among Broadway and London's West End audiences, was dropped from the film.

He worried about the opening number, called by Loesser, *Fugue for Tin Horns* which begins with Nicely Nicely Johnson and a couple of his pals discussing the prospects for their favourite horses, beginning with the famous line, 'I've got the horse right here.'

On stage, the number had been recited in a hotel room. Sam insisted it should be by a news-stand. Joseph Mankiewicz was the director and he wanted to keep that scene faithful to the original book. As he said, when these kind of guys discuss horses they do so in a hotel room. Sam got furious at this. 'I paid $2 million for this film. I didn't pay $2 million to shoot in a hotel room.' When Mankiewicz began to get angry over this, Sam got angrier still. Finally he said, 'Look when it's your $2 million, you can shoot in a hotel room.'

The scene was shot by the news-stand and was one of the most memorable in the movie.

As we have seen, Sam was often confused and never more so than with people's names. He kept thinking that Michael Kidd was, in fact, Michael Todd, the producer who introduced the Todd-AO wide screen system and later married Elizabeth Taylor.

One night, he told Frances to get hold of Michael Todd, whom he had seen earlier in the day. 'Mike Todd is in Arizona,' she told him. 'He's making *Oklahoma*!'

'Nonsense,' said Sam. 'I saw him this morning in New York.'

'No' his wife said, 'that's Mike Kidd.' In his office, he would continually call Kidd, Todd.

'It happened again in Lindy's,' Kidd told me. 'We are having lunch and I spot, several tables away, Michael Todd. He was coming towards us, stopping at a whole load of other tables on the way. He gets to our table and Sam gets up all excited. "Say Mike," he says. "It's good to see you. How are you?" I'd like to have you meet . . .".' At that point, Goldwyn was totally nonplussed. His mouth remained open. He did not know what to say. Finally, his voice dropped and he said, "You know, it's a funny thing. I was just about to call you Mike Todd." After that, we both gave up.'

Others learned to do much the same thing. Joel McCrea, the star of *Dead End*, and a member of the Goldwyn stable for years, was always 'Joe McCrail.' An executive had the temerity to try to put him right. 'The name is Joel McCrea, not Joe McCrail.' Sam was furious at being told.

'Listen,' he said, 'for seven years, I've been paying this man $5,000 a week. And you're trying to tell me I don't know his name?'

So to emphasise the fact when McCrea himself dared to correct his boss, he asked him to look out of his window. 'See that car,' he said, 'it's a Royce Rolls. What do you drive?'

That was an old showbiz trick. Al Jolson used to take a bundle of 100-dollar bills out of his pocket when an underling tried to correct him or dare to suggest he sing a song differently. 'I made this in show business,' he would say, 'show me yours.' And then he'd hit the man over the head with the bundle.

Sam didn't know the name of Shirley Temple, either. She was Ann Shirley – just as the director King Vidor was Harry King (perhaps that was a Freudian slip; it is possible to doubt that Sam would like anyone else in Hollywood to be known as King).

The writer Everett Freeman was another of his tongue-twisting victims. When he wanted to speak to Freeman, all he could get out was, 'Hey . . . Whatsisname.' That was OK – till he introduced him to someone with the immortal words, 'I'd like you to meet Everett Whatsisname.'

Even Groucho Marx suffered from Sam's machinations – although not in the same way. 'Every time we meet,' said Groucho, 'you always ask, "How's your brother Harpo?" But you never ask me how I am.'

'Next time I will,' promised Sam. 'But for the moment, how's your brother Harpo?' Groucho could not have dreamed that one up for himself – and used it on his radio programme.

Melville Shavelson worked regularly with a partner, Jack Rose. Every time he saw them, Sam would call out, 'Hi, boys.'

'One day,' Shavelson told me, 'I was on the lot, walking by myself. Sam saw me. He still called out, "Hi, boys".'

Guys and Dolls was highly successful at the box office, even though the casting seemed to have got mixed up in the studio laundry. The part of Sky Masterson, the professional gambler who, for a wager, promises to take the Save-a-Soul doll (played by Jean Simmons) to Cuba, was played by Marlon Brando. The part of Nathan Detroit, proprietor of the 'Oldest Established Permanent Floating Crap Game in New York', played brilliantly in the original show in both New York and London by Sam Levine – who was as much cut out for the role as were his suits – went to Frank Sinatra. (Sam said that 'having a Jew play a Jew wouldn't work on the screen'.) It would have made more sense for Sinatra to have played the part of Masterson and for Brando (if not Levine) to be Detroit.

However, it was still a delight, even though the streets of New York could have looked a little more like real thoroughfares and not resembled something out of a comic book. But there were plenty of compensations – not least the wonderful Stubby Kaye telling how he dreamed of getting on a boat to heaven, while the others on board told him to sit down to avoid 'Rocking the Boat'. Sinatra's ever-patient fiancée (engaged for 14 years, a fact which gave her a permanent cold), Adelaide, was portrayed, as on the stage, by the superb Vivian Blaine.

As if to compensate for the loss of 'A Bushel and a Peck', Loesser presented Goldwyn with a new number for the film, 'Ever-Loving Adelaide' sung by Sinatra. There was also one other new number – this time for Brando, 'A Woman in Love', in which Jean Simmons as the lass at the centre of the bet, joins in.

Despite the efforts of Brando and Simmons, 'Woman in Love' became a big hit, along with other *Guys and Dolls* numbers like 'If I Were a Bell', 'I'll Know' and the iconic 'Luck be a Lady', all of which had a second outing in the hit parade, as the music charts were then known.

Transferring Damon Runyon to the screen was comparatively easy. Characters like Masterson, Detroit, Nicely Nicely Johnson, Harry the Horse, Big Julie and Benny Southstreet, were gifts to any screenwriter.

But Sam Goldwyn was never satisfied with what could be easily done. Even if he had an idea of his own, he played with it before it became something he wanted to talk about. As he confessed on one occasion: 'I had a monumental idea this morning, but I didn't like it.'

He always wanted to tread where no shoes had been before. Which was one reason why, during the playwright's life, he was constantly chasing George Bernard Shaw. He went to see him in England, full of ideas for the one Shaw play he knew well – *Pygmalion*. He wanted to turn it into a musical. *Pygmalion* had already been filmed virtually as originally written and highly successfully, starring Leslie Howard and Wendy Hiller. But Shaw wouldn't budge. He had terrible memories of when his *Arms and the Man* had been translated into the filmed *Chocolate Soldier* musical and he had no desire to repeat the experience. No, he said, there would be no *Chocolate Pygmalion*, or whatever it was that Sam wanted to call it, despite the producer's assurances of treating the subject tastefully and artistically.

Shaw tried to soften the blow. 'You see, Mr Goldwyn,' he explained. 'You're only interested in art – and I'm only interested in money.'

There was another celebrated writer whom Sam *did* manage to ensnare – and then learned to regret that he had. Maurice Maeterlinck was a Belgian poet who had earned an international reputation with his story, *The Blue Bird.* Maeterlinck's English was even worse than Sam's. When the two had a conversation together it must have been something to overhear. The charitable thing would be to say that they misunderstood each other. But not before Sam signed a contract and parted with several thousand dollars. Once he had heard the poet's ideas he knew he had been on the wrong wavelength from the start. It all came to a head at a meeting from which Sam stormed out, screaming: 'He wants to make a film about a bee.'

Sam himself made a beeline for his lawyers and quickly got his driver to take Maeterlinck to the train to New York, on his way back to Brussels.

Sam was definitely interested in both art and money – which was one of the reasons why his employees – even those writers, directors and musicians who were constantly on the phone to their lawyers with him in mind – respected him as much as, despite all, he respected them.

Porgy and Bess

A quiet life was given to but a few of Sam's employees. Never was that more apparent than when he decided to tackle what turned out to be his most difficult project of all – the Gershwins' *Porgy and Bess*. This was beset with problems not to be wished on a person's worst enemy (although in Hollywood you could leave out that little word 'not'). Certainly, they were difficulties that a man now 80 years old, could have well done without. For one thing, it was difficult to find a Porgy. He dearly wanted Harry Belafonte, but the Jamaican-born calypso singer thought it was demeaning for a black man to play such an obviously subservient role. After much persuasion, the most popular black artist of the day, Sidney Poitier, agreed to take the part of the cuckolded black cripple. Bess was played by Dorothy Dandridge, reasonably fresh from her title role in *Carmen Jones*. 'I spoke to them all and told them how I would present it to show the dignified Negro life,' Sam said.

This was to be the filmed version of the 'folk opera', with music written by George Gershwin and a libretto by Ira, which in turn had been based on the play *Porgy*, by Dubose Heyward. The critics were always unsure whether it was actually an opera or a musical. One critic, though, thought it had marvellous music – 'marvellous Jewish music'.

The cast list was inspired and Goldwyn actually did feel inspired himself. Not only were there Poitier and Dandridge, but Pearl Bailey (who said she would only appear if she didn't have to wear a bandana, which she said was a symbol of the coal-black mammy, who should have been laid to rest after *Gone with the Wind*), a young Diahann Carroll and Sammy Davis Jr, in what could have been the tailor-made role of his career as Sporting Life, who gave out with 'It Ain't Necessarily So' with all the verve of a preacher on Catfish Row – a preacher, that is, who had lost his faith.

Goldwyn knew exactly how he wanted his *Porgy and Bess* to look. And he knew who he wanted to direct it – the veteran Rouben Mamoulian, one of the most respected men in Hollywood, whose distinguished career on Broadway had included the first production of *Porgy and Bess* on the stage of the Alvin Theater in October 1935. Mamoulian told me that it had been his dream to film the show for years. But he pretended he had to be won over to the project. 'Goldwyn was much more subtle than some of the other studio bosses,' the director told me. 'I found him at times very lovable. He was a terrific wooer. Indeed, he could be very charming, you know. For a long time, I was very fond of him.'

But not when it came to making *Porgy and Bess*. 'I have always thought that the music of Gershwins' *Porgy and Bess* is one of the greatest contributions ever made to the American theatre. But it turned out to be a very sad film.'

It was particularly bad for Mamoulian. 'My agent, Charlie Feldman, said that no one else had wanted to make that film, but I was desperate to do so when the opportunity arose. What I didn't realise was that Goldwyn was suffering from the effects of old age.

'He could have had the rights three years earlier for $25,000. But by the time we spoke, he had had to pay $1 million. I am used to being asked to do films, not to run after the moguls. One day, Sam called me into his office, asked how I was, asked if I wanted to do anything. I didn't say I wanted to do *Porgy and Bess*. He said, "Is there anything that interests you?" I said, "Yes, a film of quality." I knew that he wanted me to say I wanted to do *Porgy and Bess*. But I wouldn't. Eventually, I said, "Sam, nice to talk to you. Goodbye." So he then *asked* me about *Porgy and Bess*. I said I would do it but I wanted to do it my way. I then worked on it for eight months. I had told him that I saw this as a very stylised film. It was not enough to reflect life, it was to reveal what was *behind* life. The whole thing would have a stylised texture, showing gestures; the sets were not realistic, but gave the impression of houses and so on. They had to have a poetry about them.

'He said, "Oh, you mean cheap sets?" I said the sets were cheap, yes, but that wasn't the reason. They are right for the idea I have for *Porgy and Bess*. He said, "Wonderful, wonderful!" In those eight months, I did all the music and supervised the sets. The newspapers knew the connection between me and *Porgy and Bess* and Sam didn't like that. He told me had been in Washington and had talked to the President. He said, "You know what, he talked to me like he was a carpenter and I was the boss. He listened to me. I am a very important, strong man in Hollywood." I told him, "Sam, I know who you are. You are Goldwyn and I am Mamoulian. Come to the point."

'Goldwyn came out with what he really felt. "It's all this publicity," he said. "You're giving interviews about showing films on TV, which I want to do. But you don't."

'I told him that if you show a film on TV, you lose audiences and the whole point of theatre is the audience, a lot of people all seeing the same thing and sharing their emotions.

'Goldwyn told me: "In future, you don't give interviews." I told him to jump out of the window.'

It was the beginning of the end of the relationship between Sam and his director – and between the director and *Porgy and Bess*. But that wasn't immediately clear.

'His wife came on the set one day, when I was recording music. She told me: "[Sam] is very sorry. He's apologising."' That, of course, was not the truth, but he was using his most persuasive 'shmooze'. He invited Mamoulian and his wife to dinner – with 25 other guests, all there to pay tribute to the *Porgy and Bess* director whom Sam said was doing such a wonderful job with his movie. And he made a toast about *Porgy and Bess*.

'It was not that he didn't like the film. What the hell did he know?' Mamoulian told me. 'He hadn't seen it, but he made a very nice toast. I made a comment, saying, "The son of a bitch has some redeeming features."' The next day all the local newspapers wanted to talk to the director. He had no idea why. But the *Hollywood Reporter* man told him. There had been a letter from Goldwyn. It said: 'I have the greatest respect for Rouben Mamoulian. But he and I could not see eye to eye on various matters. Rather than go on with basic differences of opinion between us, I have relieved him.'

Mamoulian was stunned: 'Is that what he says? Last night he gave me a banquet. There has not been one iota of dissension concerning the film between Mr Goldwyn and myself. Mr Goldwyn's bland statement hides a story of deceit and calumny. It will be necessary at long last to expose his publicity greed, his professional hypocrisy and selfishness.'

He then issued a formal statement: 'Goldwyn is a liar, an intriguer, a hypocrite.'

To his surprise, every newspaper published his letter – all except the *New York Herald Tribune*, which was very friendly towards Goldwyn. 'I thought he was going to sue me. All he would do was repeat again that he had the greatest respect and admiration for Mr Mamoulian.'

Mamoulian was replaced by Otto Preminger, which turned out not to be a good idea at all. Or at least, that was what Mamoulian thought. 'Preminger ruined it. He was the most giftless director – in my opinion.' The one who had to take the blame for Sam's worst flop in years was Goldwyn himself.

The *Los Angeles Tribune* wrote: 'Not even Mr Mamoulian, who is supposed to have done something truly phenomenal in transmitting the original novel to the stage could direct it so that it would be anything except a smear, a stereotype, a disgrace and an embarrassment to Negroes. We have taken account of Mamoulian's statement detailing his spat with Goldwyn and we aren't surprised. The whole atmosphere at the Goldwyn studio is calculated to impress you that you are in the presence of a "Great I am", the High Lama of Celluloid. The place is dotted with the private preserves of Mr Goldwyn. "Mr Goldwyn parks here". "Mr Goldwyn drinks here". "Mr Goldwyn goes to the potty here".'

It was hitting Sam Goldwyn below the belt more violently than had ever happened before. The movie was a disaster at the box office.

'Hollywood Owes Me Nothing'

Sam, who had supervised, with all his usual care and authority, a publicity campaign for *Porgy and Bess* more lavish than any for years, was quite literally heartbroken. The 1959 film, released under the auspices of Columbia – his hated rival Harry Cohn had died the year before – was to be the last that Sam made.

He now had time to reflect on the situation of his business and the town it created. 'Hollywood,' he declared, 'has swaggered and boasted and shouted from the rooftops, to be sure, and admittedly been guilty of a variety of imperfections, exaggerations and misrepresentations. But despite all the superficial faults which it has been intellectually fashionable to point to from time to time, Hollywood has nonetheless been the most influential and universal purveyor in this country of the potpourri, the hodgepodge of all the many influences and cross currents that go to make up that thing we call American democracy.'

The words were probably written for him, but they certainly expressed his sentiments. He also said: 'The creators of motion pictures – the producers, writers, the directors, the actors and all the other artists and technicians involved – have always been interested in all the same things which interest most Americans – telling stories, making money, owning cars, having families, talking, singing, dancing, loving, history, sports, laughter – the entire catalogue of interests and emotion that is America. Overall, Hollywood has expressed America and in so doing it has created an art form which is a real embodiment of the American democratic spirit.'

Nobody could quarrel with that. In fact, when it was all analysed, there was a great deal about Goldwyn's work with which people could agree on. And that could serve as an epitaph, although it never did.

In old age, he played poker and croquet and watched the movie industry virtually committing suicide by continuing its boycott of writers and actors who had been blacklisted by HUAC – while at the same time trying to fend off the competition of television, which he still believed he would have been better off by joining rather than (failing to) beat.

To mark his 80th birthday, the Producers Guild gave him a celebratory dinner. Melville Shavelson went up to him: 'Mr Goldwyn,' he said, 'I don't know if you remember me, but I wrote a few of your films.' He looked into Shavelson's eyes and said, 'You done me proud.'

Sam suffered a series of strokes and by the time President Richard M. Nixon did an extraordinary thing and personally came to call on him at home in California – to present him with America's highest civilian decoration, the Congresssional Medal of Honor – he hardly knew what was happening. It was before Watergate and the president was enjoying a honeymoon period. Not that anything would have made the occasion less welcome to Frances – if not to Sam himself. She didn't tell her husband anything about the projected visit. She just made sure that he would be in his best suit as he sat in his wheelchair. When the president arrived, Sam was no longer making people laugh with a diagnosis of his own, like: 'I have been laid up with intentional flu.'

There were muted celebrations for what was billed as Sam's 90th birthday. At least, for a man who never had a birth certificate, it served as that. Frances wasn't going to repeat the 'fiasco' of his 89th birthday. The party she had given him then was a disaster. Frances said at the time: 'I don't lie any more. He has the heart and blood pressure of a young man. But nothing else seems to work – except his appetite.'

In January 1974, he was taken to St John's Hospital in Santa Monica – to undergo treatment for a kidney ailment. A few days later, on 3 January, he died.

With him died, not just those Goldwynisms and the stories people loved to tell about him, but a vital part of the history of Hollywood and the contribution it made to 20th century culture. When he said in his last years that 'Hollywood owes me nothing; I owe Hollywood everything,' he was speaking the truth.

There are not many movie producers who are still talked about in this new century. But Sam Goldwyn is one of them; and he's better known than most. Strange, considering that he made fewer films than any of the other moguls. The reasons are clear. For one thing he was a huge personality, full of quirks and eccentricities, but also because of that search for – and frequent discovery of – quality, of perfection. He took the not unreasonable line that if he liked a film, there was a good chance other people would like it, too. He once declared: 'My idea of making motion pictures, the idea that fascinated me originally, was that films are family entertainment, a place where everyone can go and not blush over what they see on the screen. I never made a movie that would embarrass a father who took his family to see it. People knew that when they saw the Goldwyn name on a picture, it was a family picture. I've proved that fine things, clean things, can be fun.'

The statement, 'I make my pictures to please myself', was true enough. And that's a quality that is missing today. The fact is, there are still people around who say they miss him. Even though they've all passed a lot of water since he was last around.

3

THE WARNER BROTHERS

Each of the Hollywood studios had their own trademark – and I am not talking about lions, shields or ladies holding torches. Much more, it's about what they made themselves stand for. MGM was the most glamorous. Universal specialised for a long time in the horror movie. Republic was at the lowest level in movie production, making the Marlborough Man – or hundreds like him – Westerns.

The Warner Brothers (the studio was always known as Warner Bros., complete with final full stop) were without much doubt the most interesting. And that wasn't simply because of the colourful personalities of the brothers themselves – ranging from the serious, eldest, hard-nosed Harry Warner (born Hirsch) at the head of the family to the mercurial, comic youngest brother Jack Leonard (a middle name he gave himself because he thought that adding a third initial spelled class) Warner, who revelled in the title Head of Production. In between, there was the more boring Albert, born Aaron, but known to the studio employees as 'the major' – he had been in the army in World War I and reached the rank of sergeant. 'You couldn't call a Warner Brother "Sergeant", so he adopted the rank of major,' his nephew, the Warner Bros. producer Milton Sperling, son-in-law of Harry, told me. To the family and his close friends, he was 'Abe' who, Sperling said, would have been much happier as a coat and dress manufacturer, although as the treasurer of the company and ostensibly head of sales he did exert a strong control on finances – just so long as his other brothers let him. 'He didn't have to do very much and lived in New York.' The technical expert was Sam, the brother who would before very long be responsible for the studio's biggest triumph – which was to make it a money-making concern, but that's for later in this story.

To tell the story of the Warner Bros. studio, you have to tell the story of the Warner brothers themselves. The studio succeeded because of how the brothers put their individual stamp on what their enterprise produced. It succeeded, too, because that stamp gave the studio in the Los Angeles suburb of Burbank its own personality. The eldest and the youngest brothers hated each other. And not just because Jack liked to see the funny side of most things and Harry believed by doing so – and much else – he was denigrating the name of the family. Harry was concerned about the morality that his studio represented. Jack, he decided, had no morality whatsoever – which was why he was seen on one occasion chasing his brother through the lot. That might not be such a cataclysmic event in itself had Jack not been stark naked and Harry not been carrying a crowbar, shouting as he ran, 'I'll get you, you son of a bitch, you see if I don't.' As Milton Sperling put it to me: 'That's an example of true brotherly love.'

Where the brothers did agree was in the morality of their films. It proudly emblazoned on its stationery the motto: 'Combining good citizenship with good picture making'.

But that good citizenship didn't extend to the family. Milton Sperling told me: 'It was an open secret that they absolutely detested each other – which culminated in Jack Warner betraying his brothers when it seemed that he had sold his stock in the company as they did, but in fact bought it back immediately afterwards for what he had paid for it.'

As a newcomer to the family, Sperling knew them all intimately. 'Harry, as head of the family, took his responsibilities very seriously. He invented nepotism in Hollywood. He felt that if you were in the family of the Warner Bros. you were owed a living. He looked after his sisters, he looked after his brother Sam's daughter after Sam died, cared for all the distant relatives, gave jobs in the theatres to all the husbands of third cousins' wives. He had a great family sense.

'Albert was essentially a man who never wanted to be in the movies. He loved the stock market and the races and was, indeed, a New York cloak and suit manufacturer at heart. He had a big staff and could delegate, so he rarely came into the office and was protected by Harry – as a brother. He always wanted to sell out. He felt that making movies was an illegal business, not quite right. Whenever Warner Bros. was in the money, he wanted to sell – to get out while they were ahead. He was a fine athlete as a young man; played football and baseball. He was very strong. They were all physically big and strong. They were like farm boys essentially. There was jealousy on both sides – because people, including Jack's own children, would go to Harry for advice; and, on the other side, because Jack was credited with being *the* Warner Brother.

'Jack was essentially a self-centred hedonistic man, great fun to be with. He was an enchanting personality, vulgar on many occasions, treacherous, all the qualifications of a studio tsar. He really belonged to his period. He had a satrapy at Warner Bros. It was his domain and he ruled it as Harry Cohn ruled Columbia and Louis B. Mayer, MGM. He modelled himself on Al Jolson. He adored Al and trained himself to have the same deep voice. Since Jack had been a hoofer and a singer in his early days, he found in Jolson the man he really wanted to be, an entertainer.'

Jack was an entertainer whose greatest form of self-entertainment was to make speeches – speeches that were (and this is putting it kindly) usually confused. He spoke in sentences that might have had beginnings and endings, but generally no middle sections.

George Jessel, who revelled in the title of America's Toastmaster General, once introduced a Warner 'performance'. He commented afterwards: 'What he said tonight, only God will know . . . How the hell did you become the head of a great studio?'

At a dinner for Gary Cooper, Jack began by telling the audience that Jessel who, once more, was the master of ceremonies, had ordered him to be quick with his talk because 'he has a dame in Glendale to go to. Well, I've got a dame to go to in Glendale. I hope to hell it's not the same dame.' Having said that he then explained that he had got his pages mixed up – 'because I've forgotten my glasses' – and should have begun, 'Mr Toastmaster, ladies and gentleman . . . wait a minute, I'll get my glasses back on . . . Everybody says that "I am very delighted". I wrote "proud" but everybody says "proud", so I'm making it "I'm very delighted". I heard two guys say "proud", so I made it "delighted" . . . to pay tribute to a real two-fisted guy, Schlep Cooper. I've always had great faith in Schlep Cooper . . . who the hell wouldn't have great faith in a guy who earns twenty Gs a week?'

That good citizenship already boasted by the studio was demonstrated by what they liked to describe as 'Movies straight out of the news'. Darryl

F. Zanuck, who was in charge of production at Warner Bros. at the time, wrote in the *Hollywood Reporter*: 'It is my sincere belief that the moving picture public will continue to respond to the "headline" type of screen story that it has been the policy of Warner Bros. . . . to produce during the past two years.'

That is why in the days of Prohibition and all the shootings in Chicago, Warner Bros. produced so many gangster films. On the other hand, in his piece in the *Reporter*, Zanuck said that was not part of the deal – something that was constantly being confounded by the studio output. 'A headline type of story must not be confused with the gangster or underworld cycle of productions that have flooded the theatres in the past. Somewhere in its make-up it must have the punch and smash that would entitle it to be a headline on the front page of any successful metropolitan daily.'

Say what he would, the gangster film – with its punch and smash – was Zanuck's creation. Gangsters, shooting into the windows of innocent shopkeepers who wouldn't pay the so-called protection money were worrying the American nation and were one of the reasons for the setting up of the FBI. Prohibition was proving to be more of a curse than a blessing and the brothers agreed with Zanuck that they would be fulfilling both of the criteria in their motto by making movies that showed how bad things were, and how the police were being corrupted at the same time as fighting a losing battle.

Warner Bros., through *I am a Fugitive from a Chain Gang* and similar films, really was proving that gangster movies could have that 'punch'. But, despite what Harry Warner said about leaving messages to Western Union, as we shall see, that one really did have a message.

The use of 'headline' topics led to it being the first studio to think seriously about spies working against the American way of life. *Confessions of a Nazi Spy* awakened a nation to a threat which most Americans were glad to think was more imagined than actual.

None of that fitted easily into the character of Jack Warner, who in many people's eyes really did seem to be *the* Warner Brother. He was a hedonist and a comedian (in his own eyes, if not in those of his employees and other citizens of Hollywood, whose daily diet after breakfast frequently consisted of the latest Jack Warner story). People made fun of him just as they did of Sam Goldwyn. The difference was that they knew Sam could be bitter, but at the same time had the interests of his studio (and thereby that of his employees) in mind most of all. Jack was difficult to take seriously at any time. Well, how could you take seriously a man who established a radio station just so that he could tell jokes and impersonate his idol, Al Jolson? The jokes were terrible; the impersonations dreadful. But people clapped and cheered because Jack was their boss – and more than just appreciative of their response. But it was puzzling just the same.

Certainly, his humour was execrable, never more so than when he welcomed distinguished guests to his private dining room, which had the reputation of serving the finest French food in California. He loved having guests as much as he loved having his French chef and he spoke about them both ad nauseam. But the welcome ceremonies at Warner Bros. were also as much part of Tinseltown's gossip as the films the company produced. Like the time Albert Einstein sat next to Warner and smiled politely as, over the *filet mignon* and the finest claret, Jack harangued him with the latest off-colour jokes (supplied by his writing team), which he always managed to get wrong. But the big moment was when Jack made his speech. 'I'd like to welcome you to Warner Bros. professor,' the producer declared. 'You know, I have a theory about relatives, too. Don't hire them.' (As we shall see, that was a true Jack L. Warner philosophy.) Even worse was when Madame Chiang Kai-shek, wife of the Chinese Nationalist dictator, came to Burbank. 'I'd like to welcome you to Warner Bros., Madame Chiang,' he declared.

At which point, he paused, looked around at the serried ranks of Chinese dignitaries around him and said: 'That reminds me. I must take my laundry in.'

There were others who wished he might launder some of his own habits. And yet, he could be prudish. Gregory Peck told me about the time he made *Captain Horatio Hornblower* for Warners. Virginia Mayo was slated for the female lead. Peck thought that Margaret Leighton, 'who was beautiful in a refined British way', would be better. The director Raoul Walsh came back to him and said, 'No soap with Leighton, kid. It's got to be Mayo.' 'I asked why,' said Peck, 'and he said it was Jack Warner's ruling, "No tits," he explained.'

Hal Wallis, who became head of production at First National after Warners acquired it and was a long-time studio executive, said he always knew where Jack was when he phoned him. He was sitting on the toilet. As Wallis said, 'He would phone me and I'd hear the sound of flushing. I always knew where he was. He was sitting on the john.' No more than one should expect, I suppose, from a man who once said:

'Don't pay attention to bad reviews. Today's newspaper is tomorrow's toilet paper.'

Wallis handed Jack a book that he thought would make a great film. It was *Anthony Adverse* by Hervey Allen. The following week, he stopped his boss in the middle of a party. 'Jack, have you read that book yet?'

'Read it?' said Jack. 'Hell, I couldn't lift it.' But then Jack found weights difficult. As he once said: 'Uneasy lays the head that wears the toilet seat.' What he meant by that, nobody has ever worked out.

None of that should, however, give the impression that Jack wasn't totally committed to his business – and that of his brothers – a fact he would do his best to change.

The three eldest brothers and their sisters Anna, Rose and Fanny were born in Krasnashiltz, Poland. Their father Benjamin and mother Pearl had decided to leave a country where they believed there was no future. Poland was constantly the centre of pogroms and other anti-Jewish measures – not least, the law operating in all parts of what was then the Russian Empire that Jewish boys were expected to serve 25 years in the Army. Ben began working life as a peddler, selling needles, threads and pins. There was another brother, Henry, but neither he nor Fanny survived their fourth birthdays. The remaining family came over to America, like the millions of other Jews who left the empire of the Tsars, to find new opportunities. Jack was born in Ontario, Canada, on the way to Youngstown, Ohio, a destination they chose because Ben had heard there was a sizeable Polish-Jewish community there. Was the family name always Warner? Jack's son, Jack Warner Jr, told me that as far as he knew it was. Not for him the notion that an ignorant or lazy immigration official changed it because he couldn't write the real name. However, it seems unlikely that they were called Warner in *der heim*.

There's an argument to say that Benjamin – or Ben, as he began to call himself soon after crossing the Atlantic – was the fifth Warner Brother in the business. He was always treated as such by Harry, consulted about plans and deals, even if his opinions were never acted upon (there were later two other brothers, Milton and David (David was mentally retarded and both he and Milton died young) and another sister, Sadie. Jack Warner Jr told me that the nicest of the bunch was always Rose. 'Everyone's favourite aunt,' he told me.

Right from the beginning, Ben was regarded as the most important element in the business. After all, he had financed the operation – by pawning his watch. So he was the founder of the family fortune – the one who established the idea of running an American business. Or, rather, three businesses – at least. He sold bicycles and he was a butcher but more often, he was a cobbler. When he went to Youngstown, it was to open a shoe-repair business. He was a tough, strong man who was well suited to the trade. In fact, if his sons had ever thought of casting the role of a blacksmith in one of their movies, they could have done worse than have Ben in the part – a man for whom no problem was too hard. He could also have been a tailor. Maybe not a perfect tailor, but he knew how to make a suit for his boys – usually by laying them on a bolt of cloth and cutting around them.

At the age of 18, Harry, the eldest son and heir, made it clear that he had no interest in mending shoes or riding bicycles (although he dreamed of having a horseless carriage), let alone selling them. Meat was something he wanted to eat – and in greater quantities than the family had been able to do hitherto – but not to sell. On the other hand, he had heard about the nickelodeons and the primitive theatres showing movies. That was much more exciting. Entirely coincidentally, Abe was thinking about films, too. He had seen a 'flicker' at a Pittsburgh nickelodeon. As he said in 1929: 'I began to figure out the attraction. If those pictures have such an appeal for me that I never miss one, I thought, then it must be a pretty good business to be in.' Yes, Abe said he was going to show films for a living – and his brothers agreed that they wanted a part of it.

Starting Out

The brothers bought a projector, made a deal by which they could get hold of films, and were in business. They began by showing short subjects in the nearest place they knew that had enough seats to accommodate an audience – the neighbourhood funeral parlour. It became a very popular place for people to visit, far more happily than most who went there for its original purposes. The only trouble was that, come a funeral, even if in the midst of *The Great Train Robbery*, the audience either had to turn themselves into temporary mourners or get out as the screen was rolled up.

When there were problems, it was Jack who was called in. Right from the beginning, he was the one with the audacious ideas: like snipping a few feet from the film he hired from the renters. When people complained they weren't seeing the picture they expected, he apologised and said it was a mistake easily rectified: since the film he had cut up and kept always included the opening titles, all he had to do was cement the title they wanted to see on to the existing movie – and no one was any the wiser.

It was a policy well worth extending, because they also opened a film exchange – a centre at which films could be rented in exchange for another one. It was a business previously in the almost complete control of Thomas Alva Edison, who believed that as the man who – he claimed – had invented the movies in the first place, he had a right to take every cent out of his invention. But that was, before long, deemed to be a trust and thus, thanks to legislation initiated by President Theodore Roosevelt, an illegal organisation.

It was a good time to be in the movie business. It required very little capital outlay and the word of mouth was strong about the magic of the magic lantern. But like all successful businessmen, the brothers were anything but satisfied with the little that they were doing. At about the same time that Europe was engaged in fighting the Kaiser, they decided to fight the others in the film business – and start making pictures of their own, not just show them.

Their first project was – putting it kindly – a Western, called *Peril of the Plains*. The real peril was the competition – or the fact that they were in danger, in one fell swoop, of putting a whole nation off the idea of going to the movies at all. But they kept going, operating in California as well as St Louis, where they discovered a big old warehouse for sale. Since in those days they didn't have to think of extensive sound proofing, it was a worthwhile – and cheap – proposition.

They were in business as Warner Features Inc, operating from a bungalow in Hollywood, close to the area known colloquially as Poverty Row. Sam was the one who used the camera and stood in for what served as a director. Jack was there to help him – and to play some of the parts, leading or otherwise. He wasn't exactly the most reliable kid on the block. On one occasion, Sam left a message for his younger brother, telling him he was filming at Santa Monica. 'Jack, you were supposed to meet us at 7*am*, not *pm*. Left without you, so have a good alibi ready, Sam.'

They made a giant-sized flop called *Passions Inherited*. The trouble was that their passions concerned making money, not losing it, and the director Gilbert P. Hamilton [Sam could now afford to bring in a professional and not play director himself] had a passion of his own – taking $20,000 from the brothers and spending it on women, usually two in a bed. Jack wasn't averse to taking young women to bed himself, but the threats he made to Hamilton convinced the director to finish the film – although it might have been better had he not bothered.

The brothers volunteered for war service – in the US Signal Corps. Abe did the best, and so became the sergeant for ever after honoured with the rank of 'Major'. The other two were told they would best serve their country by staying out of the army – or, at least, by making films. As things were, they only produced one picture for the troops – about venereal disease. Jack played the victim himself, which might have taught him a lesson: to be careful.

Harry, however, was a born entrepreneur. Once the war was over, he was determined to go back into business. He heard that James W. Gerard, the former American Ambassador to Berlin, had written his memoirs. How about filming them? Gerard, not sure what his next ambassadorial post would be, said yes. With the rights of the movie on Harry's desk, the brothers made *My Four Years in Germany*. And, in so doing, made enough money to carry on.

The results of that war were indeed profitable for the Warner Bros. For it was in the trenches of France that they benefited from a discovery made by a professional dog handler called Lee Duncan. He had found a German shepherd dog that followed instructions so beautifully, he thought he had potential to be in films; enough to make it worthwhile to ship the animal back to America with him.

In Hollywood, he hawked him around the studios. Only Warners, who couldn't afford much else, took the bait – and so created what Jack L. Warner always said was his favourite actor: a star called Rin Tin Tin. Jack called the dog 'the mortgage lifter', because he was so popular with audiences.

Rinty, as he was known, was to be featured in a whole string of movies, and Jack loved him – not least because he was so undemanding. 'He never bothered me for a raise,' Jack declared. 'All I ever had to do was throw him a hamburger over the transom and he was happy. He was the only one of my actors who never gave a bad performance.'

Sound – a 'New-fangled Invention'

Warner Features Inc. was a new studio in the right place at the right time. But after the first glories of *My Four Years in Germany*, things weren't exactly going the way the brothers would have wanted them to go. They made films, but none of them amounted to anything very much. They weren't Sam Goldwyn; they weren't Metro. But they were enthusiastic and resourceful. Which they needed to be, since there were people around who were not exactly sympathetic to an infant organisation which was living as close to a breadline that a film studio could be. In fact, this was a breadline without many crumbs for the Brothers Warner.

The men who were seemingly operating that breadline were the studio's bankers. Thanks to them, the resourceful studio discovered negotiating skills they hadn't previously known that they had. Seemingly they were a lot more efficient talking to Wall Street than they were at making profitable movies. However, things were so bad that they had to look carefully at the way they did their banking. Their answer was to draw all cheques on New York banks. It was a useful ploy that took a little understanding on the part of the firm's employees. Try to explain to them that it took three days for the cheques to reach their banks, another three days for them to clear and then three more days for them to get back by train to California – where, somehow or other, they frequently managed to get lost for just a couple of days.

Somehow, they kept their employees – including, on contract, actors – waiting for weeks for money. It wasn't that they distrusted their employees, but they distrusted their banks even more. It was Milton Sperling who told me the banking story. He explained: 'You know, they hated the men in the starched collars in Wall Street. They were all part of an anti-Semitic conspiracy as far as Warner Bros. were concerned.'

The brothers weren't going to let things go on as they had. They held a meeting and decided that, unless something radical was done, they were on the point of bankruptcy. For once, 'something radical' didn't mean a bookkeeping exercise; it meant doing something very different in the way films were made and the way they were shown to audiences. Eyes were focused on Sam, the third brother, and the one to whom his brothers looked when it came to technical advice.

Everyone seems to have got on with Sam, but Jack more than the others. The reason was probably quite simple – like Jack, he had wanted to perform. He had been a carnival barker in his time, although he spent more money running a floating crap game (and when things were bad, selling ice creams). But they all respected his technical expertise. Harry, Abe and Jack wouldn't have known how to mend a fuse, let alone change a light bulb (although Harry knew how to turn lights out; night after night, he would walk through the Warner lot, extinguishing lights in toilets and in offices which he couldn't understand weren't being used 24 hours a day). For them, technical activity was limited to which fountain pen to use when they signed a contract.

Sam, however, knew his way around laboratories as well as boardrooms. He knew that ever since the days of Edison, there had been experiments with the idea of making films that could offer sound as well as vision. But even the great inventor, the man who dreamed up the idea of recording sound in the first place – to say nothing of electric light and, by his own judgement, moving pictures themselves – couldn't get his head around the idea of amplifying a sound system. It was an idea that was simply filed away in the imaginations of the more adventurous moviemakers. But Sam initiated talks with the Western Electric Company – and came to a deal. At the same time, he initiated a revolution.

Sam's nephew, Jack Warner Jr, described his uncle to me as 'the nicest of the Warner brothers', and, so, an easy man with whom to do business. That business was summed up in a newly manufactured word, 'Vitaphone', a system for recording sound on discs, just like the kind that people bought every week and played on their wind-up gramophones. The difference was that these were 16 inches in diameter, revolved at 33.3 revolutions a minute, just like the LP record 20 years later, but were played out from the centre, instead of from the outside in.

With Vitaphone, a mechanism had been perfected that, by a series of gears and pulleys, could synchronise the sound on those records with the picture being projected on to the screen.

The brothers discussed the new invention, played with it secretly and then decided to go ahead using their Vitaphone offshoot. When they thought about it, they agreed they had just the right project in mind: a film starring John Barrymore and Mary Astor with more swashbuckling than had previously been accepted as wholly decent – *Don Juan*. It was not going to be all that different from the film already scripted and sold to exhibitioners. No one was going to talk in it. But there was the New York Philharmonic Orchestra playing background music; a distinct improvement on the honky-tonk piano that up till then had been *de rigeur* in the world's cinemas. Not just that – and here, Sam persuaded his brothers, was the real revolution – every time a sword was fenced (and they were often), every time a chair was thrown and every time a coach trundled over a cobbled road, the audiences could actually hear it.

The film opened at Warners Theater on Broadway on 6 August 1926 and the Brothers Warner waited to hear what the critics had to say.

Strangely, they heard very little. The movie caused none of the amazement they expected. The Warners' competitors quietly laughed over their daily Scotch and soda. They dismissed it as something with all the technical expertise and sophistication of a fairground peepshow. Had it not been for a series of shorts in the same programme – but which the critics took their time to notice – that might have been that. Sam might have gone to another meeting with Western Electric, shaken hands and put it all down to an expensive experiment. But the shorts changed all that.

Giovani Martinelli, the principal tenor of the Metropolitan Opera, sang 'Vesti La Guibba' from *Pagliacci*, Efrem Zimbalist and Misha Elman played their violins – and Al Jolson sang 'April Showers', 'When the Red, Red Robin' (Jack Warner's favourite, that) and 'Rock-a-Bye Your Baby with a Dixie Melody' in a film entitled *A Plantation Act*. Before long, word seeped out that the Warners might have something.

The other studios professed not to care a hoot and, indeed, took no steps to copy them. But Sam was still convinced that this was the way out of their financial stranglehold.

The Jazz Singer

The brothers agreed that sound was the way to go and went through their stock of prospective scripts. They came up with one that had recently been put on the shelves. The rights had been bought for a Broadway show that was proving to be, if not a box office sensation, then certainly a moneymaker. *The Jazz Singer* was based on a story by Samuel Raphaelson about the son of a synagogue cantor who chooses the stage rather than following in his father's voice prints.

The obvious choice for the lead role was the star of the Broadway show, George Jessel. According to Jack Warner Jr, when I spoke to him, Jessel's laughter at the idea could be heard for 100 yards down Broadway. He made it clear – so Warner remembered – that he wasn't going to risk his career on this new-fangled invention. Eddie Cantor was the next to be asked and gave them the same answer. But it was, once more, Sam who came up with the solution: a solution called Al Jolson. (One story at the time was that Jessel had been willing to take the part in the first place, but wanted $100,000 to do it. Darryl F. Zanuck, a senior Warners executive at the time, said, 'For that money, we could get Jolson.')

It was such a good idea that, afterwards, it would seem obvious: that is, once the negotiations had been completed, with Jolson accepting

$75,000 – $40,000 more than they offered Jessel – plus 25 per cent of the gross. It was a deal the like of which had never been attempted before.

The star himself was to say that it wasn't just money that convinced him to take the plunge into *The Jazz Singer* pool. (Indeed, he fell foul of the Warner policy of using banks 3,000 miles away. While he was in Hollywood, like everyone else in the studio, his cheques were from New York banks. On the other hand, when he was in New York, which was usual for him, the cheques came from a bank in Los Angeles.)

To Jolson, who was without doubt the most popular and exciting entertainer on the Broadway stage, this was an exercise in autobiography. It was his own story, even if Raphaelson didn't know it. He really was the son of a synagogue cantor who more than anything wanted his son to be one too (there was also an older brother who went on the stage but that shouldn't be allowed to spoil a good story).

Jessel himself told me that Jolson signed the contract the day that both were staying at the Biltmore Hotel in New York. They had planned, on a Sunday morning, to go out together for a game of golf. 'Jolson knocked on my door and said, "I don't fancy playing today. I'm going out for a walk. You go back to sleep." The next day, I read in the papers that Jolson had signed with Warner Bros. to make *The Jazz Singer*. Is there any wonder I always felt bitter? I felt sick. It was *my* part. Jolson got the role because he put money into it.'

Whether he did actually put money into the project, or just took a small fee and that share in the box office take, is now a matter for conjecture. But it resulted in a serious fissure in the previous good relationship between the two 'Js', Jolson and Jessel. But when we spoke, Jessel was, if grudgingly, more generous than he had been known to be for years: 'He was better at it than I would have been,' he told me.

If nothing else, it was a great publicity move for Warner Bros. for whom it couldn't have happened at a better time. The studio publicity machine was putting more into the story than it had for any other project. Not only was there the story of a new 'talkie' – a Warner word that henceforward entered the dictionary – but also the entry of the big stage and recording star into Hollywood was a huge event. Jack Warner, with Darryl Zanuck hovering in the background, was at the station to welcome him to Los Angeles. Charlie Chaplin and his United Artists partner, Douglas Fairbanks, joined the welcoming party and this great picture opportunity was grabbed eagerly by the press. The fan magazines went overboard – praising Warner Bros. for their great coup.

Nobody expected this to be a great picture. For one thing, there would be no spoken words – just a few songs by Jolson and by Bobby Gordon, the boy who played him as a child. But the studio was spending more on the film than it ever had before. It did things like going to the Lower East Side to shoot scenes on location (a very rare event that added to expenses).

Warner Oland, who was to play the jazz singer's father, Cantor Rabinowitz, went to Orchard Street and mingled with the pushcart vendors. He went dressed in rabbinical garb, complete with long beard and skullcap, so that he could more effectively learn how to meld into the surroundings of what was called in the film, the New York ghetto. (The Swedish-born Oland would make a speciality of ethnic roles; his most successful one was as Charlie Chan, the Chinese detective, which, combined with his part in *The Jazz Singer*, made him a kind of United Nations of an actor.)

Designers went to the Orchard Street synagogue and copied every detail so that it could all be reproduced in the Burbank scenery workshops. They did the same thing with the Winter Garden Theater, scene of Jolson's biggest Broadway triumphs.

Sam Warner knew what he wanted and he passed on the instructions to Alan Crosland, the director. It would be an essentially silent picture, complete with titles between the scenes. That might have been an easy brief for any other star. 'You emote,' was what Al was told to do. Emote? This was a man who would emote in a phone call to his milkman, who could make the bricks of a huge theatre vibrate without using a microphone – who gave his all, singing songs that held audiences spellbound. Now he was being asked to mime conversations like Valentino or John Gilbert. Not him at all. And, indeed, if Sam Warner had not allowed an unexpected event to go ahead, the movie might have been a complete disaster. The point was you couldn't confine a man like Al Jolson to the limitations of a movie set – particularly one where the microphones themselves didn't move and where the cameraman was stuck in a soundproof booth, so that the whirring of the cameras wouldn't be heard.

He sang his first song, 'Dirty Hands, Dirty Face', a lachrymose tune that was all the rage at the time, and one through which, remarkably, Jolson was making a fortune selling gramophone records. Then, came the big number, a trademark song that was guaranteed to get audiences all over the world singing along and tapping their feet, 'Toot Toot Tootsie

Goodbye'. But that was not the only reason why, in this first talkie, the song was remarkable – and historic.

The cameras were ready to go, the sound equipment was switched on. The idea was that the mikes would go 'live' with the sound of diners in a nightclub, banging their spoons and clapping. But, with the orchestra all primed to go, that was when Al Jolson stepped in. 'Wait a minute, wait a minute,' he called to the bandleader, Lou Silvers. 'You ain't heard nothin' yet. Wait a minute, wait a minute, I tell you. You wanna hear 'Toot Toot Tootsie'? All right, hold on. Lou, listen. You play 'Toot Toot Tootsie'. Three choruses, you understand, and in the third chorus I whistle. Now give it to 'em hard and heavy – go right ahead.'

So Lou Silvers gave it hard and heavy – and so did Jolson. Crosland would have asked him to do it all over again. But Al wouldn't have done it again. He never repeated himself. Every time he sang a song, it was slightly different. And Sam ordered him not to do it again. Most history books recall the first words spoken in film to have been simply, 'You ain't heard nothin' yet.' Jolson wouldn't have been satisfied with that either. And nor was Sam. He ordered a new scene to be written – with Al playing 'Blue Skies' to his aged mother (an old Warner star, Eugenie Besserer). But not just singing. Not just playing the piano, but Jolson telling his old ma that he's going to buy her a new black silk dress; take her to Colney Island and buy her a new home in the Bronx. The French-born actress was heard – just about caught by the mike, which was on Jolson – laughing and protesting. But what was really fascinating was when the cantor enters the room, hears the singing and shouts: 'Stop.' It was a thunderclap of a moment – and the sound recording stopped.

Audiences were overwhelmed. In the one night of 6 October 1927, the silent movie was pronounced dead. Alas, not just the movie.

There were four absentees at the premiere that night at the Warners Theater. Three Warner brothers were in California around the deathbed of Sam. He had had an operation for a mastoid condition, an operation that went wrong. The film premiere went ahead just the same – on the day after Yom Kippur, the fast on which the movie was centred. (The cantor dies and his son gives up the first night of his show to sing the sacred *Kol Nidre* in his place.)

The film made a net profit of $3.5 million. Jolson's share of the take amounted to an astonishing $4 million. If the Warners claimed to have anticipated the effects of *The Jazz Singer,* they would have been lying.

Not only did they not realise that they, and their studio, would go virtually overnight from being close to penury to being the possessors of riches, they could not have anticipated the effect it would have on the film business.

A Revolution in the Film Business

Of course, in retrospect, such a revolution was precisely what might have been expected of the Brothers Warner. They never cared much about the film business. They cared about Warner Bros. (as they were now known). As Neil Gabler says in this book, *An Empire of the Own*, 'Where other Hollywood Jews wanted desperately to appease the establishment, the Warners set themselves against it and challenged its legitimacy. It would be years before they finally became members of the club.' After *The Jazz Singer*, they owned the club – or the only part of it that they really cared about. Major Albert Warner was the one brother who was more chary of things. He not only didn't understand what was happening, he went on record saying so – much to his brothers' disgust.

He told *The New York Times*: 'As rapidly as theatres throughout the country are being fitted for the audible films, it is preposterous to suppose that the time will ever come when all houses, the length and breath of the United States, will be so equipped. The sweep of the talking picture does not necessarily mean that all filmgoers will want nothing else. An occasional audible picture will suffice for some audiences whose steady and uninterrupted patronage will continue to be accorded to the silent picture. Neither field conflicts with the other.'

The statement conflicted totally with the studio's policy that dictated they had caused a revolution – and nothing was going to change that. In truth, Abe's brothers were beside themselves – but, when they saw the takings at the Warner's Theater, they were more than slightly soothed.

Even Jack Warner was aware that the opposition they faced over the birth of sound films could be difficult to overcome: 'The motion picture has advanced tremendously from the short films that were shot at the start of the century,' he said. 'There was a general belief at that time that motion pictures had progressed as far as they could go as a means of dramatic expression and satisfying entertainment. My brothers and I believed otherwise. We were determined to break the barrier of silence to bring full life to the screen by giving it a voice that would be heard throughout the whole world. To this goal we devoted the full resources of Warner Bros. with possibly the destiny of the motion picture in the balance.' And then he added, tellingly: 'There was criticism from doubters who were annoyed with us for not leaving things alone.'

The other studios continued to play innocent in public and did all they could to see that their scorns were published. But once the headlines proclaimed 'Talking Pictures Sensation' they betrayed their anxieties. They didn't feel any better when Mordaunt Hall, writing in *The New York Times*, noted, 'On opening night, one almost forgot that the real Jolson was sitting in a box listening to his own songs, for it seemed as though in the darkness Mr Jolson had crept behind the screen and was rendering the songs for his black and white image.' (Which, it has to be said, a lot of people actually did think.) Orders went out to 'wire for sound'. Different systems were put into operation. Existing films were changed so that they could be made 'talkies'. Others were scrapped entirely.

Even Warner Bros. realised they had created a chalice containing its share of poison: for one thing what would happen to their international audiences? Titles could easily be changed from one language to another. But soundtracks? That was a question to be asked once they had affected the synchronisation of voices with film (and then not always successfully; there's a wonderful moment in the movie *Singin' in the Rain* when the record and the picture get disjointed; the cavalier shaking his head while saying, 'Yes, yes, yes' and his lover nodding while being heard to say 'No, no, no' was drawn from life; microphones were hidden in bushes that rustled at the most inopportune time, footsteps were recorded loud while voices were too soft.) For a time, the solution seemed to be to film the same movie half a dozen times in half a dozen languages – the sets and the costumes, the crowd scenes and the music were the same, but different actors and actresses said the same lines as the originals, although in their own tongues. That didn't last long, but the talkies were there to stay.

One of the first developments was that Warner Bros. themselves were there to stay. *The Jazz Singer* had made the Warner company, and the Warner brothers, rich. Within two years, they had bought 500 theatres all over America – which absolutely guaranteed that the talkies were now a permanent phenomenon. They were not going to sabotage their own efforts by showing silent films. Just as significantly, they had bought the entire business of First National Pictures – which not only gave them access to studios, actors and libraries, but also provided them with another section that in some ways could operate separately. Other deals like that in the industry usually suggested that a second division would mean second-rate output. Not in this case, however, unless in a dozen years or so you thought of *Casablanca* being second-rate.

Warners had not only given birth to sound movies, they had created a new genre – the film musical. They immediately followed *The Jazz Singer* with another Jolson production, *The Singing Fool*. It was a terrible picture with a terrible song, 'Sonny Boy' – written by the team of De Silva, Brown and Henderson as a joke; they couldn't believe Warners were serious in asking for a number sung by a distraught father to his dying little boy. As George Burns told me: 'They were so ashamed of the song, they couldn't bring themselves to post it. They got a hotel bellboy to mail it for them.'

It may have been a terrible picture and a terrible song, but they were both mind-blowing international successes. The clever thing about the brothers was that they appreciated the value of the star, even at a stage when the quality of either the film or the technique was, to say the least, questionable. The New York opening of the second Jolson film was held at Al's own stamping ground of the Winter Garden Theater – highly appropriate for a new 'sensation'. That was how the critic Pare Lorentz saw it. 'Obvious and tedious as the climax is, when the black-faced comedian stands before the camera and sings 'Sonny Boy', you know the man is greater, somehow, than the situation, the story or the movie.'

Without Sam to advise them, the other brothers – and people like Darryl F. Zanuck – had to decide what they should do next; what was their role going to be? Zanuck, who became studio manager after *The Jazz Singer* and then Head of Production once *The Singing Fool* proved to be so successful, was now in effect the fourth Warner Brother. He was the one whose judgements were almost always accepted in the Burbank boardroom. (When, in 1933, they no longer *were* accepted, Zanuck resigned and founded Twentieth Century Pictures – later to be the root of Twentieth Century Fox). But it was a young man called Brian (Briney) Foy, who had been one of the famous Seven Little Foys vaudeville act, who solved the matter for them. As Jack Warner Jr told me: 'The brothers, having made enough money from *The Jazz Singer*, were on vacation in Europe and had put the studio in the hands of Briney Foy – who, against instructions, made a film called *The Lights of New York* into a full sound picture. It was really wonderful for audiences.' Wonderful because this first all-talking Warner film was very much the *sounds* of New York: car horns, guns, telephones and speeches by gangsters who pronounced every syllable, to make sure they could be understood.

It may not have been much of a movie, starring the now completely-forgotten Helen Costello and Cullen Landis but, because it was the first ever movie not to depend in any way on titles, it became part of history. In 1928, it was what, seemingly, everyone wanted to see – and provided another tick on the Warner Bros. chart.

It was Zanuck who suggested the motto 'Combining Good Citizenship with Good Picture Making'. Jack Warner said: 'I want all our films to sell America long, not short. My brothers and I are examples of what this country does for its citizens. There were no silver spoons in our mouths when we were born. If anything, they were shovels. But we were free to climb as high as our energy and brains could take us.'

Louella Parsons, to whom Jack said this, regarded it as a typical example of how the wonderful patriotic moguls (who provided her bread and butter; without them she would have had nothing to write about) were flying the Stars and Stripes.

They began making every conceivable type of film in sound, but before long were demonstrating the value in speciality, in having their own trademark, and that there were some things that might, eventually, be left to others. Warners agreed that there might be other studios that were better equipped to make the musicals they had given birth to, but that was never more than a half-hearted thought.

There was a string of Warner musicals, mostly featuring the songs of Al Dubin and Harry Warren and with the choreography of Busby Berkeley. The film *42nd Street* in 1933 was the most notable of these – especially since its numbers remarkably featured a stage scene that miraculously turned into a Broadway street. It had musical numbers that became Tin Pan Alley standards, like 'You're Getting to be a Habit with Me', 'Shuffle Off to Buffalo', 'Young and Healthy' and '42nd Street' itself.

Then there were the *Gold Diggers* series, which had sort of begun in 1929 with *Gold Diggers of Paris*, but found their dancing feet with *Gold Diggers of 1933* (which featured more numbers that earned their place in popular music legend, like the opening song, 'We're in the Money' and 'My Forgotten Man', followed by *Gold Diggers of 1935* and *1937*. There was a new repertory company for these – not just the songwriters and Berkeley, but performers like Ruby (Mrs Al Jolson) Keeler, Dick Powell and Joan Blondell. When the 1933 *Gold Diggers* opened in New York, the message was that, with Franklin D. Roosevelt in the White House and the nation singing 'Happy Days are Here Again', the Depression was virtually over – although no one had told the millions of unemployed. The premiere was organised to underline the studio's optimism. As the *New York Sun* commented, having looked into its crystal ball: 'Chorus girls will sweep up and down Broadway on roller skates for an hour before an automatic girl, whatever that may be, will play a phosphorescent neon-lit violin, whatever that may be, in front of the theatre. It promises to be another of those dignified Warner openings.'

Gangster movies, however, were going to have equal billing with the musicals in the studio catalogue. The sound of gunfire was startling to people who didn't live in Chicago and who were used to regarding going to the movies as a silent experience. There was something else that went so well with the kind of talkies that Warner Bros. were planning: the telephone. Eighty years later, it is impossible to imagine the impact made by this symbol of twentieth-century progress, which people were just beginning to take for granted by the 1920s. Film after film concentrated on a desk with a phone on it. That always gave out the signal that it was going to ring.

Warner Bros. had risen from the bottom to the top of the heap. Jack was having the time of his life, playing the fool and taking the credit for so much that his studio was producing. Abe was in charge of the growing number of cinemas – motion-picture theatres in America – owned by his brothers and himself, theatres that guaranteed an outlet for the films that their studio was churning out at the rate of a movie a week. Harry was seemingly only interested in making money. ('I don't want 'em good; I want 'em Tuesday,' he declared.) Jack paid him due deference for that. 'He has the toughness of a brothel madam and the buzzing persistence of a mosquito on a hot night.' (He probably never actually said it; but like the way all the words were put into his mouth by someone in his publicity department, they certainly summed up his sentiments.)

The Trouble with Family . . .

Harry had one other major worry – his family; which was why he was so concerned with his youngest brother's behaviour. But he thought that the future of the studio was in good hands. He had a son, Lewis, ready to step into his shoes. But then, at the age of 22, Lewis developed blood poisoning while on holiday in Havana. His gums became infected and, in those days before antibiotics, the treatment he received only made things worse. Harry flew to Cuba to bring his son back, but Lewis developed pneumonia and after a few days died.

Harry was not just distraught, he was deranged. One night, soon after Lewis's death, he walked into the bedroom of his 18-year-old daughter, Doris, ordered her to get dressed and, at four o'clock in the morning, drove her to his New York office, sat her down in his leather chair, and declared: 'You're going to take Lewis's place. I'm going to teach you the movie business.'

For two hours, he harangued her with the ins and outs of picture making, bombarded her with statistics, none of which she would have understood after a full night's rest, but in the middle of the night was totally unintelligible to her. She wasn't the only one to be a victim of her father's sorrow. Milton Sperling told me: 'He walked into the office of Adolph Zukor at Paramount without an appointment. He just sat himself down in front of Zukor's desk and for two hours said nothing; in fact did nothing but weep uncontrollably.'

Nothing Harry did could console him. He took it upon himself to carry out all the duties expected of a head of the family – even though Ben and the brothers' mother Pearl were still alive. He made it clear to Jack just how much he hated all that his youngest brother was doing. Not least, how he detested his brother divorcing the former Irma Solomons for the young, beautiful, dark-eyed Catholic, Ann Page Alverado.

Jack Warner Jr, in his autobiographical novel *Bijou Dream*, recounts a conversation between the two brothers who are central characters in his book. It reprised a talk, which he told me actually took place between his father and uncle. 'The conversation was as I remembered hearing it from Uncle Harry when he was in one of his most exasperating moods.'

As the novel recounts, it went like this: 'This may be none of my business, but I've been hearing some very disturbing things about you. It embarrasses me even to bring it up, but this is something that concerns our whole family and as your older brother I must talk to you. You have to realise you are being looked at. You're getting to be better known all the time – and if you pull anything in your personal life that's . . . well . . . tawdry . . . cheap . . . it is going to reflect on all of us. I'm talking about women. You're a married man, happily I would hope. You and Irene have a son.'

'You're right,' [said the younger brother] 'it's none of your business. None of your goddamned business at all.'

Jack didn't marry Ann until Pearl died. Ben wasn't told about the marriage. (When Jack wrote his memoirs, *My First Hundred Years in Hollywood*, he didn't even mention Irma – or his son, Jack Jr.)

Unfortunately for Jack, Harry *was* told and persisted in calling his new sister-in-law the worst names he could think of, not least of which was 'whore'. The whole business rankled with a man who considered that his own role as acting head of the family was being compromised irreparably. It was not for nothing that he was the only brother – and one of the very few moguls in Hollywood – who followed, if only to a limited extent, religious rituals, like conducting a Passover Seder ceremony at his home. Jack would never have done anything like that, although he would say – in private and just so as he would not be in danger of influencing people's views of him – how proud he was of being a Jew. It was telling that his son Jack Jr chose as a quote for the beginning of *Bijou Dream*, 'Better to be a decent human and not a Jew than a Jew and not a decent human.'

Jack had no such compunctions. As we have seen, firing his own son was no more a problem for him than making sure the waste-paper basket in his office was emptied. Just so long as he had someone to empty it for him. Jack had someone on hand to do both jobs. It didn't matter to him if it was family – the number one sin for Harry – or any other employee. Indeed, he kept an executive on hand to do this particular bit of dirty work for him.

Steve Trilling would be called into Jack's office and given a piece of paper bearing a single word – a name. At which point, Jack would announce that he was leaving town – or the country. 'When Jack left,' said his son-in-law, Bill Orr, 'we knew that someone was for the chop.' As for Trilling, he knew that he had the responsibility of firing the person whose name was on the paper. One day, Jack flew off to the South of France. At an agreed time when the studio boss knew he would be in mid air, Trilling was called into another executive's room – and told that he himself had been fired.

Jack Jr always claimed that he never found out why his dad wielded the axe in his own case. But there could be two reasons – one, that he was the product of his father's first marriage, the memory of which was to remain a thorn in the sides of both father and son; or two, Jack had been a lieutenant-colonel in the US Signal Corps during World War II and his son had been a full colonel. When the two men met in uniform at the studio, Jack Jr had the temerity to suggest that his father should now salute him. The older man was not impressed – and immediately resigned his commission. Milton Sperling had another explanation for that resignation. 'Jack thought he would be called in to meet the joint chiefs and do no more than walk around wherever he was wearing his uniform, which had been made for him by Eddie Schmidt, the by-appointment Hollywood tailor. He loved to have the rank of lieutenant colonel – although he dropped the "lieutenant" part. The important thing was that he was called "Colonel" and, more important, he out-ranked his older brother Abe, who had been a sergeant in the First World War, but was called "the Major" by everyone.' But then he heard that he had to have training and would be possibly shipped overseas. That was too much for him. He quit.'

Despite her father's entreaties, Harry's daughter Doris didn't enter the movie business, apart from marrying Milton Sperling and drawing some very nice royalty cheques. Had she done so, she would have been part of taking on the new array of Hollywood personalities, like James Cagney, Edward G. Robinson and George Raft, the leaders of the Warner stable of dependable gangster stars.

Mega Stars

Cagney was the most difficult star as far as his employers were concerned. Jack called him 'the professional againster', a nice combination of Hollywood English and Yiddish, which led to some hilarious exchanges. Cagney wanted his contract with Warners changed. He said they couldn't keep their word about anything. 'I told him that they could argue all they liked,' he explained to me when I was writing my Cagney biography. 'I said I would go off to my farm and come back when they had honoured our agreements.'

Cagney was making four and sometimes five films a year for them and he thought that was too much. However, audiences didn't think so and both Jack and Harry were determined to keep him on the Burbank lot. Unfortunately, for the two brothers, their methods of dealing with him could have benefited from the advice of experts in human relations – if such creatures had existed at the time. And it was in one such escapade that the language problem came to the fore.

Jack had forgotten that Cagney, brought up in Yorkville, New York, had learnt Yiddish so that he could talk to the immigrant Jewish boys in his class. On this occasion, the two moguls were discussing the professional 'againster's' latest demand for more money. In his presence and in the language of their fathers. Cagney had stormed into Jack's office, demanding a better deal. Immediately, they began their diatribe against the ingrate whom they had rescued from the chorus of a so-so show. And then, it happened. Jack was suddenly struck dumb. '*Shvegan, shvegan,*' he said to his brother, '*der goy vershtate* Yiddish.' [Quiet, the gentile understands Yiddish.] And the 'goy' really did understand, too. He never forgot the incident and revelled in telling me about it 40-odd years later.

Cagney stayed with Warners and made some of their most notable movies of the period, *Footlight Parade* (a musical, which gave him a brief respite from the gangster movies and a chance to sing and dance), in 1933, in the space of a year, *Lady Killer*, *Smart Money*, *Other Men's Women*, *The Crowd Roars* and perhaps the best remembered of all, *The Public Enemy* – the one in which a trussed-up, bandaged figure stands at the front door of his mother's house. As that door is opened, he falls flat on his face, dead, dead, dead. It was a scene that was re-enacted in a hundred comedy routines (even Frank Sinatra would say how he scared his mother by copying the moment; Dolly Sinatra was not impressed). It also earned a niche in Hollywood folklore by being the one in which he pushed half a grapefruit into the face of Mae Clarke. He went on making gangster films for Warner Bros. right up to 1949, when, in the film, *White Heat*, he uttered the immortal words, 'Made it Ma, top of the world.'

This was a studio that seemed to celebrate famous lines almost as much as famous players. Cagney was also at the top of the Warner Bros. world. But he had competition. Edward G. Robinson's last words in *Little Caesar* became even more famous than Cagney's. 'If [the film] succeeded at all,' Robinson told me, 'it was because the construction of it was that it had a beginning, a middle and an end. It was like a Greek tragedy in which the main character, the villain, dies but doesn't know why.'

'Mother of Mercy,' he stammered in the film, 'is this the end of Rico?' 'We had to say "Mother of Mercy",' Robinson added, 'because we weren't allowed by the censors to say Mother of God, as we wanted to.'

There were even more famous lines in *Casablanca* – about which more later – a more famous collection of quotes than any since those penned by William Shakespeare 300 years before. If the Hollywood censors had their way, it might have been a lot less notable. Joseph J. Breen, head of what used to be known as the Hays Office, officially the Production Code Administration, wrote to Jack Warner: 'The present material contains certain elements which seem to be unacceptable from the standpoint of the production code. Specifically, we cannot approve the present suggestion that Capt. Renault makes a practice of seducing the women to whom he grants visas. Any such inference of illicit sex could not be approved in the finished picture. The suggestion that Ilsa was married all the time she was having her love affair with Rick in Paris seems unacceptable and could not be approved in the finished picture. Hence, we request the deletion of Ilsa's line, "Even when I knew you in Paris".'

Julius Epstein, the writer, laughed at that when we met. 'I think this film was important for a reason no one seems to have made anything out of. We just told the office where to get lost – and never heard another word about it.'

There were constant rows between Warner Bros. and the Breen Office, which was what the censors were now called. In 1941, Breen wrote to Jack saying that his film *King's Row* was 'quite definitely unacceptable. A picture, following on the lines of this script, would, necessarily, have to be rejected. Before this picture can be approved under the provision of the production code, all the illicit sex will have to be entirely removed; the characterisation of Cassandra will have to be definitely changed, the mercy killing will have to be deleted and the several suggestions of loose sex will have to be completely removed from the story.' In the case of that film, Warner Bros. surrendered.

With *Casablanca*, however, the studio was sticking to its guns. Unusually for the time, Warner Bros. knew there was something very special in its hands here – even though the script hadn't been finished before filming began; no one at that time – not even the writers – knew how it was going to end.

It was the film that made Humphrey Bogart one of the very few actors who could in those days have justified the title 'mega star' – long before the term had been invented. Bogart was to be Warners' crowning glory, even though it took a few years for him to rival Cagney and Robinson. The brothers were very circumspect in not declaring actors to be stars until they could be sure their names alone were guaranteed to bring silver coins rattling on to box-office counters. So Bogie – they hadn't yet coined that nickname either – had had to be satisfied with smaller, also-ran roles, usually of unpleasant individuals who came to the kind of sticky end audiences wanted. The exception was *The Petrified Forest*, in which he played Duke Mantee, a part originally offered to George Raft, who rejected it. It was not so much a starring role as one to be classified as 'important'. It showed he was on his way, although it took 26 films for the journey to end with the kind of stardom we now associate with him. The fact that it did, was due to the 'other Warner Brother', the one who took over from Darryl Zanuck, Hal B. Wallis, who said that the lad (a lad too old to serve in World War II, just before his big moments began) ought to be given a chance.

Films like *They Drive by Night*, about a truck driver who gets involved with a murderess, *Crime School* and Cagney's epic *Angels with Dirty Faces*, seemed to seal his fate, of a player who would end up in jail or as a gentleman baddie in a dinner jacket. You knew it was a Bogart film because he was the one you could only see after banging on the hatch of a speakeasy.

Even then, that was part of the Warner genius. Complaining about typecasting is all very well. But there was a lot to be said for it, too. The actors were in parts they could be guaranteed to do convincingly and the audiences got what they came to see. No problems about deceptive advertising in a Warner Bros. film to the extent that the company were justifying their self-assumed trademark every time a projector whirred.

George Raft, who shared top billing with Bogart in *They Drive by Night*, was in that mould – a gangster in spats; a gangster whose patent-leather hair (so much like Valentino, whom he seemed to emulate) went so well with his other speciality, dancing the tango. He was known as a man with strong links with the underworld. I met Raft in the 1960s, just before he lost his gambling licence in London. I asked him what the real gangsters thought of his performances. 'They told me they enjoyed what I did on the screen,' he said, 'but they said, "Why do you always have to die?" I said, "Well, I have to have some redeeming quality".'

Cagney told me he based some of his characters on people he actually knew in his childhood – like the guy he played in *Angels with Dirty Faces*, who kept saying, 'Whatda ya hear? Whatda ya say?'

'Several of them ended up in the hoosegow [jail], as we used to say. One boy caught me reading [a comic] and he said, "You'll go to jail if you keep reading this stuff." He went to the chair.'

The Prohibition-era crime wave made for good movies for a studio that made good money. And even when they couldn't use their own stars, they borrowed from other studios to get the right man (or woman) for a gangster role. From MGM, Spencer Tracy was brought in to make *20,000 Years in Sing Sing*, a story made to measure for Cagney, who was originally earmarked for the part of an escaped criminal who takes the blame for a murder committed by his girlfriend. The girl was played by

Bette Davis and the film bore the mark of a Warner gangster picture from the first frame.

The studio was constantly branching out, though. They made their share of Westerns – starring a young man named John Wayne. *Ride Him Cowboy, The Man from Monterey* and *The Telegraph Trail* didn't do much either for him or for the company, but were useful experience. They didn't matter in the scheme of things – Warner Bros. was now one of the big studios. They were all B pictures – part of a six-movie series, all made between 1932 and 1933. Which demonstrated just how hard the studio expected its employees (a word Jack Warner liked to use, particularly when referring, much to their disgust, to his big stars) to work.

And the men you loved to hate (a slogan coined about the non-Warners actor/director Erich von Stroheim, but which is convenient to borrow in this context) weren't all hateful. Paul Muni, one of the most important stage actors of the 1930s came to Warner Bros. and found in them the perfect hosts for his talent of being able to act in the minor key, taking advantage of every crevice in a sad face, which you just knew had to have a lot of good in it. He was a one-man justification of that 'Good Citizenship' title the studio awarded itself. (Harry liked making philosophical announcements, particularly when issuing what these days would be called a 'mission statement' about the studio. 'The motion picture,' he declared in the midst of the gangster era, 'presents right and wrong, as the Bible does. By showing both right and wrong, we teach the right.' That might have seemed pretty presumptuous, but the fact was it was true.

Muni summed it all up. He could play murderers along with the rest of the gangster rep company members. The 1933 *Scarface*, based on Al Capone, and produced independently by Howard Hawks, sent him to the top of the ratings. But also in that year, he came to Warner Bros. to make the iconic *I am a Fugitive From a Chain Gang,* based on the true story of the abominable treatment suffered by a wrongly-convicted man. The resultant film sold as many handkerchiefs as cinema tickets. He came – and he stayed. Jack saw how he poured out sympathy for what was perceived as the iniquitous practice of chaining prisoners for 24 hours a day – while they ate, while they slept – and while they did backbreaking work smashing rocks. Muni made the fact that his character was innocent – and had been struggling to prove that innocence while enduring not just the chains but also the whips of the taskmaster and the barbs of fellow prisoners – an important argument for a reform of the system. He was nominated for an Oscar for his role in *Fugitive*. It was a tearjerker, but also a document of extraordinary importance.

Whether the brothers themselves had that target in mind when they made that particular movie cannot be proved. The fact that the Warner campaign, as it seemed to be, brought money into the business does prove that it took issues like the chain gang into the public consciousness.

Meanwhile, Muni had an extra string to his bow. He gave Warner Bros. another trademark – the movie biography. In his early years at Burbank, he starred in the title roles of *The Story of Louis Pasteur, The Life of Emile Zola* and *Juarez*. The French government were so grateful for the first two of these that they awarded Jack the Legion d'Honneur – which annoyed Hal Wallis tremendously. 'I was angry because he took it. He told me – he not only did not make those films, he didn't want them to be made. They were made by me.'

When Paul Muni did take time off from the biographies, he starred in *The Good Earth*, a tremendous hit in 1936, in which he played Wang Lung (a remarkable feat for the Polish-born actor who began in the Yiddish theatre and played Frenchmen and a Mexican). Three years later, for Twentieth Century Fox, he went back to true-life stories playing the French explorer Pierre Radisson in *Hudson's Bay*. In 1945, he was Joseph Elsner, the teacher of Chopin in *A Song To Remember* (Columbia). Those last two may have been made for other studios, but the stamp of ownership – virtually the patent – of the biographical movie, bore the initials 'W.B.'. Edward G. Robinson got in on the act, too, playing the title role in *Dr Ehrlich's Magic Bullet*, the story of Dr Paul Ehrlich, discoverer of an early cure for syphilis – a brave Warner Bros. move at a time when such things were not spoken of in polite society.

But then the art of making biographies was itself fairly brave, too. Jack, after all, went on record as saying to one of his writers: 'Don't bring me any more scripts with people writing with feathers.'

Jack pioneered the use of 'sneak previews', the results of which he took very seriously. When he saw *The Maltese Falcon*, Jack wrote to Hal Wallis: 'Last night after the preview, I thought for about an hour and believe we should positively make over the opening close-ups of Mary Astor and tell the audience what the hell it is all about, instead of picking up with a lot of broken sentences with confusing words. Many of the cards stated they were very confused in the beginning and I am sure we throw them off. Therefore, why be so clever, as we have a hell of a good picture? We should do these retakes the first thing Monday.'

He had discovered some restlessness about that film at a preview. He was wrong, but he said he always had an infallible guide to audiences' preference – their bladders. While people in the theatre watched the film, he watched who got up from their seats – and how many times. 'That movie's no good,' he memorably said once. 'It's a two-piss picture.'

Difficult Divas

Bette Davis was another of the studio's stars to complain about being overworked and underpaid. It was a long, angry battle – which ended in 1937 with Ms Davis fleeing to London and then being sued by Warner Bros. – in the (British) High Court, where Warners' barrister, the famous Sir Patrick Hastings, told Mr Justice Branson: 'I can't help but think, my Lord, that this is the action of a very naughty young lady.'

The trouble was that Bette, who had gone on suspension for refusing to submit to the 'slavery' of Warner Bros. had accepted an offer from Ludovic Toeplitz – who had produced *The Private Life of Henry VIII* for Alexander Korda – to make two films, one with Maurice Chevalier, the other with Douglas Montgomery.

Bette signed the contract while on honeymoon with her new husband, Harmon Nelson. Her timing, always a Davis quality, was completely wrong on this occasion. It just happened that Ann and Jack Warner were in London at the same time. Also on honeymoon. Rightly, Jack decided that fighting his case in the High Court of London, complete with its lawyers in wigs and gowns, was a wonderful theatrical experience to relish. The fact that it was 'billed' outside the courtroom as 'Nelson v Warner' just completed the picture for him. The idea of a Warner fighting a Nelson was too good to miss. This was going to be his Trafalgar – only he was sure Nelson was going to lose this time.

Bette thought she was on stronger ground, if not on a stronger ship. She was advised by her barrister, the eminent Sir William (later Lord) Jowett, that, since she was away from American soil, her contract could not be enforced.

It was, indeed, slavery, said Jowett. 'This slavery has a silver lining,' Sir Patrick Hastings, for Warner Bros. retorted, 'because the slave was, to say the least, well remunerated.' Until 1942, he pointed out, she would receive $2,400 a week. 'If anyone wants to put me into perpetual servitude on that basis of remuneration, I shall be prepared to consider it.'

If she were a naughty young lady, she had gone to the top of the class and done all her homework. From the moment she joined Warner Bros.

in 1932, playing opposite George Arliss (another star who specialised in biographies – notably *The House of Rothschild* for Twentieth Century Fox) in *The Man Who Played God*, she was their biggest female star. Three years after her arrival, she won an Oscar – for the film *Dangerous*. A further three years later, there was another Academy Award, when she starred in *Jezebel*, which she regarded as compensation for losing out to Vivien Leigh in *Gone with the Wind*, a part she craved. In between, she had been in *The Petrified Forest*, along with Leslie Howard and Humphrey Bogart.

Now, by order of Mr Justice Branson, she would have to go back to do more. He granted Warner Bros. their injunction.

Sir Patrick Hastings, meanwhile, thought that Jack would show his appreciation in more than the 'remuneration' he received for conducting the case to its victory. He handed Jack a script he had written. Warner said it sounded marvellous – put the script in a pile on his desk and never bothered to read a word of it. After all, he had plenty of stories – and he had Bette Davis to star in any number of them.

There were some particularly classy films in the late 1930s and early 1940s. *Dark Victory* in 1939 was one of the archetype Bette Davis roles, a weepy about a woman who discovers she has a brain tumour. She wasn't immune to Warners' biography fad, either. She co-starred with Paul Muni in *Juarez*. Then came *The Private Lives of Elizabeth and Esssex*, in which she played the Virgin Queen, co-starring with Errol Flynn. But it was with *The Letter* and, above all, *Now, Voyager* – about an ugly duckling of a woman who discovers she can be a swan; a movie most famous for the scene in which Paul Henreid lights two cigarettes in his mouth and then hands her one – that she established her position as the Western world's favourite woman star. They found her gutsy and as Jack Warner discovered, gustiness was very popular among women who were used to being tied to the kitchen sink.

But there was always that reputation for being a stormy petrel on the Warner lot. If there was trouble at Burbank, it was a fair bet that someone would find Bette Davis at the centre of it. Nevertheless, about Jack L. Warner she would write: 'No lecherous boss was he. His sins lay elsewhere. He was the father. The power. The glory in the business to make money.'

Julius Epstein, who, with his brother Philip, wrote the film *Mr Skeffington*, directed by Vincent Sherman in 1944, told me of a wonderful example of the Davis power. 'Actually, it was Bette who was doing most of the direction. We were getting late in the production, missing deadlines. Jack came storming on to the set. "Why are you running so late?" he asked. "We're late," I told him "because Bette Davis wants to direct the picture and she's a slow director. And she won't do retakes."

'"She won't do retakes?" Jack screamed. "What do you mean she won't do retakes? I'll tell her she has to do retakes. Whose name is it out there on the water tower? Who built these soundstages? Who the fuck does she think she is? Does it say, 'Bette Davis' or does it say 'Warner Bros.'?" At which point, he stormed off the set and walked his way through the lot, all the time screaming, "Bette Davis says she won't do retakes! I'll tell her . . . She has to do retakes. She's making us lose money. She's got to do retakes." Quite unexpectedly, while he is still shouting, Bette Davis comes out of a dressing room. "Bette, darling!" he greets her. He changes instantly.'

In that film, Bette played the wife of an American Jewish businessman (Claude Rains in one of the most inappropriate bits of casting in Hollywood history) who goes back to Europe and is instantly put into a concentration camp.

'Does this man have to be a Jew?' Jack asked, following the by-now familiar pattern of the Jewish moguls being – to put it kindly – over sensitive about their own origins. It was not a particularly bright comment, since there would have been no story otherwise. Would a White Anglo-Saxon Protestant have been put into a concentration camp?

Jack had another complaint: 'Too many people are saying "Fanny",' said this man whose love of morality wasn't exactly a byword in Hollywood. 'Well,' Epstein told him, 'that's her name, you know.'

As far as Warners was concerned, Bette Davis's name was spelt T-r-o-u-b-l-e. However, when her contract finally came to an end and she went on to make *All About Eve* for Twentieth Century Fox, she was dearly missed.

One of the best-known parts of Hollywood lore stated that Ms Davis and Joan Crawford were like oil and water. They would never mix (although, as we shall see, they later did just that) simply because they hated each other.

It might not be straining things too far to say that signing Joan to a Warner Bros. contract in 1943, after she had been unceremoniously dropped by MGM, was not just a good commercial decision, but a marvellous way of paying Bette Davis back for all the wrongs Jack was certain she had wrought on him. In 1945, she justified Warner's commercial faith by winning an Oscar for *Mildred Pierce*, about an inconsequential housewife who, when her marriage breaks up, is forced to work in a restaurant – then buys her own café and ultimately runs a restaurant chain – in between being involved in a murder (actually committed by her daughter, played by a very young Anne Blyth).

The fact that Jack Warner survived Ms Crawford's contract is testament to his fortitude. He had to daily suffer her insults, usually on the phone, and always using the foulest language heard coming from a female star in Hollywood (and that was saying something). During the making of *Mildred Pierce* she was constantly complaining, most frequently about the cameraman who didn't know how to get the best out of her beauty. As Jack's son-in-law, Bill Orr, who heard some of these exchanges, told me: 'She was right about that. It was true. The cameras were not getting any younger. But she was insulting, excoriating, using foul language. I hated to hear her, not because she was talking to Jack but because she was using that terrible language. Jack was holding the phone away from his ear so that I could hear. After the call, I asked him why he had been so soothing to her, promising to do what he could, to re-shoot scenes if she wanted them to be re-shot. He said, "We have to get her to come into work tomorrow".'

Olivia de Havilland's name was not usually spoken of in the same breath as that of either of the other two divas, Crawford and Davis. But she was a bundle of trouble, too. She had played in the Max Reinhardt version of *A Midsummer Night's Dream* in 1934 and was given a seven-year contract with Warners – with a break (a word to be used in both senses) to play, on loan, Melanie in *Gone with the Wind*. When that film was finished, she returned to her 'home' studio and refused to take a role that Jack Warner had earmarked for her. As a result, she was put on suspension for six months – which the law allowed to be added on to the seven-year agreement.

That wasn't a law that Ms De Havilland wanted to honour. For three years, she fought in the Los Angeles courts, complaining about her slavery – which was with what she, along with every other successful actor who had made a fortune from it, continued to call the contract system. Warners responded, not unreasonably, by saying that she was one of the lucky ones.

Warners, however, made mistakes – and fighting Ms De Havilland was one of them. The contract system, allowing time on suspension to be added to the seven years, was ruled illegal. It was the beginning of an end, which was still a time-a-coming.

Errol Flynn

Jack made other mistakes. Once, he castigated his son-in-law, the eminent producer Mervyn LeRoy: 'How could you waste $500 of mine on giving a screen test to that big ape?' The 'big ape' was a man called Clark Gable. (It proved that he and Sam Goldwyn had something in common.)

Who knows, he might have been as famous as the swashbuckling star Errol Flynn, who, thanks to Warner Bros., had established himself in roles like that of the pirate in *Captain Blood*, for which he would be famous. He co-starred with both Olivia de Havilland and Bette Davis in *The Private Lives of Elizabeth and Essex*; with de Havilland in both *The Charge of the Light Brigade* and in one of Warners' most popular films of the pre-war years, *The Adventures of Robin Hood*, still regarded today as the definitive Robin Hood story. (The 1938 film was the most expensive the studio had made to date – costing more than $2 million.)

Flynn himself, who had begun his film career in the Warners film, *The Case of the Curious Bride*, in which he played a corpse, had an unusual relationship with his boss. He spoke to Jack Warner as though he were one of his drinking pals – which no one else would have dared do. During *The Charge of the Light Brigade* he approached Jack with the words: 'I think I need some more money, chum.'

Jack was not fazed, which was surprising, since any other actor would have been shown the door with the suggestion that he call his agent. 'Sure, Errol,' he said. 'Let's just get the picture over and we'll talk about it.'

'No,' said Flynn. 'Let's do a deal now.' They talked money there and then and shook hands, Jack twisting the cigar in his mouth, with apparent satisfaction. 'The dirty son of a bitch,' he whispered as Flynn left.

Flynn would do all he could to show his contempt for his boss – the star's anti-Semitism was partly responsible for this, most of the people who knew them both agree. Sometimes, his friend Raoul Walsh would aid and abet him. Like the time he and Errol were in New York and the actor, to most people's amazement, was finding himself unlucky in love. Walsh said that the answer was to send the lady in question a dozen red roses, which he ordered on Flynn's behalf. And then, the next day, Errol himself sent her two poodle puppies. 'Your name, sir?' asked the shop-keeper. 'Jack L. Warner,' he answered. 'Address: Warner Bros. Pictures Inc. 321 West 44th Street, New York.' It didn't do much good. The girl jilted Errol, who then threatened to throw himself out of his hotel window – which would have been a revenge of sorts. It wouldn't have pleased Jack at all.

Errol had a good war – he was one of the Hollywood actors who actually never put on a uniform to fight. But like John Wayne, who also failed to sign up for military service, Flynn was always ideal casting when it was necessary to show a brave soldier in a foxhole. He looked marvellous in battle scenes, a helmet slightly askew, mud on his face.

The Tasmanian-born actor (a fact that Americans didn't like to talk about in those days) began the war years on film with a lightly disguised attack on fascism and the Nazi idea of mastery of the world. *The Sea Hawk* was ostensibly about the Spanish Armada, with Flynn playing a pirate called Geoffrey Thorpe, a part that suited him perfectly, as it did the director Michael Curtiz, his partner in *The Charge of the Light Brigade* and one of the great characters in the Warner stable. Curtiz could have easily competed with Sam Goldwyn in his misuse of the English language. It was he who spoke the immortal words during the making of that movie, 'Bring on the empty horses.' During one row with Jack Warner while *Charge* was made, Curtiz stormed out of his boss's office, with a farewell that's still talked about: 'Don't call me back until you're not ready.'

But the film was no laughing matter. It was an enjoyable epic, but it was also a notable polemic exercise. For the Spanish, you read the Germans. The speeches by Flora Robson, as Queen Elizabeth (an incredibly popular character in films of the time, not least for Warner Bros. who had already given their public *Elizabeth and Essex*) were, without too much strain on the thought processes, stirring attacks on what the Nazis were doing at the time.

There could be no doubt that Flynn was unambiguously up-to-date in his other war films, *Dive Bomber*, *Northern Pursuit* and *Objective Burma*. The last of these got him into considerable trouble with British audiences, who believed that their own 14th Army, virtually alone, had fought the Japanese in the Burmese jungles and had suffered appallingly. Warners, under the direct instructions of Jack, mounted a campaign to show how accurate the movie was in its background (although not in the story itself) and in defence of its star – who needed all the defence he could get.

Controversy over the film was nothing in comparison with his private life. He was at the centre of a group of friends, collectively known as the

Roustabouts, heavy drinkers like the actor Alan Hale and the director Raoul Walsh. Their big moment had come when the actor John Barrymore, who was regarded as the patron saint of the set, died. Hale and Walsh broke into the funeral parlour and stole the body. They then took it back to Flynn's house. Flynn walked into his living room, said, 'He doesn't look well,' and ran in flight into his garden, crashing into an oleander bush.

Flynn had escaped jail in 1943 on charges of multiple statutory rape (he had a good lawyer). That was well-publicised in the press at the time. What was kept more secret were the FBI inquiries into the seemingly patriotic star's loyalties. He was suspected of Nazi sympathies; paintings last seen on the walls of Jews in Occupied Europe were mysteriously noticed in Flynn's Los Angeles home – a fact that has never been accurately explained. There were other questions asked – about why Flynn took photographs of the US Pacific Fleet at anchor in Pearl Harbor, shortly before the Japanese attack. The never-proved charge was that he sold pictures to the Japanese. For their part, it was in Warner Bros.' interest to protect their star at all times – a gesture which Flynn returned by saying the most insulting things he could think of about his employers. And throwing stones from Mulhulland Drive down on to Jack's house.

The studio itself also did well in the war. If for no other reason that, for the first time in living memory, Harry and Jack came out in public together, smiled together and seemed to be singing from the same song sheet. They even did broadcasts together, appealing for greater public help for the war effort.

Casablanca

No film Harry and Jack ever made compared with the picture that earned Julius and Philip Epstein an Oscar. I saw the statuette myself when I went to see Julius at his Hollywood home. While he left the room to get a couple of drinks, I looked around the big lawns at the back of the house, studied the over-sized pool and then turned my attention (as I always do) to the books surrounding the room where I waited patiently. As Epstein returned to the room, I could see a piece of brass protruding from behind one of the volumes on movie history. I was nosy and looked further. This was an Oscar. 'What's it for?' I asked him.

'Oh, just for something I wrote.'

'What was it?' I pressed.

'Oh it was a long time ago. I wrote it with my brother.'

Again, I wouldn't let it go. 'What did you write?'

'*Casablanca*,' he replied, as though revealing the winner of a rather boring football game.

Casablanca figures on most people's lists of the perfect film. When it was shown in 1943, it was seen as the movie that contained every single aspect of the ideal war picture. It was a great love story (with great lovers, Ingrid Bergman, Bogart and Paul Henreid), it was topical, it was very patriotic – if with Bogie being more cynical than most actors in parts like his would be. Then there was the wonderfully convincing performance by Claude Rains as the Vichy French police chief with a nice line in supplying exit permits for young ladies who agreed to sleep with him, which, as we have seen, caused a few sleepless nights for the censors. And there was, over and above everything else, the writing – the script, the dialogue and all those quotes, 'We'll always have Paris', 'Here's looking at you, kid' and 'Of all the gin joints in all the towns, in all the world, she walks into mine'.

People still talk about Bogart's order to the pianist, Dooley Wilson: 'Play it again, Sam' – a line which, of course, he never said, although both he and the beautiful Ms Bergman got close to it. As for Wilson's song, 'As Time Goes By', it became a hit forever, more than a decade after it was written by Herman Hupfeld in 1941 for the Broadway show *Everybody's Welcome*.

Above all, it fulfilled that other wartime criterion for the perfect film: it was a huge boost to civilian morale. As for Bogart himself, he found himself a job – driving people to doctors' offices or hospitals. That was when he wasn't before the Warner cameras.

If there had ever been doubts about Bogart's staying power as that mega star (what a pity it wasn't a term used in his day; he deserved knowing that it could be said about him), *Casablanca* dispelled them all. There had been hints of how brilliant he could be in those second-banana roles for Warners before the war. But it had been *High Sierra* written by John Huston for the studio – planned, first of all with Paul Muni and then with George Raft in mind – that put him in the running for a film which, legend has it, was also slated, again not for him, but this time for a certain Ronald Reagan.

However, what really delighted Jack Warner was the fact that there was now much, much more to come.

The movie won more than its share of Oscar nominations – best film, best director (Michael Curtiz), best actor (Bogart), best actress

(Bergman), best supporting actor (Rains), best screenplay, best cinematography (Arthur Edeson), best film editing (Warren Marks), and best scoring of music (Max Steiner). A healthy clutch. But, surprisingly, there were, out of those, only three actual Awards, for Michael Curtiz; then the one I spied out for the Epstein brothers, which they shared with Howard Koch and, finally, the statuette that delighted Jack Warner most. As the compère Jack Benny opened the envelope with all due deliberation and suspense, the Warner party sat, crossing as many fingers as they could reach. 'The Academy Award for best picture of 1943 goes to . . . *Casablanca*.'

Hal Wallis, 'in charge of production' for First National Pictures, jumped out of his seat to collect the award – as was his right – and fell flat on his face. Jack Warner, wreathed in smiles, had positioned himself with his family at the end of an aisle so that he could get up to collect the Oscar. Wallis got up to take it – and tripped over his boss's leg. He got back to his feet and then sat down, furious. Jack smoothed his moustache and moved out into the aisle, down which he walked up to the podium at Grauman's Chinese Theater to collect the Oscar.

Wallis told me: 'Jack had no right to take that Oscar and I detested him for it.' But he needed his job. 'It was a terrible situation to be in. I had to show that I really didn't care.'

He certainly managed to do that. At least, in public. In March 1944, he sent a telegram to the *Los Angeles Times*'s critic and movie editor: I HAVE BEEN WITH WARNER BROS. FOR TWENTY YEARS AND DURING THIS TIME IT HAS BEEN CUSTOMARY HERE AS WELL AS ELSEWHERE FOR THE STUDIO HEAD TO ACCEPT THE ACADEMY AWARD FOR THE BEST PRODUCTION. NATURALLY I WAS GLAD TO SEE JACK WARNER ACCEPT THE AWARD THIS YEAR FOR *CASABLANCA* AS HE DID FOR *THE LIFE OF EMILE ZOLA* STOP I AM HAPPY ALSO TO HAVE CONTRIBUTED MY BIT TOWARD THE MAKING OF THAT PICTURE STOP YOUR COMMENT IN YOUR COLUMN THIS MORNING ON OUR RIVALRY AT WARNER BROS. [ARE] TOTALLY UNJUSTIFIED.

It is possible that Jack Warner himself instigated the telegram.

In his autobiography, Wallis came out of his self-imposed shell and wrote: 'I couldn't believe this was happening. *Casablanca* had been my creation. Jack had absolutely nothing to do with it.'

It all didn't do too many favours for his relationship with the boss – and it was only to get worse. Jack wanted to ease Wallis out of the business and so take over himself as head of all productions. He wasn't exactly subtle – unless you include arranging for a truckload of manure to be emptied under his producer's open window as being subtle.

Jack was smiling every time he heard Wallis squirm. Bogart may have been disappointed at losing his chance of an individual Oscar for *Casablanca*, but he tried not to show it. The ceremony was 'meaningless', he declared. What was the point of competition between actors 'unless they are playing the same part?' he asked. But then he had compensations – and Jack Warner, in particular, was around to make sure he himself got all of the ones that were available to him.

Bogart, wearing white tuxedo at the Awards, looked as good in *Casablanca* in a trench coat, with the collar turned up, a snap-brim hat on his head. It proved to be ideal garb for the private eye he now also settled down to playing in a series of landmark films for Warners.

The great success of the Hollywood studios, especially those who were under the direct control of the founding fathers was that they knew how to use their stars to their best advantage – and Jack L. Warner knew that better than most. The fact that he didn't always show it to his players (or to his other employees) was beside the point, or at least the point as he saw it. As far as he was concerned, his word was law and breaking that law was nothing less than treason. Bogie was to have to atone for his alleged treachery to King Jack in a few years, but for the moment seeing the name 'Sam Spade' painted on to the glass above the doorknob outside a decrepit San Francisco office had been sufficient compensation to him. Three years before *Casablanca*, Bogie as Spade, the private eye in *The Maltese Falcon*, had left all doubts about him behind. He might not have got the part of Rick had he not convinced Warner in that movie that he was Big, Important and Box Office.

Jack, who was the most intolerant of men, loved the idea that Bogie was a man's man, so different from some of the other people with whom he had to deal. He knew how to exploit that, too. Which is how, Rick and Sam Spade metamorphosed into Philip Marlowe, Raymond Chandler's creation, who was fairly interchangeable with the man who searched for the Maltese Falcon. Similarly the part he played in *Key Largo* in 1948 could very easily have fitted into that of the sea captain in *To Have and Have Not*, which, in turn could have served as a sequel to *Casablanca* – if you imagined what might have happened to Rick after he had gone away with Louis, the head of police and then left him. No one, however, was going to make him leave the female lead in *To Have And Have Not* – a discovery as potent as a bottle of Scotch and as enticing as a gallon of

Chanel No.5. It was the film that introduced Lauren Bacall to the cinema-going public – and, in turn, as a wife to Mr Bogart. She was with him in *Key Largo*. Well, even Jack Warner wouldn't have dared to split them.

Eventually Bogie did split from Warner Bros. and almost (almost) regretted it. 'I kind of miss the arguments I had with Warner,' he would say. 'I used to love those feuds. It's like when you've fought with your wife and gotten a divorce. You kind of miss the fighting.'

Difficult Family Relationships

Jack would never have initiated a divorce with Bogart – at least not to his face. It would have been out of character for the man who got underlings to fire the people he wanted to get rid of – including, as we have seen, his son, Jack Jr.

That wasn't exactly calculated to make for ideal father-and-son relations. Indeed, they only saw each other once or twice after that humiliating event. 'He never saw my daughters,' Jack Jr told me. 'Except once when we were at a doctor's office.' They also bumped into each other in the street and the senior Warner invited him to have lunch. 'It was a stiff, difficult occasion,' he said.

The younger Jack told me he had no idea why the breach occurred. His father had never liked the idea that he had to surrender his bespoke-tailor-made uniform when Jack Jr jokingly suggested he salute him. The Warner brother took the alleged slight very seriously, even though the Warner son did not. Another reason for the split could be that the younger man resented the fact that his father had divorced his homespun mother and taken a new wife who gave him a new daughter. Wife Number One had been complaining for years about the time he was spending away from home. At first, she believed it was, as he claimed, a matter of working late at the studio. But before long it was obvious that there was another woman – another woman called Ann. She had been told that he was seeing a dark, Latin beauty, but somehow it was worse when she had a precise identification. It made something that had previously been ephemeral into a definite can't-be-changed situation.

'I wasn't happy about him forsaking my Yiddisher Momma for a *shiksa*!' Jack Jr said, laughing. A Yiddisher Mama who practised Christian Science but was, nevertheless, Jewish. Ironically, Jack Warner would say that some of his biggest rows were over that devotion of his wife to Christian Science. Now, though, he had gone full circle himself and his brothers were less than happy about it. 'None of the family were,' Jack Jr told me. 'In fact, it led to still more rows between my dad and Uncle Harry.'

There are many other suggestions for the rift between the two Jacks. One was that the older man resented the statements his son made at the time he himself had a serious road accident. He thought Jack Jr had told the press that he was about to die. And then there was another complication at that same time – the son refused to pay court to his stepmother when he went to visit his father in hospital. Ann, on the other hand, always resented the fact that her husband had never seen fit to introduce his son to her – or to let the younger Warner meet his stepsister, Barbara, the daughter Jack had with his second wife.

But things were not always totally bad between them. 'You can't imagine how much I wanted to have a good relationship with my dad,' the younger Jack told me. 'I had hoped he would warm to me after one incident in his office. Uncle Harry and he were having one of their spirited arguments. I saw Harry pick up a heavy paperweight on his desk and he was about to throw it at Dad, who ducked. I, though, grabbed it from my uncle before he could do any damage with it. I think Uncle Harry, who cherished family relationships, even though he and Dad hated each other, appreciated what I did.'

Jack Jr told me that he dreamed of building up a relationship with his dad. 'I would like to have felt that he loved me,' he told me. 'But there was never any warmth there. I think I detected that he would have liked to have been closer at one stage, but it wasn't in his nature to do so. He was proud of me, I used to think. But maybe afterwards, he thought I was going to be something of a threat. Or perhaps he just didn't think I was up to his standard of ruthlessness. I certainly couldn't have done some of the things that he did.'

Harry, on the other hand, had given up his dreams of having his own daughter run the business after his demise and was determined that it wouldn't fall into the hands of anyone from Jack's line. That could be another explanation for Jack Jr's departure – especially since the general feeling was that the 'boy' was not fulfilling his potential. If rough ruthlessness was a quality demanded of the successful Hollywood mogul, then Jack Jr wouldn't have easily stepped into either his father's or his uncle's shoes. But he had a good brain and understood the business, sprocket by sprocket.

The War Years

Jack Senior's attitude suited the films he was making – and which, grudgingly, received his eldest brother's approval. The style of Warner films didn't change for a decade. Jack had someone in his publicity department to craft a statement about its sense of responsibility for America. 'More and more is the realisation growing that pictures can play an all-important part in the cultural and educational development of the world,' he said. 'We should strive for pictures that provide something more than a mere idle hour or two.'

Even if they weren't all the hard-bitten Bogart-Cagney-Raft heavy-weight type movies, there was something of the same gritty quality, even about the musicals, which, though no longer a Burbank speciality, were still being made – and still succeeding. Sammy Cahn told me: 'Warner Bros. had brought in Erich Wolfgang Korngold, Hugo Friedehofer and Ray Heindorf. Jack Warner said he wanted to have music from the first title saying "Warner Bros. Presents" to "The End". If a film started to slow down, Warner would say, "Bring in the music department," so that we could fill in appropriately.'

Yankee Doodle Dandy in 1942 had fulfilled the qualifications that Jack himself laid down as studio policy: it was wartime and, therefore, Warner Bros. had to do its bit in fighting both the Japanese and the Nazis. After previously kowtowing to German pressure and even keeping an office open in Germany throughout the early years of Nazism, Jack L. Warner was now making the war a personal crusade. Nevertheless, he closed the Berlin office only when the SS stormed the building and killed its director. Like every other Hollywood studio, there were talks with Dr Josef Goebbels, the German propaganda minister, to be sure that nothing would be done to offend Nazi sensibilities. But that was now in the past. After insisting that he didn't want any Jewish content to his films – a lingering sentiment, which is why he was so unhappy with *Mr Skeffington* – he now made it clear that he was deeply offended, as if Hitler had declared war on Warner Bros. alone.

That was the first criterion – be patriotic. The second criterion was how to manifest it. Sure, there were to be the war films of which Errol Flynn was proving to be undoubtedly, if embarrassingly, the master, but there were also going to be movies which made the people who put their ten cents or shillings over the box-office counter and waited for the tickets to sprout up from a hidden slot, feel better.

Yankee Doodle Dandy was as patriotic as the American flad, which seemed to be flying ever time James Cagney opened his mouth or danced a step. The movie began shooting the day that the Japanese invaded Pearl Habor – which was a good omen as far as the film was concerned. 'What publicity opportunities!' said Jack – and he was right.

Joan Leslie, the teenage actress who the studio had succeeded in grooming as their big new star, recalled that first day for me. 'We heard President Roosevelt on the radio, speaking about Pearl Harbor and Jimmy said: 'I think this is the time for prayer.' All Jack Warner was praying for was a hit.

The film was the story – highly romanticized, as was the usual way with Hollywood biographies – of the song and dance man George M. Cohan, who not only had half a dozen Broadway shows that he was producing on at the same time, but was writing the popular ditties of the First World War, like 'Mary's a Grand Old Name' and the archetype show number, 'Give My Regards to Broadway', in addition to 'Yankee Doodle Dandy' itself. He also wrote the stirring 'Over There', the most patriotic of all the patriotic World War I songs. Jack Warner himself saw the beauty in that. He told the director Michael Curtiz to keep going back to the First World War – because that would stir people to win the second.

Thanks to the persistence of Hal Wallis, Jack had started thinking on those lines as far back as 1940, when Europe was engulfed in the war and when – in an example of prescience he couldn't always claim – Jack thought America getting into the conflict was inevitable. And so had Cagney – if only because his boss had told him so. More than a year before Pearl Harbor, he starred in *The Fighting 69th*, about a recruit who thinks himself too clever for the trenches, then becomes a hero and is killed as a result.

It turned out to be not such a good idea as far as certain members of Congress were concerned. In 1941, questions were asked about the role of the studio when they made *Confessions of a Nazi Spy*. The isolationist members of the House alleged that Warner Bros. were guilty not just of scare tactics, but of 'war propaganda'. Harry defended his studio. Everything in the film, he insisted, was just 'factual'.

He issued a statement to the US Senate's Sub-committee on Interstate Commerce. 'Reckless and unfounded charges have been made before your committee against Warner Bros. and myself. These charges are so vague, that, frankly, I have great difficulty in answering them. However, they have been widely disseminated and may be believed by the uninformed.'

Nor was he, as was vehemently charged, trying to 'incite people to go to war'. As he said, on that question: 'This we deny. Warner Bros. has been producing pictures on current affairs for over twenty years and our present policies are no different than before there was a Hitler menace.' There was no doubt that the studio's output was accurate. 'They were all carefully researched. They show the world as it is.'

The committee had made an astounding charge – that Warners were making films that the public did not want to see (as if any business could possibly do that). 'The proof of the pudding is in the eating,' he said. 'All of the productions complained of have been profitable.'

As for the *Nazi Spy* picture, 'If Warner Bros. had produced no pictures concerning the Nazi movement, our public would have had good reason to criticise. We would have been living in a dream world.'

It was all very strong stuff. Not just that. It was contrary to what all Hollywood was doing. Harry emphasised his policy by saying that Warner Bros. cinemas were no longer going to show German-made newsreels that gave the impression that the Nazis ran a 'peace-loving country'.

Pearl Harbor stopped that row.

By the time *Yankee Doodle Dandy* was in the theatres, there was no doubt that the studio had been on the right wavelength. It not only did extraordinarily well at the box office, it was the biggest hit of the year and Cagney – 'once a song and dance man, always a song and dance man,' he told me – got an Oscar for his trouble. The film itself was nominated for best picture, but failed to win, although there was one for music direction (Heinz Roemheld).

The idea of going back to World War I in the battle for coming out tops in the new conflict gave rise to the other big, big musical of 1942-3. Jack led the fight to get the screen rights for Irving Berlin's all-Service show, *This is the Army*, which was staffed by 350 servicemen, none of whom drew more than their military salary. The Warner cast refused to take any extra money, with those on contract salary just doing it as another job.

Even though he wasn't going to make too much of a profit on a film for which all the royalties would go to military charities – $9 million in the end – it was more great publicity for the studio. In a way, it was the film of the show which had not only wowed people on Broadway with the same kind of patriotic fervour Jack was trying to bring to his films, it had made history, by going round the world. As in the live show every scene was played by servicemen; most of them totally unknown – although a certain Major Ronald Reagan starred in the linking storyline, along with Joan Leslie again. In pursuing the World War I angle, Irving Berlin – whose idea it all was and who, of course, wrote all the songs, words and music – put on his old (if finely tailored, just like Jack Warner's) 1917 uniform, complete with Boy Scout style hat and sang a song with which small boys all over the world could identify – 'Oh How I Hate to Get Up in the Morning'. (After Berlin recorded this song, he overheard a technician saying, 'If the guy who wrote this song could hear the way this guy's *moidering* it, he'd turn over in his grave.')

But the really exciting number and one that probably did more for the Army recruitment campaign than any other was the song 'This Time' in which a soldier in full battle dress, surrounded by seemingly a whole battalion of singing soldiers, led them in an aria proclaiming,

> 'This time, we won't say curtain until
> We're certain
> we ring it down in their own home town.'

The message was that since the war wasn't finished 'last time', America was going to do it now – 'so we won't have to do it again'.

There were other allusions to the First World War and to America's resolve to get it all finished once and for good. *Wilson* in 1944 was ostensibly a biopic, celebrating the life of the US President of the first war, Woodrow Wilson, the man whose campaign slogan had been 'He Kept Us Out of War' and then not only did go in, in 1917, but also laid down the terms of the Armistice a year later. The war gave it all new resonance, which it might not have achieved without America being in the midst of the big fight. Like *Sea Wolf,* it superimposed a previous conflict on to the one being fought at that moment. But more than that, the Democratic Party was ecstatic – because they knew that the underlying message was: for Wilson read Roosevelt. And the President was about to fight his fourth election campaign. Had there ever been a better election message?

That was all Jack's doing. The film may have starred Alexander Knox in the title role and he was splendid in it. The photography may have been perfect. The direction by Henry King couldn't have been better. But it was Jack Warner's creation from start to finish.

As much as anything, he made the film because he wanted to remain in President Roosevelt's good books. Could there possibly be, he asked himself, a better person to have on his side than the leader of the Free World? How useful could that be in the future? He knew the answer. Just as he knew the answer when he responded to Roosevelt's call for a movie that would help convince the American people that the Soviet Union was a trusted ally, a friend who needed help.

Warner's response had been to make *Mission to Moscow,* the film with the most realistic lookalikes (for Roosevelt, Churchill and Stalin) ever put on to celluloid. In a way, it was reminiscent of the studio's first big project, *My Four Years in Germany*. Like that film, *Mission* was based on the diaries of an ambassador, Joseph E. Davies, envoy to the Russian capital. It wouldn't bear much scrutiny today and it won no Oscars, but it did surprisingly well at the box office. Surprisingly? Perhaps not so surprisingly. Warners themselves, under the guidance of Major Abe, had enough theatres to ensure it got reasonable playing time, and the international mood was such that it could be chalked up as a financial hit in the rest of the allied world, too.

One of Hollywood's great contributions to the war effort was to set up the Hollywood Canteen, a converted livery stable, at which troops stationed in Los Angeles, but about to be shipped off to some battlefield or other, could dance with real film stars who also served them with sandwiches, coffee and doughnuts.

Warners decided that they could make a film around the plainly most patriotic thing that the film industry was doing. People like Bette Davis, Eddie Cantor, the Andrews Sisters, John Garfield, Barbara Stanwyck, Jane Wyman and Janis Page took part in the film – much to the annoyance of the Screen Actors Guild, who said that their members were not being paid enough. Halfway through the movie production, they called a strike and stopped work on the project. All those taking part, said SAG, were paid a total of half the fee that would have gone to a contract star.

Warner Bros. sued the Guild and claimed that between 750 and 1,000 extras would be put out of work. Not only that, the studio had promised the Canteen $250,000 which they would not now get.

A compromise was worked out and filming recommenced. But it was a good deal for the studio. Warner Bros. had a mass of actors available – still for much less than they would normally have to pay – a simple script and virtually no expense on making a set. They had similar rewards from *Thank Your Lucky Stars,* which featured almost every player on contract to the studio and available to appear before the cameras at the same time as the picture was being filmed. There were no problems about using Humphrey Bogart, Joan Leslie, Errol Flynn, Ann Sheridan and Olivia De Havilland among dozens of others – because they were under contract at the time. The most notable feature of the film was the appearance of Bette Davis, singing her only song on film – 'They're Either Too Old or Too Young'.

'The Nicest Man in the Country'

As a result of their war work, Jack Warner and his brothers were hailed as the perfect Americans – immigrants who showed a loyalty to their adopted country and its government that all too many native-born citizens couldn't match. Jack's trouble was that he believed his own publicity. He began to talk about himself as though he were the nicest man in the country – which is why his employees should show him full respect. It was also why he decided that there had to be ways of ensuring that while he paid his staff for a full-day's work, that was precisely what they should give him. Saturdays were regarded as a normal working day, although writers tended to think that was a penance and frequently failed to turn up – until Jack ordered that the gateman keep a record of who came in and left, and when.

There was to be no nonsense about lunch breaks, for instance. His writers, on the other hand, the people who were clever enough to dream up plots for his films, were equally clever in finding new ways to get round his regulations. Melville Shavelson revealed one of them to me: 'We were told we couldn't go out during the day, but we wanted to do so. We wanted to go to restaurants or to bars or to play golf – like the stars did. So we arranged for a truck to be parked outside the writers' building – with a tarpaulin. When one o'clock came, we all clambered into the truck and hid under the tarpaulin, so that we could go to our favourite restaurant for an hour. We were, needless to say, never discovered.' If they had been, Warner Bros. would have been without any writers at all. Jack didn't tolerate disobedience and if he found there had been any, there would have been the letter delivered in person by whichever underling had been deputed that day to do the firing.

The tarpaulin gag wasn't the only one used to defy Warner's instructions. Julius Epstein told me of another with even more laughable – and effective –consequences. There were murmurings that the writers were producing their own material for their own devious purposes in the course of their working hours. Jack decided that was not just a breach of discipline, it was immoral – to the extent that he claimed (and could have been right in law) the copyright to everything produced during that work time. Epstein's answer was to go to his boss and tell him: 'Jack, you know I had a great idea for our film yesterday.' 'Really,' said Jack, 'what is it?' 'A super idea,' said the writer. 'One that will make all the difference to the picture.' 'So,' said Jack, 'tell me about it.' 'I can't,' Epstein answered. 'I thought of it in the bath at eight am. Yesterday. Since we don't start work till nine, it's my own idea, not yours.' At that point, even Jack Warner had to surrender. But he was exasperated. He once said to Epstein's brother Philip: 'I want back all the money I've been paying you.'

Philip replied: 'I'd love to help you but, you see, I've built a pool with the money. However, if you're ever in the neighbourhood, you're welcome to come and use it.'

He rarely did that, as we have seen. Nor did Jack accept the norms of decent behaviour. Not, that is, if the publicity value of one of his stunts was involved. Joan Leslie, who made a remarkable transfer from young adulthood to old age in *Yankee Doodle Dandy* celebrated her 16th birthday while working on the film. 'Jack called in all the press and then took me to one of the sound stages. There, I saw a beautiful brand new car. "This," he told everybody, "is my birthday present for Joan."

'Then he gave me the keys for the car. I was so excited.' She kissed him and looked over the new gift. It could only happen in Hollywood. So could what occurred next. 'When everybody left, he asked me for the keys back – and I never saw the car again.'

You could say that was an indulgence on Jack Warner's part. He did a lot of that. Indulging himself in things that were not only immoral, but which occasionally brought his studio – which deserved credit for so many ground-breaking ideas – into disrepute. The press steered clear of printing stories that might be considered too unflattering; the stunts, the jokes. They may have known about the Joan Leslie car fiasco, but never said a word. But the jokes sometimes got just that little bit too jokey.

Sometimes, however, those indulgences of Jack's were good for business. Jack was ready now to put his passion for Al Jolson to effect. In 1945, he indulged both his love for business and that for Jolson together with what he hoped would be a definitive cine biography of George Gershwin. *Rhapsody in Blue*, the perfect title for the perfect film devoted to the man who was the epitome of the perfect 'cross-over' composer, the song writer of beautiful melodies like – his last – 'Love Is Here to Stay',

Partners, but not for long – Sam Goldwyn, left, and Charlie Chaplin in Paris in 1953, long after they had ceased to be in business together.

The Warner Brothers – Jack, left, Harry, centre, and Albert (the ex-sergeant who liked to be known as 'Major'). Sam, the technical genius of the family, died on the day of his biggest triumph – the opening of the first talkie, *The Jazz Singer*. The picture was taken to mark the sale of the studio. Jack didn't tell his brothers that he was about to buy back his share of the stock – for the price at which he sold it.

Jack Warner loved to show his patriotism. Here he is in 1943 with Captain Edward MacAuley, Deputy Administrator of the War Shipping Administration. The pennant is the US Maritime Service's victory flag.

'So this is where your work goes?' The young (17-year-old) Joan Leslie, left, in the Warner vaults with her mother, Mrs Agnes Brodel, and her sister, Betty.

Thousands (make that millions) did cheer, but nobody more than Arthur Freed, the head of the MGM musicals unit, Judy Garland, Louis B. Mayer himself and Irving Berlin – who didn't smile that often.

Harry Cohn, the iron dictator of Columbia Pictures, at the controls. He was usually happier pressing the buttons that 'hooked' him into the private dressing rooms of his stars.

Jesse Lasky was not too choosy about his friends – here he is, right, with Joseph Kennedy, bootlegger, boss of RKO and father of the future president, in 1924.

Thinking about the old days – the movie pioneers Cecil B. De Mille, left, Adolph Zukor, centre, and Jesse Lasky. The occasion: a celebration to mark Zukor's 80th birthday and his 50th anniversary in show business.

of an acclaimed piano concerto, the folk opera *Porgy and Bess*, and the 'Rhapsody' itself.

Robert Alda – father of Alan Alda – played Gershwin, and Alexis Smith and Joan Leslie were there, to provide the love interest in entirely fabricated roles. Interestingly, Ms Smith would play virtually the same part the following year in *Night and Day*, supposedly based on Cole Porter's life. Porter was a noted homosexual (Alexis played his wife; Porter did actually marry), Gershwin decidedly was not, but in addition, there was not much in the *Rhapsody* film that could be said to have actually happened. On the other hand, Oscar Levant was on hand to play one of George's close friends, which he certainly was, and to play the piano, which he did brilliantly, notably in the final performance of the 'Rhapsody' at the end of the movie. He also had a chance to use his own dialogue – reprising the bright witty things he was delighted to remember he had said in real life, including the unforgettable 'Tell me George, if you had a chance to fall in love with yourself again would you still do so?'

A weak Jolson, who, newly recovered from a serious illness after entertaining the troops, sang George's first song, 'Swanee', with all the verve he could muster. And, inevitably Paul Whiteman, who had been the conductor at its first performance of 'Rhapsody in Blue', reprised that historic moment.

The idea for the film had come from Jesse L. Lasky, the kind of entrepreneur filmmaker who would never let a good idea go. As we shall see, long separated from Adolph Zukor, he was in business on his own and producing the *Rhapsody* picture was the answer to his dreams. The film was exactly the way he planned it – with Jack Warner's intervention.

If you could excuse the fictionalisation of the story, which was good enough and certainly strong enough to tell without making so much up, and despite Warner's constant determination not to talk about Jews in his movies – Gershwin's father, played by Morris Carnovsky, said lots of Jewish things in the movie without mentioning the three-letter 'J' word once – it was an entertaining project. Why it was made in black and white remains a mystery. Colour was always reserved for films that were either considered spectacles or were decreed to be 'special' and this movie should have certainly been in that second category. But it was in black and white.

That was one of the reasons why, surprisingly, Warner Bros. lost the opportunity to make a biopic of Jolson himself. The firm, and Jack himself in particular, were seen as the obvious and logical home for the movie that the columnist Sidney Skolsky was beginning to hawk round the Hollywood studios. As he told me: 'I wanted to make a film of the life of the King of Broadway and Entertainment and I knew that Jack Warner was as smitten with Jolson as I was.' But not smitten enough to commit himself to a big enough budget – which would have meant colour.

Jolson would have wanted Warners to do the picture. He fancied James Cagney playing him. But, despite (or maybe because of) the success of playing George Cohan in *Yankee Doodle Dandy*, he didn't seem right, either to the studio or himself.

Skolsky, as we shall see in another chapter, found a home for what became *The Jolson Story* at Columbia – where, coincidentally, Al had recently taken an honorary job as a producer – although the only thing he seems to have produced at the studio was an extravagant phone bill.

McCarthyism

Jack Warner, however, was moving on to other things. There were opportunities to appear in the public prints. In May 1947, those appearances in newspapers and on radio illustrated that other trait to which people who knew him recognised all too easily: his cowardice. When HUAC, the House Un-American Activities Committee, held its first hearings in Hollywood, Jack Warner proudly stepped up to the witness table and declared his loyalty to the United States, the committee and to himself. Unlike Sam Goldwyn, he had no compunction whatever in appearing to take the committee's party line. He had a reputation to live up to – not the one that everyone said he had as a hedonist but as a real patriot, who had been awarded the Medal of Merit for his work during the war.

John Huston asked him what he had told the committee. He said he had 'given them some names' – and then added, 'I guess I shouldn't have done, should I? I guess I'm a squealer.' He was, in fact, squealing loud and clear. Later, he would explain it, as a case of being 'emotional in an emotional business'.

The hearings were, at this stage, in private, but transcripts of his evidence both at the Biltmore Hotel in Hollywood and the public sessions in the caucus room at the Capitol in Washington later, revealed the extent of his support for J. Parnell Thomas's committee. He would never knowingly employ a Communist, he declared. In fact, he had failed to renew the contracts of 11 writers who he was sure were reds. As far as he was concerned, they were all termites and when he had termites in his building, he made sure he would destroy them. 'My brothers and

I will be happy to subscribe generously to a pest-removal fund,' he declared. 'We are willing to establish such a fund to ship to Russia the people who don't like our American system of government and prefer the Communistic system to ours.'

As always when making public statements, Jack dressed in his best Schmidt-made suit, a flower in his buttonhole, with his moustache duly trimmed, and warmed to the opportunity to emote to his heart's delight. 'If there are Communists in our industry, or any other industry, organisation or society who want to undermine our free institutions, let's find out about it and know who they are.'

He then declared war on writers. 'Communists inject ninety-five per cent of their propaganda into films through the medium of writers.'

That was followed up by the most unforgivable sin of all: he gave a list of Communists working for him, a list published on all the front pages of the newspapers circulating in California. At the top of the list were the Epstein brothers who had given him *Casablanca*, *Mr Skeffington* and much more.

'Looking down the list,' Julius Epstein told me, 'we found that they were all people he either wanted to get rid of or who wanted to get out of their contracts. If you didn't want to work any more for Warner Bros., you had to be Un-American.'

A little while later, when Congressman John Wood was chairman of the committee, the Epsteins were sent a questionnaire. Among the questions were: 1. Have you ever been a member of a subversive organisation? 2. Name that organisation.

'We wrote down: "1. Yes. 2. Warner Bros." We never heard another thing about it.'

But they did hear from Jack Warner. He wrote the brothers a letter, apologising. Not that that was always the end of the matter. The question of Communists in the studio was, hardly surprisingly, the main topic of conversation at the writers' table in the Warner commissary. As a result, one man reported Philip Epstein to Harry Warner, who called the writer into his office – in the presence of the 'spy'. 'I understand you have been talking communistic,' said the studio presence. Philip saw the man who had fingered him – and punched him to the floor. 'Shush,' said Warner, 'I have the same thing in my own family.'

Jack heard about the commissary conversations, too. One day he stormed into the large room himself, poking his fists at the men who he tried to tell himself owed more loyalties to Moscow than they did to

Warner Bros. One by one, that lunchtime they suffered from Jack's verbal jousts as well as the physical onslaught. 'I can do without you!' he shouted. 'I can do without you.' 'I can do without you.' He was about to make the same statement to the producer Jerry Wald, busily engaged in making a film for the studio at that very time. 'And I can almost do without you.'

It is fair to say that Warner wasn't just worried about what HUAC would say. For the first time in his life he was worried about publicity – the sort dished out by the American Legion. The do-gooders (or do-badders as it later became evident) were ready to picket theatres that were booked to show films involving the writers, directors or actors that the committee had charged with being reds.

Harry worried even more than Jack. One man pleaded with the head of the company to allow him to stay in his job. 'I am an anti-Communist,' he protested. 'I don't care what kind of Communist you are,' yelled Harry. 'You're fired.' It was funny, but it was also frighteningly part of the Hollywood way of life, although 'way of death' might be more appropriate.

Without the Warners' cowardice and that of most of their fellow producers, McCarthyism, as it came to be called, would never have got the hold that it did on the film industry and hundreds of careers – and not a few lost lives – would have been saved.

Jack Warner bit off his nose to spite his face and lost the potential of those writers whom he convinced the committee he hated for their red-coloured views. People like John Huston, who had introduced *High Sierra* to the studio, and Robert Rossen, who went on to make *All the King's Men*, were told that their Warner Bros. days were over. The eminent director Vincent Sherman walked towards his office to see his name being erased from the door. Of course Jack didn't tell him about it first.

One of the saddest stories was of that staple of the Warner repertory company, Edward G. Robinson. He had joined no political party, had written no political articles or made any political speeches, but because he had played 'unsavoury' characters on the screen, he was named. Charges that he had been a Communist couldn't be made to stick but he was known as a 'leftish liberal'. That was enough to have him put on a 'grey' list, not the familiar 'black list', which would have made him entirely unemployable, but a list which ensured he would be relegated to bit parts – quite a humiliation. So was the article that Robinson published under his name – but which he later disavowed – 'The Reds Made A Sucker Out of Me'.

That was part of the Warner Bros. deal to partly get him off the hook. He wasn't the only one to do it.

In fact, you could say that Jack Warner's biggest contribution to HUAC's case was not so much the evidence he gave to the committee as the threats that emanated from his office. In October 1947 Jack, who had been chosen to represent all the moguls, and Gary Cooper – who had made the archetypal First World War film, *Sergeant York*, for Warners – sat at their table and became 'friendly witnesses'. It was a sobering sight. *Sergeant York* had been a movie that fitted perfectly with Jack's dictum that reprising the 1917-18 (US) conflict was the ideal morale booster for the second war. So having the two men, studio boss and star, 'on stage' told the nation that HUAC wasn't a bigoted group, but one that was going to emphasise the good things about Hollywood. The fact that they – and people like Robert Taylor and Adolphe Menjou – said how much they hated the dirty Commies was just what the men from Washington wanted to hear. Before long, ten Hollywood figures – nine of them writers, along with the director Edward Dmytryk – also appeared before the committee. The 'Hollywood Ten', as they became known, were all ultimately jailed for contempt of Congress.

While they attempted to argue their case, another group of Hollywood personalities hired a plane to take them to Washington, where they delivered a petition and attempted to lobby the committee. They also took part in a radio broadcast, *Hollywood Fights Back*. The group called themselves 'The Committee for the First Amendment' – the First Amendment of the American Constitution being the one that guarantees freedom of speech. Among them were John Huston, Larry Adler, Danny Kaye, and Humphrey Bogart and his new wife, Lauren Bacall. They all made speeches saying they were there to defend the rights of decent Americans who just wanted to be able to carry on their working lives.

But, as soon as they got back, the flak began to fly and unprintable results of human living hit the fan. Jack Warner went berserk and, more than any of his competitors, sought to distance himself from the Committee for the First Amendment's activities. He made it clear that unless there were retractions – like Robinson's – they would be out of work. The first to cave in were the Bogarts. They issued statements that, if anything, were more cowardly than Jack's own. Bogie declared his part of the proceedings had been 'ill-advised, foolish'. He added: 'I detest Communism.' Worse, he said that he had been 'duped'.

To ingratiate himself more with the mogul, he now made sure that, just as in the war, he called his boss, 'Colonel'. There was no better way of flattering him – unless it was to play tennis – or 'studio tennis' as the locals called it. Some of the really serious battles between the brothers occurred on the tennis court. To say nothing of rows with executives who knew where their bread was buttered. The studio tennis games were on Sunday mornings and Jack employed a former champion player to co-ordinate the game on his own magnificently maintained court and its landscaped surroundings. It used to be said that he cared more about the court than he did about the game – he almost hit a partner in a doubles match who decided to eat a sandwich between games, dripping juice on to the surface. When his partner slipped and found it difficult to get up, all Jack cared about was the damage to the court. He didn't even inquire after the injured player. The pro would be no help. He just did what Jack wanted – including telling players just how often they were expected to lose. The mogul was proud of his backhand and liked to believe his 'victories' were entirely due to his own prowess. 'That was typical of my dad,' said Jack Jr.

New Stars of the Screen

Of course, there always were battles over something. In the late 1940s and early 1950s, Jack Warner personally declared war – on television. He saw the little box in the corner of the living room as the principal enemy of the movie business – to the extent that he refused to allow a television to be seen on a Warner set. He banned the use of the song 'I'm in Love with the Girl on Channel Nine' when he saw it featured in a script.

He refused to allow Warner films to be shown on what America was already calling the Tube. What was more, he said no to any suggestion that his company offer films to its renters that had first been shown on the small screen. After all, why should he bother? He now had Marlon Brando on his books – to say nothing of all the controversial publicity engendered by his film, *A Streetcar Named Desire*. Jack loved the publicity, but the man who believed that women should be seen in satin dresses and men in smart double-breasted suits with flowers in the lapel (he once ordered Ronald Reagan to change his shirt because the collar looked untidy) bristled at the new 'fashion' that the picture inspired. No,

Brando's dirty vest didn't go down well with him. Nor did he fancy taking Vivien Leigh to bed when he saw how old and dissipated she looked in *Streetcar*. But the film caused a sensation and made a box office fortune and there was little more that he could ask than that.

Later, he saw the obvious error in his ways and ordered that the studio should start making TV films themselves. Though to say he was wary would be an understatement, as going into TV would be seen by his competitors as eating a hefty dose of humble pie. There had to be a face-saving operation as well as a pocket-filling success. The first would come if he achieved the second. But Jack wasn't taking any risks before he could boast new Warner Bros. triumphs. His TV staff were ordered to keep everything totally secret, as if they were working for a government on a new weapon. Which was precisely what they were. Everyone involved had to report directly to Warner himself. They weren't even allowed to use their own secretaries to type letters or memos. At a pinch, they could use the typing pool at the studio, but if they could employ stenographers from outside, so much the better.

Jack put Bill Orr in charge of the television operation – which had considerable success. Among the first projects was – say it not, you cinema purists – a TV serial based on *Casablanca*. It was a better success than it deserved to be. Then there was *Dragnet* and *The FBI Story*, *Maverick* and a series called *Days of Wine and Roses*, which later became a landmark big-screen movie with Jack Lemmon and Lee Remick and a great success for Warners.

Lemmon himself had had a highly successful introduction to Warner Bros. with *Mister Roberts*, also starring Henry Fonda and William Powell.

It was once again a good time to be Jack Warner. He was introducing another new star to the public, who became one of the most popular personalities in America – Doris Day. From the black and white *Young Man with a Horn* (or *Young Man of Music*, as it was known in Britain, for reasons which many young boys would have understood), through *I'll See You in My Dreams* (a biography of the songwriter Gus Kahn, played by Danny Thomas) and *By the Light of the Silvery Moon* to *The Pajama Game* and *Lullaby of Broadway*, right up to the iconic *Calamity Jane*, she made a fortune for the studio.

Warner Bros. was now also celebrating a whole swathe of new multi-coloured, wide screen movies that have become part of movie legend.

Judy Garland made her most notable film since *The Wizard of Oz* in 1954. *A Star is Born* was a remake of the 1930s Janet Gaynor-Fredric March movie, but was much more powerful, thanks not just to Judy's singing a clutch of great songs like 'Born in a Trunk' and 'The Man Who Got Away', but because of the heavyweight acting of her co-star James Mason. Though Garland herself was no slouch when it came to acting honours for the movie.

Then there was Frank Sinatra in *Young at Heart*, cashing in on his amazing rebirth as a record star with best-selling albums like *Songs For Swinging Lovers* and *A Swinging Affair*. Of course, the comeback was mainly the result of his Oscar-winning performance in *From Here to Eternity*, and Warners milked the chance of tying in the new film with that success.

More significant than even these, was the discovery of a young, dishevelled actor who was instantly dubbed the 'New Brando'. In just three Warner Bros. films, James Dean became a cult figure. No one was more surprised at the success of *East of Eden, Rebel Without a Cause* and *Giant* (with Elizabeth Taylor, borrowed for the movie from MGM) than the brothers themselves. They couldn't understand much about the scripts (Jack still said he didn't want to read books that he couldn't lift and Harry was still keen on seeing films ready by Tuesday), but they could read the balance sheets.

Not that everything they touched turned to gold. Gregory Peck, who was one of the great heart-throb leading men of post-war American films and would go on as such for another generation, flopped badly in one of his few Warner films, *Moby Dick*.

Final Curtain

Film purists say the change in fortune had something to do with the change in the Warner Bros. logo. The dignified shield formed around the company's initials got wider along with the screens. Despite the big successes of late, there were plenty of people who said that the Warner Bros. quality went down with the end of the black and white era, in which they had formed such an important part.

In 1957, the rumours were rife that the brothers were going to sell out. Errol Flynn went on record with a telegram he sent his boss. 'CHIEF DON'T SELL WHO WILL I FIGHT WITH?' As Bill Orr told me: 'Jack liked people to stand up for themselves.'

But there was indeed a problem that Hollywood saw coming. Jack's fights were seemingly as important a part of Hollywood as were his movies – and his jokes. He was still regarded as the village idiot of Hollywood. But a very, very clever idiot.

But then something happened that fitted as well into the Jack Warner story as virtually anything he ever did. The brothers announced that they really were selling out. The Warner Bros. without a Warner brother? Could that possibly be true? Indeed it could, if the newspaper financial pages could be believed – and everybody did believe the newspaper financial pages.

The story was correct. The truth was that the company had sold 800,000 shares – for $22 million. The buyer would be a Boston banker by the name of Serge Semenenko.

Jack had always had complaints from his brothers, protesting at not being told about film projects. Now, Harry and Abe were grumbling about the sale they knew nothing about. They first heard about it in the form of whispers in the Wilshire Boulevard Temple in Beverly Hills on Yom Kippur. They knew that Semenenko had bought the shares. What they did not know was that Jack had immediately bought his own shares back again – for the price at which he had sold them. Neither did they know that part of his agreement was that Jack become president of the company – with roughly his old power. His two brothers were given places on the board, but with no authority whatever.

They never spoke to Jack after that. Which suited the youngest Warner Bros. just fine. Particularly since he knew the effect it was going to have on Harry.

Jack Warner was really the boss now. As for Harry, 'I've got the old bastard by the balls at last,' Jack said. 'He can't do a goddamned thing.' Soon afterwards, Harry had a heart attack and a stroke. 'I have no doubt my father was the cause,' Jack Jr told me. Harry died in 1958 at the age of 76.

Rabbi Edgar Magnin said at his funeral, which Jack didn't attend: 'He was a plain, simple man who loved above all else being a farmer.' That was a secret few knew about, although he did have a ranch and used to breed horses. On the whole, however, Harry was a man who liked to keep things to himself. That was one of those things. Abe lived on until 1967.

Jack, meanwhile, showed that as President of Warner Bros., he was very much the boss. He had an idea and no one was going to deflect him from it. It was the same idea that Sam Goldwyn had had – to make a musical based on the *Pygmalion* story.

My Fair Lady had been the most successful Broadway show of all time and there were hefty negotiations before Jack secured the film rights. But the boss spoke and the rights were his. Rex Harrison rejoiced in being able to recreate his own role as Henry Higgins on screen. Stanley Holloway was again to play the part of the dustman father of the 'Fair Lady', Eliza Doolittle, portrayed by Julie Andrews in the stage show. Julie waited for the phone call. It didn't come. Jack Warner thought she was too much of an unknown. Only those who had seen her on stage in New York or London had even heard of her. It would prove to be perhaps the first indication that Jack Warner was beginning to lose touch. Instead of Julie, he signed Audrey Hepburn for the role of Eliza Doolittle. She looked beautiful, but it was the voice of Marnie Nixon (who had already done the same thing for Deborah Kerr in *The King and I* and for numerous other actresses) that sang 'Wouldn't it be Loverly' and 'Oh, Henry Higgins' and 'I Could Have Danced All Night' – just as Julie would have sung them. But Ms Andrews had her compensations – like almost immediately after hearing that Warner had rejected her, being offered her Oscar-winning role in Walt Disney's *Mary Poppins.*

But Jack had little to worry about. His judgement in making the film was affirmed by its winning the Best Picture Academy Award at the 1965 Ceremony – as well as Oscars for Harrison, the director George Cukor, Andre Previn for his score, and for Harry Stradling for his photography and for the costumes and sound. There were also nominations for Stanley Holloway and for Gladys Cooper, playing Higgins's mother.

Nevertheless, things weren't anything like they had been. Jack did manage to put those two grande dames of the cinema, Bette Davis and Joan Crawford together – in fact, put on screen their real-life hatred for each other – in *Whatever Happened to Baby Jane?* There were also *Gypsy, Look Back in Anger* and *Who's Afraid of Virginia Woolf*? Big projects for anyone's money. But there were the failures, too. Certainly, Laurence Olivier's *Othello* wasn't exactly calculated to bring in the audiences.

In 1966, Jack did finally decide to sell out. Warner Bros. became part of Seven Arts productions. He unloaded his 1,600,000 shares for $20 each. He thought it was a good deal – until someone told him he could have sold the rights to *Casablanca* alone for precisely that figure.

So did that mean that he was out of the movie business? Not quite. He was becoming one of those (to him) hated beasts, an independent producer. He made two movies, neither of which amounted to anything at the box office – *1776* and *Dirty Little Billy*. But he could at least claim he was still in the business.

That didn't mean that he was content. He most certainly was not. He was concerned about his reputation above all else. Jack Warner needed to be in the public eye. So he went out of his way to achieve that. Mel Shavelson told me that he told the mogul: 'Jack, what are you so sad about? You're now a free man.' Warner looked at him and said, 'Yesterday, I was Jack Warner. Today, I'm just another rich Jew.'

He had his magnificent Beverly Hills mansion in Angelo Drive, a place he delighted in showing to guests to the finest detail. It was built on the site of a house that Jack had created for Irma, the first Mrs Warner. Ann had insisted on building, at least, *something* new on the same land. The something new was a poker room. Jack Jr told me: 'I was never invited there, but I know the poker room was my dad's favourite place – although I could swear that one night he lost the equivalent of the cost of the house in one game. But then he always said he paid three times more for it than he should have done.'

The question of why the moguls so loved poker isn't difficult to work out. They were in a gambling business. When they played poker, they gambled, just as they did on a new project or a new star – but without the hard work that always involved. And the results were instant. And sometimes they won – even when they were playing at the Warner house.

Melville Shavelson told me about his visit to the house. Jack proudly pointed to the wall panels, which he said he had bought from a British stately home. The parquet floor, he said, had come from France. 'If you look carefully,' he told the writer, 'you can see the old bloodstains. It came direct from Versailles and the blood was from the French Revolution.' 'Gee, Jack,' said Shavelson, 'I could have sworn it came from your office.'

There was another house of which he was doubly proud in Cap d'Antibes in the South of France, called 'Aujourd'hui', where scenes from his films and pictures of his big stars dominated the house – and still do. But the people in the house have changed. In Warner's day, the guest list included King Farouk of Egypt and various generals and heads of industry. If it were an attempt at creating Hollywood in France, it didn't amount to more than – as Bogie might have called it – a hill of beans.

If he were going to succeed again, he needed to find something new – or at least new to him. He made *Baby Doll* in 1956, which people said was indecent and caused a huge furore, and other films that the Catholic League of Decency – and the old Hays Office – abhorred. So would Harry Warner have done if he'd been alive. As Jack Jr told me: 'Uncle Harry was a puritan himself, so he could usually agree with the Hays Office decisions.'

Jack went on making speeches that no one took very seriously. The only time that people did listen to him, they laughed him out of the TV studio – and he loved every moment of it. Dean Martin hosted a Jack Warner *Roast* – the series in which celebrities could work out how important they were by the number of insults that were hauled at them. The insult quotient when Jack was one of the victims was up to par. As Dino warbled:

> 'Jack L. Warner
> That Jack L. Warner
> He don't know nothin'
> But he must say somethin'
> He just keeps yackin'
> Keeps on yackin' a-long.'

Warner would stop a lowly office boy and ask him, out of the blue: 'What do you know about property?'

'Nothing,' was the usual answer.

'No,' said Jack, 'you should reply, "Lots".'

Most of the comments on Jack's sense of humour were less kindly intended. The actress Loretta Young put it like this to me: 'I always thought he was a clown.'

That was certainly how he appeared to the audience at one function when Jack got up and said: 'Does anyone mind if I say a few words? Who's going to fire me if do?'

Of course, the time came when someone could have done just that; but they didn't.

Jack Benny didn't get it quite right when he said that Jack Warner would 'rather tell a bad joke than make a good movie'. If people paid him to tell those jokes as much as they did to buy his movies, it might have been true.

Perhaps his greatest quality as a bad storyteller was that he just didn't care what other people said about him. As Julius Epstein said: 'The only people who really laughed at Jack's jokes were the ones who were insecure. I only remember one that was really funny. It was when Ronald Reagan first ran for Governor of California and Jack heard about it. "No," he said. "You've got it wrong. Dennis Morgan [a one-time big Hollywood musical star] is running for Governor. Ronald Reagan for best friend".' Poor Jack didn't think that his old contract player Ronnie Reagan would one day be the most powerful man in the world.

But then there were many things that Jack didn't know. He should have taken Oscar Wilde's dictum seriously: 'I never make predictions, particularly about the future.'

If he had, a Broadway show called *Jimmy* would never have happened. As it was, Jack Warner's last attempt at production was a dismal failure.

For that, he had to blame, as often, his vanity. He still had his old office; Seven Arts thought that was the least they could do. Somehow, although he had nothing to do with the business, it made the name Warner Bros. seem more authentic if he were on the lot. It was something he appreciated. He could look round the room and enjoy the surroundings, the big windows, the luxury carpeting and the antique furniture that he had always loved. There was something else that he enjoyed, another trapping of days past which he had to recreate for himself – a barber shop which he could visit every day as the only customer (apart from the few favourite friends who were granted a similar privilege). He converted an adjoining private dining room into the shop and employed his old personal barber Don to wait on him and his guests. But there was still something missing: the thrill of a new project. He thought he had one the evening in 1972 when a dining companion started talking about James – Jimmy – Walker, the colourful former mayor of New York.

It was no secret that Walker was what show business liked to call a 'character'. He had been a songwriter – most notably for the 1920s hit, 'Will You Love Me in December as You do in May?' – and became mayor in 1925. He was involved in corruption charges, complaints of immorality, left his wife for a chorus girl and spent more time, it was said, in New York's classiest restaurants and speakeasies than he did with members of the council. He was forced to resign in 1932.

His life had already been the subject of a film, made by Paramount in 1957, starring Bob Hope and written and directed by Mel Shavelson. Now, Jack was convinced it had all the makings of a Broadway show. So convinced that he rang Shavelson. Early in the show's life, the writer said he knew it wasn't going to work. When it reached Philadelphia for its pre-Broadway try out, he was certain that it was a disaster.

'I phoned Jack and said he had to close this turkey,' he told me. 'I said that nothing works. "The sets are terrible, the costumes are terrible. Everybody is in it just to get money out of you. It's one big vacuum cleaner." But Jack wouldn't listen. He was determined to go to New York with it.'

When it did open, the critics confirmed Shavelson's view. But Warner was determined to carry through with it. 'What are you worried about?' he asked his writer. 'It's only a mill.' And then he explained: 'If I close it now, who'll have dinner with me?' Actually, it wasn't a 'mill' that Jack lost. He had invested $1,500,000 in the show and lost every cent of it.

While the show was running, however, he was happy. His name was to be seen high on the Broadway hoardings and he cared more about that than anything else. He also had a girlfriend – he always had girlfriends; this time, she was a hairdresser. But he could only spend so long enjoying the office and the memories that went with it. People like Jack Warner need, in their own eyes, to be as good as their next project. The sad thing was that even he had to admit that there were no next projects for him. From the time he made that realisation, he began to go downhill, a hill that was steeper than he himself could have imagined. There was no way he was going to cope with it.

On the other hand, people had begun softening to him by then. The actor Dane Clark, born Bernard Zanville, told me: 'I may complain, but that's bullshit. They took an unknown kid from Brooklyn and made him into an internationally-known person. I bow to that.'

You could argue that what Warner really made internationally-known was his studio. It had a style that was recognised in the industry as being different from that of his competitors. The general public may not have realised that fact, but the truth was that the company stayed in business all those years right from the days of *My Four Years in Germany*, through the films of *Rin Tin Tin* and then *The Jazz Singer*, simply because Warner Bros. knew how to make what the public wanted. The fact that they made fortunes from keeping their fingers on the pulse of the film-going public was the ultimate proof.

As for Jack himself, his jokes made him a joke – but only until people analysed his huge contribution to the movies. He was not a nice man, but when did being nice mean a guarantee of success?

Ben Hecht, the writer of *The Front Page* and much else, said of the Warner Bros.: 'There's nothing much wrong with this town that three murders wouldn't cure.' Of course, it couldn't last. Jack became ill and then, on 9 September 1978, he died. Warner Bros. was now really without a brother – and Hollywood had lost a founding father.

4

LOUIS B. MAYER

The slogan at the MGM studio at Culver City, another of the sprawling Los Angeles suburbs that masqueraded under the generic name of Hollywood, was very precise: 'More stars than there are in heaven'.

Astronomers would probably take issue with that, but you've got the idea: this was a studio that boasted stars the way that other businesses crowed about profits. The fact that MGM could bracket the two without apologising gives some idea of its success. Success? That was a Hollywood byword and Louis B. Mayer, its creator, demanded and achieved nothing less than that. There was only one thing going against him – unlike the other moguls, he didn't actually own MGM. But with the company's roster of box-office triumphs and the stars who made them, why was he to worry?

'When you drove through the gates of MGM,' songwriter Sammy Cahn told me, 'you were entering a kingdom and Louis B. Mayer was the ruler of that kingdom. He had the absolute power to control it and by a stroke of pen could make or break a career in the movies.'

Mayer, the veteran director Rouben Mamoulian told me, 'was very clever, very shrewd and ran his studio with tremendous intelligence and flair.' All true. He was also vicious, argumentative and evil.

The fact remains, however, that MGM was the most glamorous of all the Hollywood studios, made so by its stars, but also by its sets, its sex appeal and in what Mayer took to be the family structure of his company. Other moguls regarded themselves – and were so regarded by their employees – as dictators. Louis B. Mayer saw himself as father of his family. It was the basis of his whole life – all the more so perhaps since he quarrelled with his own family incessantly. He and his two brothers hardly spoke – even though his younger brother Jerry was employed as manager of the MGM studio. He and his daughters and their husbands could list the rows they had and fill a shelf of books to do so. Yet, he himself wouldn't allow anyone else to say anything critical of any of them and was, by all accounts, the perfect Jewish grandfather, as doting as a new mother.

But to the outside world, the people he cared about most were his other 'children', the ones who worked for him, either as actors or producers or directors.

At least, that was the legend he wanted people to believe. He also considered he was king of all he surveyed, although that, too, was an understatement. Nothing less than the title 'emperor' would have suited him. Which didn't mean that he didn't appreciate beauty for its own sake – or, rather, for the sake of what it brought his studio.

Florenz Ziegfeld used to stress that through his stage door walked the most beautiful girls in the world. Louis B. Mayer would have been satisfied with that. But, since he was their 'father' they had to behave in the way he would appreciate – which amounted to doing nothing that would appear to be less than all-American. When he became head of the Republican Party of California, it was no more than he would consider his right. After all, who in Hollywood could more accurately be said to wrap himself in the Stars and Stripes than he? He loved his adopted country. He looked after it with all the regard and love of the father of a child who has been specially chosen rather than arriving at birth.

The fact that he was also the highest-paid executive in the United States was, likewise, no more than he saw as his due. As was that bestowed upon him by his stars in return for all that he did for them.

In 1950, when the studio celebrated its 25th anniversary, he assembled all those stars for a lunch in the biggest soundstage on the MGM lot. He made sure that the cameramen came to record what was, after all, an historic event. Everyone who was under seven-year servitude (contract) to him at that time, along with those he was currently borrowing to make an MGM film, were there. They sat in six serried ranks behind trestle tables, knives and forks poised over their plates. There was Greer Garson, whom L.B. liked to call 'my lady' (another was the haughty Irene Dunne who shared his politics but not his sexual proclivities); also Judy Garland and her partner in all those Andy Hardy 'family' movies that MGM loved so much, Mickey Rooney. Ava Gardner looked as beautiful as she had ever looked on screen. Greer Garson's film husband (from *Mrs Miniver* and other movies), Walter Pidgeon, was there and so were Hedy Lamarr, Lionel Barrymore and Gene Kelly. Errol Flynn, who was currently making *That Forsythe Woman*, was close to Fred Astaire. So were Astaire's recent partners Jane Powell and Ann Miller. Clark Gable was also there, of course. And so was Spencer Tracy, along with Jeanette MacDonald, who used to put an engagement ring on her finger whenever she thought that Mayer was about to come on to her – as he did with many of the women tied to him by contract. In the corner was a separate table bearing a bowl – for a very special MGM star, Lassie. The dog fitted in perfectly with the Mayer idea of the ideal American family.

They were there to prove that Mr Mayer, as they all called him, had been a father indeed – if a tough, stern father, whom none of them could have been said to have loved.

People like Garland, Astaire and Peter Lawford, who had recently made *Easter Parade* for Mayer, were there to do something else – to underline the fact that MGM didn't just stand for Metro-Goldwyn-Mayer. They signified that this was the studio that 'Makes Great Musicals'. Other people had a different definition for the initials – Mayer's *Gunzer Mishbocher*, Yiddish for 'Mayer's whole family'. As one wit put it, 'This is where the Son-in-Law also rises.' We shall see how true that was – not that he treated sons-in-law any better than any of his other 'children'.

The point was that he regarded any contradictions to his authority as a personal affront by naughty children who knew no better and, therefore, had to be punished for their own good. The fact that it was also always for *his* own good was beside the point. So was his own professed sense of morality. He wanted to see that his stars, his 'children', lived the sort of lives his films portrayed. They might not have been expected to have the sort of domestic bliss – and were occasionally 'naughty' – that word again – as was evident in the movies of the 1930s, but he would have liked it to be so. His ideal would also have been the kind of family portrayed in that other Judy Garland vehicle, *Meet Me in St Louis*: doting parents, sweet daughters, a cheeky dirty-faced son, a lovable answering-back maid and a dog (always a dog).

The fact that he kept mistresses had absolutely nothing to do with his self-professed duty of portraying America as the land of mothers and apple pie. Yes, he said on one notable occasion, there would be sex in

MGM pictures, but nothing that people would consider dirty – how could it be on those snow-white MGM sets? He hated the idea of buying the play *The Women* because he thought it was 'dirty'. But he managed to get the story about a socialite's divorce to seem just witty and socially correct. It had an all female cast – billed as '135 women with men on their mind' – starring Norma Shearer, Joan Crawford and Rosalind Russell; was written by Anita Loos and directed by the only man with his name on the credits, George Cukor, who specialised in what became known as 'MGM women's pictures'.

Cukor was an asset to any studio. On the other hand, Mayer began wondering just how much of an asset Joan Crawford was. All the hatred she would later show for Bette Davis at Warner Bros., was presaged by her fights with Norma Shearer, whom she resented. For Mayer, that was a big problem. So he went out of his way to boost Crawford – not least, making sure that her wedding to Douglas Fairbanks Jr had all the panoply of his latest MGM production.

Other stars would prove equally difficult. But he got to regard that as just par for his own course. If he needed them, they were pampered. If he didn't, they were shown the door.

People would kiss each other according to the rules of the Hays Office. 'As long as we have men and women in the world, we will have sex,' declared the man who liked it to be known that he spoke from experience (but only the kind of experience on display in his movies; there was never any need to talk about his private life – if there had been, it would have resulted in blood on his carpet). 'And I approve of it. We'll have sex in motion pictures and I want it there. But it will be normal, real beautiful sex – the sex that is common to the people in the audience, to me and to you. A man and a woman are in love with one another. That's sex and it's beautiful, in movies and in life.'

Was it naivety on his part – or just good business? It was business every time. He went to extraordinary lengths to make sure that his stars appeared to their public as doting married couples. He might pretend that he knew nothing about homosexuality, but he knew enough to make sure that any stars 'guilty' of such activity would either be sacked – if they were easily disposable – or married if they were still of value.

One of his most popular stars of the war and early post-war years was caught in a compromising situation with the world tennis champion, John Tilden, high on the Hollywood Hills. The fact that the two were caught *in flagrante* made it too juicy a story for the media to simply ignore. The star was called into Mayer's office and told, without any due ceremony, that the following day he was to elope with another unmarried star and would subsequently get married – 'secretly'. Of course. With just a dozen or so reporters and photographers present. Of course. That was his definition of a gay romance. He didn't want to hear of any other kind where his stars were concerned. The couple in that story, incidentally – which without that incident on the Hills would have made a great plot for an MGM film – remain happily married 60 years later. No children, but a happy Hollywood couple.

Mayer was worried that Van Johnson had never married. It was Mayer's ever-present and ever-doting secretary Ida Koverman who had the answer. She had met Evie Wynn, wife of the actor Keenan Wynn. She thought she was beautiful, funny and full of life. Just what Van Johnson needed in a wife. Wynn, son of the famous comedian, Ed Wynn, was a journeyman actor whom Mayer decided was useful to have around but would probably never be a star, at least not a big star. But in Evie, he had a beautiful wife. 'If you divorce your wife,' Mayer said to Wynn, 'you have a job here for life.' He did divorce Evie, signed a big new contract and Johnson and Evie Wynn were married and apparently lived happily ever after. So did the actor Robert Young. Mayer told him to get more sex – to leave his mother's house and get involved, preferably to get married.

There was little fun to report where Mayer was concerned. There never was any associated with the stern Victorian father that he represented. He didn't mangle the language the way Sam Goldwyn did. He didn't tell terrible jokes or impose impossible rules that made his writers prepare entire scenarios around him the way they did about Jack L. Warner.

But moguls were meant to be laughed at, nevertheless. If you couldn't laugh about them, life would be impossible. Mayer called his enterprise 'The Friendly Studio', which made not a few people laugh into their morning coffee when they opened threatening letters from him with that legend at the top of the notepaper. There were other things in which Mayer was involved that were much more in character with the man of legend. The famous Mayer crying scene – about which more later – was funny and legendary but really happened. If he thought there might be trouble in getting his way, he simply burst into tears. The damp handkerchief solved the problem his way virtually every time.

Mount Ida

If Mayer wanted his films to be squeaky clean – which he did – he ran his office in the same way. Ida Koverman was more than just the lady who typed his letters and poured his tea (specially blended). She found talent for him – including, to the regret of a number of Mayer's MGM fans and then Mayer himself, Nelson Eddy, who looked quite good dressed as a Mountie in the 1936 film, *Rose Marie*, but was known round and about as The Singing Capon, which was not intended as a compliment to the long-time screen partner of Jeanette MacDonald, who complained of his terrible breath when he sang at her.

Ida Koverman aided and abetted everything her boss did, short of acting as his pimp. You couldn't walk into Mayer's office, not only without an appointment, but also without passing muster to Koverman's eyes. Actors who had clearance to visit Mayer had to satisfy her that they were dressed properly and that their hair and make-up were just right. She was a battle-axe who acted as a doorman in an era when you couldn't say doorperson or whatever.

The mogul's biographer, Scott Eyman, quotes Evie Johnson describing her as 'Mount Ida'. But if, as Louis B. Mayer did, you had the smooth running of the studio as your main consideration, she was a mountain worth climbing – if, between telling everyone what a wonderful man L.B. was and how marvellous his studio was, you could stomach her constant missionary activities on behalf of Christian Science, a religion that became more and more popular with people in the movie fraternity.

It was Ida who checked Louis's speeches and introduced him to people of power, including politicians. She was well qualified to do that since she had at one time been the secretary of the then-future president, Herbert Hoover, who later became a great supporter of the MGM chief. The connection was important. Mayer was able to talk of Hoover being a close friend; a fact proved by a personal invitation to attend his inauguration. Later, the mogul, his wife and daughter Irene were the first guests to actually sleep in the White House after the ceremony.

Yet Mayer, unlike some of his competitors, was aware of his limitations as far as the social graces were concerned. Ms Koverman helped in that regard, too – advised on the decor for her boss's house and how she thought he ought to learn to entertain his guests. He trusted her the way he had faith only in his closest executives and it showed in how, gradually, he learned to comport himself in company. She had an office next to his and was more one of those executives herself than just a secretary.

She knew when stars were about to be fired and, if considered appropriate, would smooth the way for the final notice before her boss got personally involved. She was also his principal scout. If she spotted a potential talent in a play she had seen or maybe even waiting at table at a restaurant, she knew her duty was to report the fact to L.B. It is said that it was Ida who brought both Judy Garland and Elizabeth Taylor into the studio. They were living proof that, more times than not, Mayer respected her opinions and took her advice.

But throughout his life, the woman who was his real influence was his mother, whom he believed had fulfilled all that was required of American womanhood. The fact that he had a daily standing order in his private dining room for chicken soup – made to old Mrs Mayer's recipe – was a metaphor for his love for her, to say nothing of serving as a symbol for his respect for the all-American values of motherhood.

The soup was made to the traditional Jewish specifications. It was about the only way in which he demonstrated his religious associations. Whether Louis B. Mayer – or any of his rivals for that matter – ever went to see a psychiatrist (which would, naturally, have resulted in Sam Goldwyn telling him he needed his head examined) is unknown, but unlikely. What is not unlikely is what the man the other side of the leather couch would have told him.

The moguls' arrogance, their brutish behaviour, their paranoia and their determination to always get the better of a perceived opponent, was plainly stemming from a sense of insecurity. One of Mayer's early top stars, Maurice Chevalier, told me when I was working on his biography that he always suffered from 'a complex of inferiority'. That was as true for the mogul as it was for his star. The story is that he would frequently regale visiting celebrities with stories about his early days working in his father's scrap-metal yard. Successful people like to talk about their rags to riches escapes. What was surprising about Mayer was that he also told them of the number of times that customers would shout 'Kike, kike' at him. Like the chicken soup, it was a rare admission of his Jewish background.

Lazar to Louis

Louis was born Lazar Mayer in 1885 in Vilme, near Minsk, the now-Belarus capital which was at the heart of the Jewish pale of settlement.

While still a boy, he emigrated with his family (he had two sisters, Yetta and Ida) to New York where his two brothers Jerry and Rudolph were born. Before long, they all moved northwards to St John in Canada. It was there that his father, Jacob, a traditionally Orthodox Jew, who wore a skullcap at all times (his love of the Talmud was to be stressed in the inscription on his grave, chosen by Louis) and his mother Sara set up in the junk business, which proved profitable but which the more sensitive Lazar hated. He vowed to get out of it as soon as he could, thinking there were other things in the world than old bedsteads, tin cans or prams.

One of the reasons that Mayer wanted to leave St John was seeing the contrast between his life and that of other people. The strict religiosity of the family wasn't for him – although, at 13, he had been photographed at the time of his bar mitzvah wearing a big hat and a tallit, prayer shawl.

In a scene that could be recalled by thousands of other ambitious youngsters with seemingly nothing to be ambitious about, he told the writer Adela Rogers St Johns (the coincidence of her name and that of the city had no relevance here at all): 'There was a little hotel in St John with a dining room. I used to walk by and stare in, seeing the little tables in the windows with silver candlesticks and electric candles in pink shades. I would stand on the kerb and say, "Someday, I'm going to get in there and sit at a table and order an expensive meal." But when I finally had the money and went back to St John, the restaurant had gone. That, Adela, is the definition of the tragedy of success.' Twenty years after leaving the city, he returned there to see family and was given a civic lunch by the mayor.

As he might have added, everyone should have such tragedies. But he used something of the ingenuity he would later bring to the movie business by convincing his father that there was a world outside of New Brunswick where they could sell or buy their stock. He travelled back to the United States. It was in Boston that he met the woman whom he swore was the love of his life, Margaret Shenberg, whose father was a kosher butcher, and also dabbled as a rabbi and cantor. They married at an Orthodox synagogue. To Jacob and Sara that was a marriage made in heaven.

He promised at the wedding ceremony to honour and keep her as was befitting a Jewish husband. A husband who was no longer Lazar, but Louis – and because he was all-American, one who decided he needed a middle name. He said it was Bertram, which was very American, he considered. Later, he said it stood for Burrill. But Louis B. Mayer sounded even better. Margaret gave him his first child, Edith. When she agreed to move with him to Brooklyn, he gave her the respect he thought was due a dutiful wife. Now, he swore he would treat her the way he believed all Jewish mothers should be treated – although he could never allow anyone to take the place of his own mother. (When the second daughter Irene arrived, she merely confirmed in his mind the respect he had for all that motherhood stood for.)

He worried about the way he spoke, although by the time he had married, unlike Goldwyn, any trace of his old Yiddish accent had totally disappeared. He was already stressing his American credentials – not least by making up a birthday for himself: the fourth of July.

The old expression of several people with but a single thought never applied more than it did with the men who made Hollywood. The new 20th century was time for a new business. The new Louis B. Mayer realised that there were now audiences out there for a new form of entertainment. He had seen the movies himself and decided that this was the life for him. Showing them, that is. He heard about a burlesque theatre that was for sale in Haverhill, not far from Boston. It was called The Gem. He looked at the place and concluded it was a gem of an establishment. But he wouldn't call it that himself. No, this was going to be the Orpheum, which sounded grand and imposing, just as he agreed his theatre was going to be grand and imposing when it started showing films. Whether he thought it would confuse people into believing it was part of the giant Keith-Orpheum vaudeville circuit cannot now be confirmed, but that was probably likely. The new theatre would feature vaudeville acts as part of its entertainment. The circuits were renowned for putting on the best shows in the vaudeville business. Maybe people would think they were now putting on the best movie shows, too. Particularly when he had one ideally suited for the Christmas season when he opened the theatre. *The Passion Play* (though really an Easter play) did well, even though the story of Jesus was not what one might have expected of a nice Jewish boy – even though he would have enjoyed the comparison; as we shall see, in later years, he was indeed to be described in those terms.

He did well with his Orpheum – well enough for him to open a second theatre. Only this one was going to be brand new, built from scratch. The Colonial – then not a name to disparage – would be almost three times bigger than the Orpheum, with 1,600 seats. It was total confirmation that the film business was there to stay. And Louis was there to stay in it. 'The

Colonial is the zenith of my ambitions,' he said. However, he was also in a business that he was expanding. Ever since he peddled scrap metal he had known that expansion meant moving on. He didn't give up his theatres, but he also wanted to make sure that they were going to be operated like a highly successful store. He wanted to move on from being a mere retailer. He wanted to be involved in wholesaling, too – the people who provided him with his 'stock', the films that he was showing. He organised a number of distribution companies, Master Photoplays, the Serial Production Company and the American Feature Film Company.

He obtained the New England rights for distributing their biggest epic ever filmed, *The Birth of a Nation*, which had been made by D.W. Griffith. It made him half-a-million dollars.

He saw the film, studied the way it was made and came to a conclusion familiar to every entrepreneur: 'I can do that.'

Virtuous Film Maker

Louis was going to make films himself. He set up a new company in New York. It was called Metro Pictures. The trouble was that he and his partner in the venture, a man called Richard Rowland, had a row and he left the organisation.

He joined a new firm, the Select Picture Corporation and found a new partner, Lewis J. Selznick. It would be a surname that would play a big part in his life in later years. But Lewis Selznick was too much like Mayer himself, too much wanting his own way.

So Louis set up yet another new company of his own and found his first star, Anita Stewart, whom he would feature in his first 'big' film, *Virtuous Wives*. Another leading player in that film was called Hedda Hopper, who remained in the Hollywood business for the rest of her life, but as one of the gossip columnists who made people in that business – not least Mayer himself – shake with fear every time her writings appeared. But at the time of *Virtuous Wives* he didn't worry about that. It was the right film with the right title for the kind of movies he was going to produce at the right time.

A psychiatrist wouldn't find it difficult to work out why Louis chose that title. His whole public philosophy was his belief in virtue, not least in marriage. He expected wives to be virtuous. Husbands were something else. On film, they would never be allowed to stray. As for himself, the business and the exposure to beautiful women allowed him to take his first mistresses. Ms Stewart does not appear to have been one of those, but she was *his* star and he wanted to keep her that way. It wasn't easy since she was constantly rowing with her boss; shouting, screaming and failing to turn up for work. Eventually, Mayer sued her. She was at the centre of a court case in which she was asked if she were single or married. She said she did not want to answer the question – for personal reasons. The personal reason was that she was married – a fact that Mayer thought would reduce her appeal, which was considerable – more so than the serials that Mayer was producing in Brooklyn. He wanted to expand his business. Already, he was thinking that his features would one day be the most important ever shown in a theatre.

If those early films – in the days before the censoring organisations like the Hays Office set up operations – dealt with extramarital sex, it was no more than he was practising himself. But the public would never be allowed to know that. The most sinful thing he allowed people to know that he did was play pinochle. At least, that's what he could have told people. He was making what he called 'beautiful photographs that move'. And beautiful was the watchword. He was a moral man making and showing moral movies – films that would justify his publicised maxim, of being 'only pictures that I won't be ashamed to have my children see'. Or his mother, who proudly told her friends about the house 'my son the picture producer' had bought for her and her husband, who had begun to think of himself as part of the business too – much to Louis's chagrin when he took to going around the lots, offering advice to all concerned. He would do that until his death.

Meanwhile, his son was doing better and better. He moved his operation to California, running before he could walk. But, then, why walk when he could run? Especially, since he still had Anita Stewart on hand to star in the films he was going to make. It was all going so well that he sold his interest in his theatres. Now he was going to concentrate on providing the fodder that those cinemas would need. Let other people worry about the paying customers.

Louis quickly became part of the movie establishment, doing all he could to outsmart his competitors in the industry, but being with them when social status required it. He joined all the necessary charity organisations and benefit funds that gave the right impression of a caring business. He became a mason and showed a devotion to its rituals to an extent which he never bothered with in the synagogue, but then the people he met on the pews wouldn't tell the same jokes or have time over a drink to exchange gossip.

Above all, he knew the value of talent – and not just of people who appeared before the cameras. He needed help administering his business. And that was how 24-year-old Irving Thalberg – whom the mogul said he would treat 'like my son', hardly a surprising statement as the 'son' was paid $500 a week, a vast sum for 1924 – came into his orbit. How Mayer came back to the Metro orbit was thanks to the man who had bought that company, Marcus Loew. Loew knew more about movies than anyone else in America. That was something he claimed for himself and nobody around was there to argue the point. He owned the biggest and most successful movie theatre chain in the country and for him going into production was the obvious next step. The only problem was that he operated from New York and had no intention of moving. He also had no intention of leaving the theatre business. Like Mayer, he couldn't do both, make films and show films.

Loew offered him the chance to run his production business, not just Metro, but Metro-Goldwyn (although as we have seen already there was no Mr Goldwyn in that operation. But they did have Sam's lion – and the 40-acre Goldwyn studio complex at Culver City from which to operate.) How would Mayer like to run it for him? Loew would remain the boss and would have a majority share, but Mayer would have full control of the studio and could name his price. He named something else, too: the addition of the name 'Mayer' to the firm. So Metro Goldwyn now became Metro-Goldwyn-Mayer. The initials MGM were carved on to Hollywood history.

The title of the movie *The Big Parade* had to be carved along with them. It was 1925 and this was the picture that confirmed the vitally important part that MGM had found for itself in the centre of the film industry. The picture, directed by King Vidor, was the most successful – in terms both of box office gross and critical reaction – silent picture of all time. Vidor's huge canvas filled with men, with trucks, with despair, was one of the first anti-war films, based around the survival of a young recruit at the time of the United States' entry into the First World War when all around him are dying and being wounded.

Just before his death, King Vidor told me: 'He was very adroit at persuading people to stay when they wanted to leave. He was the papa and they were his children. They had fifty stars, twenty-five directors and made fifty films a year – all through the planning of Mr Mayer.'

None of those 'children', however, would have a firmer place in the heart of the mogul than Greta Garbo, whom Mayer discovered on an overseas tour, looking for ideas and, above all, for talent. His discovery of her in Sweden was another achievement that made his glands salivate. He would have liked to take her to bed, too, but he had to be satisfied with seeing the enormous impact she made on the people who bought tickets for her movies. Even he could never have anticipated that.

He offered the former Greta Gustafson half the $5,000 a week she said she needed to work at Culver City – she was an enormously confident young lady, even in 1926. That was when she made *The Torrent*, a hit that was followed by *The Temptress* the same year and, most notably for that era, *Flesh and the Devil* 12 months later. When she heard Mayer's original offer, she replied, 'I tank I go home.' If Mayer cried at that, he did it silently. He realised she was saying no more than what she intended to do and he was in no mood to bargain. Had he allowed her to go home, MGM would have turned out very differently. He put up with her tantrums, her arguments with her co-star Clark Gable in *Susan Lenox, Her Fall and Rise*, a film she didn't want to make. He tolerated her coming in late for work or not appearing at all – simply because the name Greta Garbo was one of MGM's biggest assets.

She was so important as a silent star that when the talkies arrived, the slogan 'Garbo Talks' was the talk of the town – and of all the film-going world. A glance at the sales figures chalked up by *Anna Christie* in 1930 and *Grand Hotel* two years later proved how clever those words were. *Queen Christina* was one that Mayer loved. 'What he loved particularly was the bedroom scene,' said the director Rouben Mamoulian. 'This is going to look marvellous,' he said, 'I can see it with Garbo in a diaphanous nightgown, black stockings. Wonderful.' It was not the reaction that people expected of the priggish Louis B. Mayer who later on would say how much he enjoyed dignified sex on the screen.

As for her relationship with Clark Gable, it amounted to very little off the *Susan Lennox* set. Gable was much was more interested in Joan Crawford, with whom he was sleeping. Crawford's husband Douglas Fairbanks Jr was encouraged not to say too much about it. The fact was that no one could win a fight with the mighty Ms Crawford. Or the even mightier Mr Mayer. When she and Fairbanks were divorced – 'We couldn't get along,' she said – Mayer used all his wiles to make sure that Gable wasn't cited. He wasn't.

William Randolph Hearst

Mayer treated Joan Crawford with great reverence – for her own sake and for that of his studio and its balance sheets. He bestowed even greater respect on Marion Davies – a fairly talentless MGM 'name' who, much to the disgust of other stars, was earning $10,000 weekly. Not because she was a better actress – she was anything but – not because she was a greater beauty than Garbo – she had a glamour girl type of prettiness, but there was no comparison with the subtler Swedish appeal, to say nothing of her bone structure. What Ms Davies had was William Randolph Hearst, her lover and later husband, 36 years her senior. The newspaper magnet – the model for Orson Welles' *Citizen Kane* – had set up his own studio to feature Marion and had come to an arrangement with MGM to distribute Davies films. Eventually, a deal was struck – her salary would be paid jointly by Mayer and Cosmopolitan Pictures, which was owned by Hearst. The two studios would share any profits. It suited Hearst, since his movie operation was virtually moribund.

Keeping Hearst happy was a big investment. Mayer even suggested that his company pay out to RKO every cent they had spent on *Citizen Kane*, to avoid upsetting the newspaper publisher, even though the movies Ms Davies was to make at MGM were usually flops – flops that he still allowed to be described with his favourite publicity adjectives of 'colossal' and 'gigantic'. His newspapers would guarantee publicity for films like *Quality Street* and *The Red Mill*, which Mayer had in mind for her.

One of Mayer's most important writers was Louella Parsons, the Hollywood columnist who could make or destroy a star's career seemingly with the rise of an eyebrow, let alone a key of her typewriter. Hearst invited her to one of their regular dinners together and broached the subject of being kind to his friend Mr Mayer's movies.

In between the turtle soup and the *filet mignon*, and after a couple of glasses of vintage champagne, she asked the 64,000-dollar question: did she always have to be kind to the pictures emanating from the MGM lot? No, Hearst answered with all the confidence of a man whose newspapers – containing Ms Parsons' column – were thrown on to the front porch of every other house in America. He just wanted her to use her judgement and to exercise that judgement with . . . judgement.

Mayer himself no doubt offered Ms Parsons the crying scene when they met. 'How can I say that every picture is good?' she wanted to know. Between sobs, the mogul seems to have replied: 'We only make good pictures, but some are better than others.'

For as long as he was friendly with Hearst, Mayer was guaranteed a good press for his films, which must have seemed a bit fishy to readers who began to think about such things. However, the more he himself thought about it, the more sense it made to L.B. to keep Ms Davies on the books – and hope not too many people noticed how bad she was.

Mayer promised not only to give her film parts, he would make her life at Culver City as comfortable as a woman now used to the luxury of San Simeon, Hearst's private castle, would expect. The phrase hadn't yet been invented, but she was treated like a super star. For some unaccountable reason for a man who had his eye constantly on his accounts, he never considered the possibility that making movies with inferior actors or actresses might rebound on him. Not only was there the assurance that the star's lover would guarantee that only rave reviews appeared in his section of the press, her flaws would be hidden in the best MGM way. She would be given voice coaches, the finest make-up artists, hair stylists and couturiers. So much camouflage that he could pray that she would be hardly noticeable at all.

Mayer built a magnificent suite of dressing rooms for her. Outside he deferred to the religious woman's desire for a Madonna statue to keep guard for her at her 'cottage'. It is said that Dorothy Parker saw it and came up with one of her celebrated verses, which was not so lovingly inscribed in the visitors' book at San Simeon:

Upon my honour
I saw a Madonna
Standing in a niche
Above the door
Of a prominent whore
Of a prominent son of a bitch.

One assumes that whoever wrote that meant Hearst. She (or he) could just as easily have been referring to Louis B. Mayer.

Ms Parker denied writing it and gave her reason: 'I would never have rhymed "Honour" with "Madonna".' Whether she thought either of the two men were sons of bitches is not on record. Chances are she did.

After ten years, Marion Davies swapped the favours of Louis B. Mayer for those of another son of a bitch. She had had a row with Thalberg because he refused to cast her in the lead of his film, *Marie Antoinette*; not just that: she had always seen herself in *The Barretts of Wimpole Street*, which was also denied her. In that, he had more courage than Mayer himself, who found it very difficult to say no to her or to anything to do with William Randolph Hearst, whose Metronome newsreel was still produced by MGM. Marion moved to Warner Bros. (On the day of her departure, she trailed a roll of toilet paper from the back of her car as the Cadillac wended its way to Burbank.)

Despite it all, the friendship with Hearst lasted for the rest of the publisher's life, which was fortunate because he was important to the studio for as long as he was in charge. That friendship encompassed the suppression of news as well as the boosting of things that Mayer wanted publicised. If it had not been for Hearst, there is a solid argument to suggest that Clark Gable would never have made *Gone with the Wind* or become the most important male movie icon of the 1930s.

Cover-ups

It was a well-known fact in the Hollywood community that Gable had fathered a child born to Loretta Young, who was spirited away for a year's 'rest' without anything ever being published about it until her death in 2000. But the most significant thing hushed up at Mayer's request concerned Gable's drinking. At Mayer's request? Rather his demand; he told a Hearst executive, along with the Chandler family who ran the powerful *Los Angeles Times* group, that should any word ever appear about it, he would withdraw all advertising for the rest of his life.

The big story that no one heard was that the star drove home from the studio one night, so inebriated that he knocked over and killed a black woman and her child. He was arrested. This led to the most demonstrable example of a movie mogul's power than anything else ever recorded. He ordered an underling, who was about to be fired, to come immediately to his home. When the man arrived in the early hours of the morning, he was certain he was to be the principal victim of the latest Mayer night of the long knives. But he wasn't going to be fired. Instead, Mayer offered him $1 million. 'I want you,' he said, 'to go to jail instead of Clark Gable.' The man was dumbfounded – but also broke and with a family to keep. He accepted the offer – to say that it was he at the wheel and that Gable was innocent. At the same time, a similar amount was offered to the district attorney to change the documentation and replace Gable's name with that of the under-performing executive – who was jailed for manslaughter for a year, with the help of a good lawyer paid for by Mayer. The deal stayed secret till Charles Higham revealed it in his Mayer biography. (A little while later, Mayer used his influence to get the young John Huston off of a similar charge – he had also run over and killed a woman while drunk.)

There were other cover-ups. In 1937, a party for MGM salesmen resulted in drunken behaviour – and the rape of at least 127 women who had been hired for the evening as 'entertainers'. Mayer, both furious and frightened that the name MGM was being sullied in this way, managed to bribe sufficient police and law officers to avoid anything coming out in public – until one of the girls, Patricia Douglas, sued Mayer. Her story 'Girl 27' was later turned into a documentary.

Despite the cover-up of his case, Gable had to be punished. Mayer was very good at punishing, as good as he was at flattery and bribery. The star was not invited to the annual brunch which Mayer organised at New Year, to which every star and executive who was in favour would have to be invited and expected to attend, as if answering a whip. Mayer then 'loaned out' Gable to the much smaller outfit, Columbia Pictures, which had previously operated, not from a palatial estate like MGM's at Culver City or an area as impressive as Warner Bros.'s Burbank layout, but from a studio in the area of Los Angeles known as 'Poverty Row'.

The role was in a film called *It Happened One Night*, which was originally going to go to Robert Montgomery, but who before the movie could get on to the studio floor, dropped out. As far as Gable was concerned, he was too valuable an asset to lose and had been ordered to go to Palm Springs and wait for further instructions. He knew he had been guilty of a monstrous offence – not the killing, which was not very nice, but upsetting Louis B. Mayer. Hence the punishment of replacing Montgomery and the ignominy of going to Columbia was constantly stressed by the studio boss, who also cut Gable's salary.

It Happened One Night was going to be a cheap movie that would be directed by the young Frank Capra and would co-star Claudette Colbert, hardly a Garbo or a Jean Harlow. It was a story which, ironically, had originally been bought by MGM, but was then turned down by Mayer, the defender of the American dream which said that people had a right to be hideously rich. He didn't like the idea of the multi-millionaire father of the heiress (Colbert) in the picture being shown in a bad light.

It happened one night that Mayer saw the film and was sick – except that he still owned Gable's contract and would give him a few other things to do. It also happened one night at the Academy Award ceremonies that the star won an Oscar for his role in the film – so did Colbert and Capra, and the writer of the piece, Robert Riskin. To make

Gable feel even worse, *It Happened One Night* won the Oscar for the best movie of 1934 – after the star caused a furore by stripping to the waist in the famous 'Walls of Jericho' scene, in which he puts his clothes on a line to act as a screen between him and Ms Colbert. The American men's underwear business went crazy because he wasn't wearing a vest.

There was an ultimate accolade for the star who learned to become more disciplined as the years went by. In *Broadway Melody of 1938*, Mayer had Judy Garland singing 'You Made Me Love You' to Clark's photograph as she writes a letter to 'Dear Mr Gable.'

Judy Garland

If Gable could be lent to Columbia, Mayer was not above 'borrowing' artists, too – and frequently with highly positive results. Which was why Paul Muni in the 1937 picture about China, *The Good Earth*, was one of the year's success stories and why Mayer loved having him around the studio. The film received an Academy Award nomination for best picture and the female star Louise Rayner had the Best Actress Oscar.

Five years after *It Happened One Night*, there was another Oscar nomination for best picture for MGM, one now starring Judy Garland. *The Wizard of Oz* didn't win, but there was a special award for Judy. It was another huge triumph for the studio, to say nothing of its producer Mervyn LeRoy (who happened to be Harry Warner's son-in-law) and, of course Louis B. Mayer himself. It would be one of those very few films which has not only lasted long past what would normally be its sell-by date but has more and more earned an iconic place in movie history.

This story of the Tin Man, the Cowardly Lion and the Scarecrow is best known for its principal number 'Over the Rainbow' and, of course, the 'little' girl who sang it, the 17-year-old Judy Garland, playing Dorothy, aged 12. It all looked so lovely – not least because of the last reel, shot in Technicolor, when suddenly the Yellow Brick Road became just that, yellow. Judy's voice was delightful, the numbers, including 'Rainbow', written by E.Y. (Yip) Harburg and Harold Arlen were tuneful and fitted beautifully into the tale of the unhappy little girl who runs away from home and finds her way to the wizard, played by Frank Morgan.

The fact that Judy Garland had such a tragic life can be directed right at the doorway of Louis B. Mayer's office. In *The Wizard of Oz*, she had to be strapped up like the Invisible Woman so as not to look as mature as she really was. And she was stuffed with drugs – on Mayer's instructions.

Her daughter Lorna Luft told me: 'I blame MGM for what happened to my mother. She was given uppers to wake her up in the mornings so that she was ready for work and downers to make her sleep at night – so that she would be fit enough to work the next day. What do you think that does to a girl?'

Not even daily doses of Mrs Mayer's chicken soup, which the producer prescribed for Judy, could settle her, but the mogul only cared about getting the work he wanted from her. He even at one time thought that threats were the real answer – when Judy asked him the identity of a pretty new girl she had seen on the set, he revealed that her name was June Allyson – who was primed to take over from Judy if she ever thought of stepping out of line. Apparently, Ms Allyson was given the same message – that Judy was ready to step into her shoes if she didn't behave herself. 'Behave' was generally meant to stand for 'lose weight'.

He watched over his stars like a sheepdog overseeing a wayward flock. If they were involved in successful series, as Judy was, there was always a bite to peck at anyone he considered ill behaved. He loved Myrna Loy and William Powell for the *Thin Man* series of benign detective stories.

But La Garland was in a class of her own. With her, Mayer helped to create a massive audience for an adolescent star who took over where Shirley Temple – whom Mayer at first wanted for the *Oz* role – left off. Unlike Temple, she continued into adulthood and made important grown-up movies that at times set the Pacific on fire – not least, Warner Bros.'s *A Star Is Born*.

But the drugs, and later the drink, had their impact on her. Mayer wanted her for *Annie Get Your Gun*, but her behaviour was so unnerving that she was dropped after recording numbers like 'I've Got the Sun in the Morning' and 'Anything You Can Do'. Betty Hutton took her part. While making *Summer Stock*, an underrated musical, with Gene Kelly in 1950, she was close to committing suicide. Her weight varied from light to heavy in the midst of making *A Star is Born*, although that was not MGM's problem. Warners had to deal with a star who looked as if she was born to be fat in one scene and thin in another. It drove the costume department mad. Mayer would have ordered that her meals be checked for calories – and contained a reasonable dose of arsenic (to take effect when her contract expired).

It was all a long, long way from the glory years of Garland and MGM, the years when she and Mickey Rooney would walk into a barn and exclaim, 'Let's make a show.' They had certainly made a big, big show with *Babes in Arms* and *Strike Up the Band.* Mayer could demonstrate that they showed everything that was good about young America. After all, they were only extending part of what everyone expected of the nice, clean American family, the Hardys. In *Love Finds Andy Hardy*, Judy is the love interest in the title – the lovely, clean girl next door, the lovely, clean American family, which took more than two million lovely, clean dollars. The movies, with Rooney as the son of Judge Hardy, played memorably by Lewis Stone (except in the first of the series, *A Family Affair*, when the judge was portrayed by Lionel Barrymore), who was old enough to be his great grandfather, showed the kind of country that Mayer told himself he was proud to live in – if more than a little sad that he hadn't experienced anything like it in his own childhood.

Mayer used his own experience and emotions in the fabric of the pictures. In an early one, Andy was seen to be impolite to his mother (played by Fay Holden). Mayer was beside himself in anger. How could anyone write a story like that? How could any film man produce a picture in which the mother is so denigrated? He ordered that this mother should be shown the same respect as her apple pie. That was why he always claimed that the Andy Hardy movies were the best he ever made. They were, he would say, 'the only pictures I really took an active hand in. They were good and wholesome. They had heart. You can't imagine how much good they did for America. I saw them in Turkey and Egypt and all over the world.' All places where he liked to believe people loved and honoured their mothers.

In 1938 Mayer called the actor Jackie Coogan into his office. Coogan was in the midst of a lawsuit – suing his own mother for the moneys he had earned while a child star. 'How can you do that?' he asked Coogan. 'Nobody sues their mothers.'

Mayer told him: 'You and I are good friends. Look, I'll give you $2,500 a week and put you under contract.' And then he added: 'One condition, you have to drop the suit against your mother.'

'I can't do that,' said Coogan.

'You dirty son of a bitch,' Mayer answered, without realising that calling a man a son of a bitch was saying even worse things about his mother. 'I'll see that you never work in this town again.' For several years, Coogan really was drummed out of the town. He couldn't get a film part for love or money – and at one stage, he needed to have both.

Mayer would say that honouring motherhood was his mission in life, which is stretching things a bit. Nevertheless, insulting mothers was always beyond the pale. When the popular silent star John Gilbert came to his office obviously more familiar with a bottle of bourbon than with the contents of his latest script, Mayer grew increasingly angry. When Gilbert dared to say that it was nothing to worry about; his mother had had a drink problem, too, Mayer grew furious. Even worse, Gilbert called his co-star Mae Murray a whore – which he then added to his mother's characteristics. That was all Mayer needed to hear – and so he went round to the other side of his desk and punched Gilbert to the floor with a powerful left hook. He was known to repeat the performance whenever he thought that kind of chastisement was required. Needless to say, Gilbert was fired and his career finished. The story was that he couldn't fit in with the 'talkies' because the glamour boy of the past had a high voice that made people laugh. It was not true. Mayer had had sufficient faith in him to get Lionel Barrymore to give him lessons in voice production. The sound that came out of his mouth might not have had the quality of a Ronald Colman or even a Gary Cooper, but there was nothing unacceptable about it. Certainly, no audiences laughed when he made love to Garbo.

Gilbert died of a heart attack at the age of 37.

Mayer also had a celebrated fight with Charlie Chaplin when he heard that the great silent star had said words about him that wouldn't have fitted in with Mayer's idea of a good publicity campaign.

None of that was obvious in the 16 Andy Hardy movies, all of them with Mickey Rooney getting into one kind of trouble or other, usually over money or girls (which was total typecasting; Mayer was always chastising him for that and for showing off – like the time, at 15, he bought a new Cadillac, and, because he was too young to drive, employed a chauffeur). Billy Wilder told me that when he and Charles Brackett were working on the Garbo film, *Ninotchka*, he happened to pass Mayer's office as he was tearing Rooney off the proverbial strip. 'I could hear Mayer tell him: 'You're Andy Hardy. You're the United States. You're the Stars and Stripes. You're the spirit of America. Stop drinking. Behave yourself!' The series began in 1937 and ended, in effect, in 1946. There was an attempt at reviving the theme in 1956, but *Andy Hardy Comes Home* featuring the naughty boy in his 40s was a one-off, even though it did end with the words 'To be continued'.

In retrospect the series should have been notable for the debuts of

Lana Turner, Kathryn Grayson and Esther Williams, and Andy's on-off girlfriend was always there in the shape of Ann Rutherford. Rutherford was a pretty girl who provided nice wallpaper for the series and was ideally cast for a role that called for little else. She asked Mayer for a rise. He said he couldn't manage it. So she took out her bankbook and showed him the small amount of cash that she owned. She said, tearfully, that she had promised to buy her mother a house and couldn't afford it. That was all Mayer needed to hear – a young girl who loved her mother. The crying scene was in full flow on both sides of the desk and she got her increase in salary.

No one could describe Judy Garland in those films as anything but very important. Judy also appeared in *Andy Hardy Meets Debutante* and *Life Begins For Andy Hardy* in 1941, set in a world before America realised there was a war out there – and it showed. For a time, the series became the most famous product of the Culver City studio, as big as the musicals would prove a decade or so later, although Judy Garland would make plenty of those all-colour spectacles produced by the iconic Arthur Freed unit. To justify the claim that she was overworked by Mr Mayer, one only has to look at the roster of Garland films in this era. There was *Little Nellie Kelly* in 1940, *Ziegfeld Girl* a year later, *Babes on Broadway* and notably *For Me and My Gal* with Gene Kelly in 1942.

The same year, there was *Girl Crazy*, a Hollywood version of the Gershwins' Broadway hit, which was another pairing with Mickey Rooney. *Thousands Cheer* in 1943 was followed by *Meet Me in St Louis*, a year later, arguably Judy's most popular musical, which featured her famous 'Trolley Song' and 'A Merry Little Christmas'. *The Harvey Girls* in 1946 was a stunning follow up if only for the song set on another of the MGM trains, 'The Atchison, Topeka and the Santa Fe'. In 1947, she was with Gene Kelly again in *The Pirate* (in which he sang 'Be a Clown', by Cole Porter, the melody of which no one has ever been able to distinguish from Arthur Freed's 'Make 'Em Laugh' in *Singin' in the Rain*). A year later, she was partnering Fred Astaire in *Easter Parade*, the Irving Berlin musical which also should have starred Gene Kelly, but he broke his leg just before filming began in earnest. It was the film that included a melange of old and new Irving Berlin melodies – for which the songwriter was paid $600,000 in lieu of royalties.

In 1949, Judy starred in *In the Good Old Summertime* with Van

Johnson, an actor who was extraordinarily popular in the war years. He might not have been had it not been for Mayer's confidence in him when an unknown. Johnson had had a serious road accident, just as he was about to make the film *A Guy Named Joe*. The year was 1942 and actors who looked good in MGM films were in short supply. But there were alternatives under contract who could have been available. Mayer decided to wait till the young man was better – and *A Guy Named Joe* was a huge hit both for Johnson and the studio.

In between, there were the occasional straight roles for Judy like in *The Clock* with Robert Walker in 1945. Whenever there was an MGM compilation film like *Thousands Cheer*, Garland was on hand to appear as a 'guest'.

Warner Bros. were not the only studio to take advantage of the stars it had under contract. Judy would not be omitted when there were fictional biopics of songwriters to be had at MGM. *Till the Clouds Roll By* in 1946 (an amazingly prolific year for musicals) was allegedly the story of Jerome Kern. It was nothing like it, although Judy charmed doing the washing up in her interpretation of Marilyn Miller singing 'Look For the Silver Lining'. When it came to the story of Rodgers and Hart as seen by the studio (but not by either Rodgers or Hart) in 1948, *Words and Music*, she was there with the rest of them, including Lena Horne and Perry Como. She sang 'I Wish I Were in Love Again' in a duet with Mickey Rooney. It had first been featured by them in *Babes in Arms*.

The fact that Judy Garland died at the age of 47 in 1969 owed not a little to Louis B. Mayer. The thought that without him she might have survived a lot longer cannot be dismissed from the mind. He, naturally enough, would just say how much he loved her. As he did her many musical partners.

Irving Thalberg

The very evident expense of an MGM picture, particularly an MGM musical, showed from the moment the first credits appeared. In the 1970s and 1980s, MGM produced a series of compilation films that consisted entirely of clips from the studio's huge output of mainly (the first of these three movies consisted entirely of them) musicals, called *That's Entertainment*. The by-then overgrown, dusty sets gave an idea of the standards to which Mayer and his Gunza Mishpocha worked and insisted others did, too. There was the now crumbling diving board and the swimming pool in which Esther Williams and her chorus of breaststroking and crawling maidens, all magnificently made up, performed the impossible, looking as though they never really got wet, while a lighted candelabra was raised from the pool.

Other studios would send teams on location, which MGM did, too – notably with the first musical ever shot outside Culver City, in the streets of Manhattan for the Gene Kelly-Frank Sinatra 1949 film, *On the Town*. When they chose not to do that, MGM could make parts of the studio lot look as if they actually were outside locations: there were the street scenes, the thoroughfares of New York, used in a dozen musicals, the ones in which Gene Kelly danced on roller skates and Fred Astaire marched with Judy Garland in *Easter Parade*. There was the railway station, complete with a streamlined train that always looked immaculate – now looking as though it had travelled through an earthquake, but still there and still demonstrating the extent of the MGM scene creators' art. The train and the station may have looked different every time it appeared in a new film. The art of those designers was to make sure that it always looked perfect. Louis B. Mayer would have expected – would have insisted on – nothing less.

Reviews of his films were like school reports given to parents. Since his employees were his children, he was sometimes inconsolable if there were reports that were summed up by the phrase 'could do better'. The 'children', of course, always knew that. Two men working for him were favourites, one of them justified that adage about the son-in-law also rising.

Irving Thalberg was the big influence on the studio and Mayer was happily going around saying that he couldn't do without him. He produced films at Culver City with an intuition that few others seemed to understand. He was the second most important man in MGM and, in a way, the second most powerful in Hollywood. Yet outside of the industry, his name was virtually unknown. Until he married Norma Shearer at a big Hollywood society wedding, you rarely saw him in the gossip columns. There were influential writers at the time who had never heard of him – because he never had his name on a film. As he said, when you reach the stage when you have the power to put your own name on a movie, which he did, you didn't need it.

The story was that Mayer dearly hoped that the young producer – who was immortalised in the Scott Fitzgerald novel, *The Last Tycoon* – might marry his daughter Edith, known as 'Edie', but he was for the moment more concerned with marrying films. There was another story about

Mayer's ambitions for Thalberg – that he would never introduce either of his daughters to him, because he knew the young man had a serious insipient heart problem, as a result of rheumatic fever.

Not that Thalberg allowed that to affect either his love of films or the way he put that love into practice in the business. He knew it was good to bring the Marx Brothers to MGM, although Mayer couldn't understand them and hated Groucho. It was thoroughly mutual. Groucho's son Arthur Marx told me: 'My father didn't like Mayer, but he loved Thalberg. After they made *A Night at the Opera*, they started working on *A Day at the Races*. One day my father was strolling the MGM lot and bumped into Louis B. Mayer. He said, "Hello Groucho, how's the picture going?" My father said, "What do you care? We're working for Thalberg." Mayer was furious. When Thalberg died, they were in the employ of Louis Mayer. He hated them after that and he would never give the Marx Brothers good writers and wouldn't allow them to go on the road with their vaudeville act, to try out new material. So that was my father and Mayer. Hated Mayer, loved Thalberg.'

A Night at the Opera, which was the brothers' first MGM movie, was a huge success, bigger than the ones that followed, but they all more than earned their keep at the studio. This was probably due more to Thalberg than anyone else. He saw the picture twice at previews and came out of each saying that it needed tightening up, with more emphasis on the humour than had first appeared. For three days, he worked in the cutting room, rearranging the whole movie to make that humour – like the famous stateroom scene – more dominant than it had been in the original George S. Kaufman and Morrie Riskind script.

Actually, Mayer didn't think much of comedy at all. The writer Melville Shavelson told me: 'MGM was a big place. They didn't have comedians to write for. They had their own staff. You had to know your way around and do it their way. You could get buried at MGM.'

Above all, Mayer distrusted writers. He was one of the most vociferous opponents of the founding of their union, the Screen Writers Guild. He tried to set up a rival union and then called in Irving Thalberg to try to bring peace. Shavelson remembered: 'Thalberg made a speech in which he said, "We know that the most vital people in Hollywood are the writers and we're doing all we can to prevent them finding out about it".'

It was Thalberg, who before the talkies arrived, had persuaded Erich von Stroheim to direct *The Merry Widow*; no easy job, forsaking the Franz Lehar score to make a silent movie. He did and it became a hit –

although 'Von' as he was known in the business, became more and more insufferable.

Thalberg also took Lon Chaney under his wing. 'The Man of a Thousand Faces', as Chaney was described (it was the title of his biopic, starring James Cagney; Chaney died from throat cancer at 47), played a circus clown in *He Who Gets Slapped*. Norma Shearer supplied the love interest. It became a big hit and Thalberg was confirmed as the 'Man with a Thousand Gifts'. Mayer loved him for it – but he could be jealous if he realised that there was no one considered more popular and kind than the physically weak younger man.

Thalberg had indeed been the fulcrum of much of what the studio was presenting, dating back to the silent era. Not least, right at the beginning of their relationship, Thalberg had been responsible for making *Ben Hur*, an epic starring Ramon Novarro and Francis X. Bushman, that was as much part of Hollywood's history as that of the studio. Mayer, on the other hand, would say that the triumph of the film – most of it originally shot in Italy – was his own.

Thalberg was the brains behind *Mutiny on the Bounty*, which he produced in 1936. In that he had to be as much a psychologist as a moviemaker, smoothing things over when the rows between Charles Laughton and Clark Gable were like the ones on screen between them as Captain Bligh and Fletcher Christian. Gable complained of being treated by the newly-arrived British actor as an extra, which might have been a polite way of putting it.

Thalberg was an undoubted presence, which Mayer sometimes felt was perhaps a little too present. He even suggested, in an unguarded moment, that life would be easier for him without the continued presence of Irving around him, dogging his every move and making great suggestions which he knew he would have been foolish to turn down. Indeed, he did regard it all as his baby, with all the results one would expect of a relationship between Louis B. Mayer and his 'children'.

When he heard that Thalberg had had a row with a star – for all his kindness and popularity, he could be hard, too – Mayer had reason to sit back in his high-backed chair and smile. Yet, he had reason to cry, really cry when, in September 1936 the pneumonia that the physically weak man developed resulted in his death. He was just 37. Suddenly the unknown Irving Thalberg became a front-page story. Mayer probably did love him – as much for himself as for what he brought to MGM. He rightly wondered if the studio could survive without him. It did. But he had to remember what Thalberg had brought to him and to his business.

MGM – Made Great Musicals

The other Big Personality at MGM was Lewis Selznick's son, David O. Selznick, who did become a son-in-law. They apparently admired and loved each other – but only after the younger man suffered from that well-known Louis B. Mayer failing – jealousy.

When Irene married David O. Selznick, that jealousy was extreme. Not that he didn't like Selznick, but anyone who threatened to take his daughters away from under his immediate care couldn't possibly be good enough. However, he found Selznick was indeed good enough. He saw in him a successor to Irving Thalberg and knew that he was a talented producer. His first film, *Dinner at Eight*, based on a successful Broadway play by George S. Kaufman and Edna Ferber, and directed by George Cukor, was a big critical and box office hit, notable for a remarkable performance by Jean Harlow.

George Sidney said of him: 'David was a real producer. He understood films in a way that Mayer never did. He knew how scenes worked. Mayer had general ideas, but Selznick knew all the details.'

The studio had good reason to be grateful to the man who brought *David Copperfield* to the screen in a version of the Dickens story that has never been bettered, and *Anna Karenina* with Greta Garbo recreating her own silent movie role.

Later, when he left MGM, after making *A Tale of Two Cities*, with Ronald Colman, still one of the best transfers of a Charles Dickens story to the (black and white) screen, Mayer was not just willing to distribute Selznick's work – including a little thing called *Gone with the Wind* in 1939, he was proud to do so. But that was only after Mayer had at first decided it wasn't a film worth making. When Selznick proved that it was, he did pretty well out of it, too.

Selznick fitted in perfectly with his definition of the kind of person he wanted for his children. He was a big man, physically and in personality, and Mayer showed respect for his achievements. Strangely, bearing in mind his own attitude to religion, he also seemed to appreciate that he was Jewish. It was something they had in common, especially since neither was observant. What Mayer really appreciated about his son-in-law, and remained appreciative of after his divorce from Irene, was the fact that at no time did he ever ask for or receive help from him. It was a fact that the mogul mentioned in his will – in contrast to Edie's husband William Goetz, who received a lot of help, both financial and professional from him.

If this was the outfit that Made Great Musicals, it needed not just actors and actresses who could sing and sometimes dance, but the right camera angles which ensured that stars didn't appear to be warbling down the throats of their partners. They needed the best music from the best composers, like the Gershwins, Cole Porter, Irving Berlin and Jerome Kern. Above all, they needed to have them produced properly, which is why this was the only major studio that had its own musicals unit presided over by the songwriter Arthur Freed (the score for the studio's musical *Singin' in the Rain*, arguably the best of the genre ever made, consisted entirely of Freed's own songs, with lyrics by Nacio Herb Brown). Freed ran what was virtually an empire within an empire and even Mayer rarely dared to interfere with what he did – a miracle in itself.

Like Mayer, Freed could find talented players, and directors, too. It was Freed who discovered Vincente Minnelli, one of the most talented directors of musicals of all time, whose best production was probably his daughter Liza. But, although marrying Judy Garland may have been good for him, films like her *Meet Me in St. Louis* as well as *An American in Paris*, *Father of the Bride* and *The Band Wagon* assured his place in the industry's pantheon.

None of that could have happened, however, without musicians. And it was here that Mayer put his own stamp on things right from the very beginning. He established not just a studio orchestra, made up of what today would be called session musicians, which would have been common in Hollywood, but an MGM symphony orchestra, consisting of and conducted by some of America's greatest wielders of a baton. A young Andre Previn became a fixture early on and won an Oscar for the studio for orchestrating *Gigi*. But the mainstay behind the orchestra was the man known as Johnny Green, who, when he became extremely famous for conducting concerts at the Hollywood Bowl and other venues called himself John Green.

Green was a man rightly sure of his own capabilities and reputation, if not more than a little pompous, but he had no doubt to whom he owed so much of that success. 'You know,' he told me, sitting round his swimming pool which looked as if it had come straight out of an MGM set, 'Mayer had this amazing personality and ingenuity. He is often portrayed as a man who knew how to use people, who understood the books – the ones with figures on them, not those of his stories – but he demanded the best and knew that he had to have the best. Since MGM was producing those marvellous musicals, they had to be the best, too and have the best ingredients. Thanks to him and his investments, you heard music the way it should be played – not always an easy thing in films.'

It was because of that insistence on perfection by Mayer himself that 'his' orchestra had an international reputation. It played outside of the Hollywood orbit, too – that is, when its busy musicians had time to travel.

Plainly, money was never going to be an object when making a movie for his studio.

That was why MGM was among the first to jump on to the talkie bandwagon once *The Jazz Singer* had proved that the silent movie would never seriously return.

Mayer had been one of the founders of the Academy of Motion Picture Arts and Sciences and, in a moment of unusual generosity to another studio, had been instrumental in making sure that *The Jazz Singer* had a special award. It wasn't simply altruistic generosity. Showing his colleagues that he thought the movie was important, raised his own status in the business and showed that he had faith in a medium he had previously denigrated as not worth thinking about. Now he had the chance for the general public to see not just that he was firmly in the game but was intending to be ahead of it.

In not too glorious, flickering black and white, *Broadway Melody* in 1929 was the first real musical. It was billed as 'all-singing-all-dancing', with a group of heavy chorus girls clumping along a stage and Charles King singing 'You Are My Lucky Star'. Whether anyone was prescient enough to think that musicals were going to be one of the trademarks of MGM is probably doubtful. Audiences just sat and marvelled at the fact that, not only were there songs to hear and music to back the dancers and singers, there were absolutely no titles between scenes.

The roar of Leo the Lion bespoke power and authority – and strength. All the qualities that Louis B. Mayer admired and demanded.

Which was why there was so much ingenuity evident in Mayer's empire. Very often, Fred Astaire was the beneficiary of that. Astaire was known as a perfectionist – it is as impossible for someone who knew Mr Twinkletoes to avoid using that word as it is to describe a spiral staircase without using hands making circular motions – and it was that search and demand for perfection that attracted him to the studio boss. It was why, in the movie *Royal Wedding*, he does a dance with a hat stand. But more remarkable, for the 1940s, long before the computerised age, what was really remarkable was the time in the same film when he appeared to be dancing upside down on a ceiling – in fact, technicians had rigged up a camera in a revolving drum that gave the impression that it was the dancer who moved, not the set.

Right back in the days of black and white, the more 'normal' internal sets had been as perfect as were the technically innovative or lifelike outdoor ones. The all-white rooms, sometimes complete with all-white pianos and all-white carpets over which was placed an all-white desk in a business executive's office were as much MGM trademarks as the lion. The art deco style that the studio pioneered was seen as the ideal in a thousand fashion and style magazines, the kind of sophistication Mayer wanted his audiences to look up to, even if few of them could emulate. Of course, he also knew that if they could have emulated it, much of the magic of his films would have been lost and he wouldn't have liked that at all.

The Crying Game

Mayer not only took films on location, even when the studio was consolidated as one of the biggest and the most prestigious in Hollywood, he still went on location himself to look for new ideas and talent. In 1939, he brought Greer Garson, the Irish-born actress, over from England, where she had been working on the stage, to join another British actor, Robert Donat, in *Goodbye Mr Chips*. This story was a saga tracing the life of a British public-school teacher, played by Donat with Garson co-starring as his wife. It was one of the most significant movies of the decade. The fact that it was made at all was due to one of the team of people in the studio whose main job, actually whose only job, was to read books and plays for him and then explain the plots. He didn't read much himself. In fact, some people doubted if he could read at all, which was untrue. It is true, however, that he didn't trust either his eyes or the part of his brain which governed taking in information in writing.

Mayer's own office, on the other hand, could have come right out of one of his movies. At various times, it was also all-white, although metaphorically it often seemed as red-stained as that of any of the moguls. Bloodletting was strictly verbal, most of the time – but not the tear-letting. Mayer would bring out his handkerchief to dab his eyes as a kind of punctuation mark to the diatribe he was aiming at an erring star. Both

Joan Crawford and Frank Sinatra were victims of the crying scene. The routine went like this:

'Ida, could we have some tea?'

If the 'guest' sitting in front of Mayer's huge desk was really important, Ms Koverman would bring in the tray herself, complete with the kind of thin translucent china which would never be seen on a film set (it would have cracked under the lights). Then the conversation would begin in earnest: 'Joan (or Frank or Mary or whoever was in front of him) your last performance for me was wonderful. How could it have been anything but? Now, darling, how long have you been with me?'

'About ten (or whatever) years, Mr Mayer.'

'Ten years, darling! Ten years! Whatever would I have done without you?'

'Well, Mr Mayer, I don't—'

'I know, darling.' At this point, the handkerchief came out of his top pocket. 'I couldn't have managed without you. You helped make MGM.'

Depending on the importance of the person in front of him, the handkerchief would then be used to either simply wipe his eyes or to mop up the results of his uncontrollable weeping.

'You know, darling, how much I respect you and love you. Yes, I love you. And I think . . .' (sniff, sniff, wipe, wipe) '. . . I think you love me, too.'

'Of course, Mr Mayer.'

'And it is true, I know, that you would do anything for me.'

'Well, of course, Mr Mayer. You know you only have to say . . .'

The eyes are now whirlpools and his guest is all ready to offer her (his) own handkerchief. Between sobs, he can hardly get the words out. 'Well, darling, I really do want you to do something for me, something very, very important.'

'As I said, Mr Mayer, anything.'

'Thank you, darling, for making this easier for me. I want you to go into your dressing room and collect your things. You're fired.'

Frank Sinatra's experience was in the same mould. He and Gene Kelly were having lunch one day in the MGM commissary, talking about the this and that of studio politics. Unfortunately, they were overheard. Mayer was not pleased. Not because they talked about the problems they had experienced in making *On the Town*. Not because they were talking about television and what MGM were going to do about the competition it offered, but because they were talking about an accident in which their boss had been involved. 'You know that L.B.'s broken his arm?' asked Kelly. 'I'm told he fell off his horse.'

'Oh,' said Sinatra nonchalantly. 'I thought he fell off his mistress.' He thought nothing more of it – until the summons to The Office and the chance to watch Louis B. Mayer's handkerchief get more and more sodden. He had the tea, shook hands and went to his dressing room and collected his things – after phoning his lawyer and agent and agreeing terms for the dismissal. Mayer would never have done that had Sinatra's popularity not taken a nosedive (he had just lost his contract with Columbia Records, too) or had he had a crystal ball which would have told him that a rival studio would, in just a few years, make a picture called *From Here to Eternity*. That film would make Frank a super star and an Oscar winner, a performer who could justify the title of the World's Greatest Entertainer of the second half of the 20th century (Al Jolson laid claim to the title before his death in 1950).

Gregory Peck told me about the time in 1942 that he experienced the crying scene. Mayer offered him a seven-year contract. 'No, thank you,' said Peck.

Mayer stood up and walked around his desk – his usual practice when trying to persuade actors to do things against their better judgement. The actor, then still in his 20s, had not yet made a single movie.

'I want you Gregory, to join my family – my family of MGM stars. I have made great careers for Judy Garland, Robert Taylor, Greta Garbo, Robert Montgomery, Clark Gable . . .' The list went on and on.

He then added: 'You must let me decide on your pictures for you and you must become one of us. I will make you the greatest star of them all.' Plainly, he had a prescient feeling about this man who was not yet a film star. In fact, Peck told Mayer: 'Sorry, Mr Mayer. I'm a stage actor. I want to continue to be one. I'm determined not to sign an exclusive contract with anyone. If I were to do it, I'd be very happy to do it with you because I know your reputation, of course. But I cannot do so. It's against my nature.'

Mayer knew what that was all about. Peck wanted more money than the $1,000 a week being offered – the same sum that, coincidentally, Sam Goldwyn had already just suggested and which had been summarily rejected in the same way.

Mayer was trying to find bright new stars to fill the vacancies left by his top actors like Gable and Taylor who had joined the Forces. But Peck insisted it wasn't the money that was causing the problem between them. That was when the crying started.

L.B. could hardly get the words out as he paced the king-sized floor, king-sized tears cascading down his cheeks. 'Please, Gregory, understand what I'm offering you.' Twice he had to take off his glasses to demist the lenses.

'Now,' he asked, 'will you sign?'

'Mr Mayer,' the young actor said, 'I'm flattered. I cannot tell you how much I appreciate your offer. But I cannot consider it.'

Outside the office, Peck whispered to his agent, Leland Hayward, 'My God, what a performance!'

'Oh,' Hayward replied. 'He does that every day and loves it. I've seen that show a dozen times.'

Certainly, it was an effective weapon for getting things done – and done his way. He did it when the 'opposition' wasn't nearly as polite and respectful as Gregory Peck. Mario Lanza was at the height of his powers when he made *The Great Caruso*, one of the first biopics of an opera singer, even of one who had had a household name like Caruso. Lanza made the 1952 movie *Because You're Mine*, which could sum up the relationship between Mr Mayer – always 'Mister Mayer', if you couldn't bring yourself to say 'Your Majesty' – and his subjects, or rather his staff. When you worked at MGM, you did what Mister Mayer said because, as he could have said, you're mine.

Lanza was a vulgar, mostly unpleasant person who respected nothing apart from himself and the food that he ate in enormous quantities. But he was extraordinarily popular. He was known to storm into The Office and call his employer a 'Jew son of a bitch'. Instead of ordering him out of the room and banning him from the lot, which he would have done with many another actor who dared to use such anti-Semitic behaviour in an attempt to get his way, the crying scene began – partly perhaps out of shock. Yet, verbally, he responded just as he would have done had he been treated with the respect of a Gregory Peck. 'Mario,' he said, 'I thought you loved me.' Retirement of (very) stout party.

Mayer would extend the crying routine as a weapon for talking stars out of demands for big pay rises (when a sock on the jaw wouldn't do it) or for persuading them to take roles they had no wish to play. Myrna Loy was determined not to do one particular role to which she had been assigned. She was summoned into the presence, but this time a handkerchief to the eyes was not going to be enough. If this were a scene from a film it couldn't have been better written.

The star protested the part was not for her. Mayer listened to her, carefully, attentively, giving the definite impression that he not only understood, he sympathised. After she had finished her argument – more an earnest plea, for this was a lady – Mayer got up from his chair and walked to the other side of his desk, taking the actress's hand in the process.

'Please, darling. This role is made just for you. It wouldn't work, it couldn't be the same without you.'

The director Joseph L. Mankiewicz told me of the scene that he witnessed. 'He fell down, as if he were having a heart attack. The studio doctor was called and Mayer was carried on to a couch. Myrna was actually trembling at this point, as people were being cleared from the room. She said, "Do you think I could have done this – by refusing to play this part?"'

By and large, stars didn't refuse to play parts that Mayer wanted them to play.

His eyelids fluttered and he said to Myrna, 'Myrna, come closer. If you don't want to play this part, you must have your reasons.' But he had his reasons, too. He made it seem that by turning down the role, she would not only be breaking his heart, but breaking up the studio, too.

The star protested more and this time, Mayer grabbed hold of his collar and fell to the floor. He was all but foaming at the mouth, as Ms Loy was bending over him, now in full retreat and in total abject fear.

'Mr Mayer, I'll do it, if it's so important to you. Of course, I'll do it.'

Mayer was now whispering to her. 'Darling, you don't have to do it, if you feel so strongly. You really don't. Please don't worry.' He was stammering out the words now, but the tears were all hers. She was led out of the room, crying as she hadn't done for a long time. The studio boss waited to be sure that she was out of sight, then got back behind his desk, straightening his collar and tie as he called to his secretary on the intercom: 'Next.' Of course, Myrna Loy played the role.

Another who faced the crying scene was Robert Taylor, one of Mayer's most important stars, he of the widow's peak and *Waterloo Bridge*, who in 1938 was mobbed wherever he went when he made *A Yank at Oxford*. He was grateful that he got tears and not the left hook he had been told he might have to expect when he knocked on L.B.'s door and asked for a rise. It seemed more and more likely when the tears turned to shouts. But then there were more tears.

Mayer told him: 'Robert, I know what you want but if I were your father and you told me you were going to ask Mr Mayer for a rise, I would tell you, "Son, don't do it. Business is not so good at the moment. We might lose our European market. When things get a little better, we will discuss it again."' When Taylor left the room, one of the friends who had gone with him as support asked if he had got his rise.

'No,' he said, 'but I have found a father.'

That, of course, was how the mogul wanted to be considered. When he had a letter from Maureen O'Sullivan's father, he called the young woman, who would later have two reasons for fame – as Jane in the 'Tarzan' series and later as Mia Farrow's mother – into The Office and chastised her for 'not being a good daughter.' It was as though he were regarding her as his own erring offspring – which in his heart he might have considered her. Had Robert Taylor been one of his female stars, he might have been expected to sit on the mogul's lap as the boss sobbed. Several women agreed to do that. Several did not. Whether Ann Miller ever sat on the boss's lap isn't exactly on the record. What is certain is that Mayer fancied her to distraction and in all probability had an affair with her. He and his wife Margaret were divorced in 1947 (at a cost to Mayer of more than $3 million, a virtually impossible figure to imagine in that decade).

Father, God or Dictator

The following year, Mayer was married for a second time, to Lorena Danka. It was the end of an interesting period in the studio's story – when executives were at times required, quite openly, to act as his pimp, sometimes organising one-night stands, at others to introduce him to more proper ladies who might one day share his life as well his bed. One young woman complained: 'He doesn't want to screw me – just to be my father.' That figured.

The girls to whom he really was father had to learn to deal with a man who cheated on their mother – a woman who could cite the studio, as well as all the other women in his life, as co-respondents. He was as strict with his daughters as he was with his stars and starlets, trying to bring them up as nice, clean all-American girls. The fact that the daughters, Irene and Edith, were Jewish was never allowed to enter his thoughts – or those of the people with whom he came into contact. It only became a relevant factor when he tried to enter the girls into a posh private school. They were turned down instantly – because of their Jewishness. Wags said they were rejected because their father was Louis B. Mayer, whom the school thought would turn the institution into a film studio.

That is highly unlikely. He would have been a tremendous asset to the school – showering it with financial help if needed, bringing stars along to school occasions. But all the girls were required to state their religion and 'Jewish' was not one they wanted on their entry forms. Instead, Mayer enrolled them at the Hollywood School for Girls, where they met dozens of other daughters of people in the industry, who had had similar experiences.

When they grew up, he was jealous of any young men who courted their attention. And yet, he was not too proud to admit that he could be wrong, which is why the relationship with David O. Selznick is so important a part of the story. It was a story repeated with Edie's husband William Goetz, who, when he realised there was no way out and that the marriage was a fait accompli, he went to extraordinary lengths to help.

Among those extraordinary steps was his financial help to a rival studio. Goetz had been working as a producer for Fox, which then fired him. Shortly afterwards, that studio merged with Twentieth Century, another studio, to form Twentieth Century Fox. Mayer put more than half a million dollars into that studio as an investment, but on one condition – that they give Goetz a job. Cynics said he thought this was an insurance policy – with Goetz producing films, the new organisation had to fail. For once, his motives were pretty certainly simply to help his son-in-law and in that way his daughter. He later helped him become an independent producer, providing millions of dollars. But the couple broke up – Edith and William were no longer on speaking terms when Mayer died and his will stipulated that neither of them would benefit from it. He had, meanwhile, piled up all sorts of reasons for hating his son-in-law – not least the fact that when he himself was doing everything he could as head of the Republican Party of California to support General Dwight D. Eisenhower's bid for the presidency in 1952, Goetz and the man who had succeeded him as MGM boss, Dore Schary, gave a mammoth party for Ike's opponent, Adlai Stevenson.

There were other actors who admired Mayer for his persuasive powers. Edward G. Robinson is quoted by Scott Eyman as saying: 'Not for an instant did I discern hypocrisy or untruth in what he was saying. He meant every word and I found him to be a man of truth. Behind his "guttta-percha" face and roly-poly figure contained in some of the best tailoring I've ever seen, it was evident that here was a man of steel – but well-mannered steel, the very best quality steel, which meant the hardest and most impenetrable steel.'

There were employees who thought of him more in terms of a combination of Dracula and Santa Claus. To some, though, he was quite simply a dictator – actually, not just any ordinary dictator, but one with distinctly fascist tendencies. This was an unfair argument, even though Mayer's love of the Stars and Stripes was equalled perhaps only by fascist organisations like the German-American Bund. The truth of the matter was that Mayer's principal god was enough money to keep him in his position as the richest executive in the whole of the United States; the first to have a salary of $1 million in one year. As he once said: 'Anyone who walks into my office now knows my name is good for a million dollars on a cheque.'

Anything that interfered with that had to be fought – even when it came to doing business with the Nazis. By 1940, it was becoming much more of a one-sided affair – German-sided, that is. Charles Higham in his Mayer biography tells of the time *Gone with the Wind* was seized by Nazis in Paris and shipped off to Berlin (after MGM paid the customs duty for the film). Like other studios, the company kept its offices open in occupied Europe for up to a year after Pearl Harbor. But there was another side to the story and one that does Mayer a lot more credit than some of his other activities. He arranged to bring over to America more than 20 MGM employees working on the Continent and gave them jobs at the studio itself.

Mayer started filming *Mrs Miniver* in October 1941, two months before the United States entered the Second World War. It was a highly romanticised view of life in a rose-cottage England where Mrs Miniver's main problem in life was whether or not to buy a very silly hat. That was until her husband, Walter Pidgeon took one of the little boats out to Dunkirk.

(Greer Garson had a problem with her role. It had already been turned down by Norma Shearer, who didn't want to be seen as the mother of a man old enough to serve in the RAF. Garson was reluctant for the same reason. But Mayer, as always, won the day.)

In one scene, a German parachutist falls on to the Minivers' garden. Mayer didn't like the way he was made to appear in the script. He ordered that the character be 'softened' so as not to offend the Germans' sensitivities. William Wyler, the director, was furious. 'This is a way of getting at the Nazis,' he protested. That was precisely why Louis B. Mayer said no. The parachutist was just a patriot for his own country, doing the job he was expected to do. The mogul's concern was all the films he wanted to show in Germany.

It all figured. In 1938, Joseph Breen, who ran the Hollywood censors office after Mr Hays left, issued instructions to all the studios saying that no movie should show anything critical of the Nazi regime, even to the point of making sure there was no filming of Germans in uniform.

The original screenplays of a number of anti-Nazi films were watered down – in one case, with the inference that the unpleasant people involved were actually Communists. For the first time in his life, Mayer, by going along with the policy, was demonstrating cowardice, a sin of which he had not been previously accused.

To soften up the criticism, he made a statement saying: 'I am a Jew and I try to be a good one. In some lands, in an increasing number, you are persecuted if you are a Jew. You cannot own anything, may not vote, be driven from your home. If you are a Catholic you will find persecution in other lands.'

But amazingly, MGM films were still being offered in Germany. When the Germans declared war on America after the Japanese bombing, Mayer changed his instructions and the Nazi was seen as someone you would have to detest.

The episode illustrates Mayer's ambivalence to both Nazism and his own feelings as a Jew. He had considerable business interests in Germany – MGM films were very popular among the hierarchy as well as with the public and it seems, with the benefit of 20-20 hindsight, remarkable that Jewish-made movies weren't subject to the boycotts (and the burnings) that were meted out to Jewish books. Mayer even asked his Berlin executive to intercede with the government to ease up on its anti-Semitism. Of course, it did no good, but it remains notable that this man who went out of his way not to appear too Jewish did go as far as he did.

Certainly, Mayer had a great deal to be grateful for in *Mrs Miniver*. The movie ended with a church sermon, stressing the correctness of the Allied cause. President Roosevelt, always aware of the power of Hollywood, asked Mayer to provide him with copies of the sermon – which he then ordered should be dropped over Germany by American bombers.

If the characters in the film had been Jews, Mayer's enthusiasm for the picture would have been much more muted.

Unlike the Warners, he did not go on record as seeing anti-Semites under every bush in the studio garden, but he was frightened of them and the effect they had on his business, just the same. He was scared of going just that bit too far.

A year before the *Miniver* film, the studio made a picture about life in Germany at the time the Nazis came into power. *The Mortal Storm*, starring James Stewart, Robert Young, Margaret Sullavan and Robert Stack, dealt with the life of a very popular college professor (played uncannily by the most gentile-looking of men, Frank Morgan, one of Hollywood's worst examples of miscasting since the screen had first learned to talk). He was plainly the nicest, kindest of men, loved by his students – until the day they turned up in their Hitler Youth uniforms and asked him about the differences between Aryan and non-Aryan blood. When he assured them there was no difference at all, they turned against him, the non-Aryan professor. Never was the word 'Jew' used in the picture. If Mayer had wanted to change that, a visit from the Swiss Consul, who said he was representing German interests in California, talked him out of it.

Robert Stack told me: 'This man said that when the Germans came to Hollywood, presumably after they invaded us, there would be a reckoning. Bob Young was walking around, shaking, saying, "Oh my wife, oh my children"!' The professor in the film ended up in a concentration camp – looking nothing like a real prisoner, but no one could know at that time anything about striped pyjama-type Auschwitz uniforms, let alone about death camps, which were still three years away. But in this instance, Mayer was brave enough – if only up to a point.

What irked the sections of the Hollywood community, who were more concerned about the fate of Europe's Jews than Louis B. Mayer, was the fact that here was a Jew who might have done so much doing so little.

Before the war, but after Kristallnacht and the Nuremberg Laws that made Jews non-citizens, stars still went from Hollywood to Europe and still were intensely interviewed. The braver ones dared to walk where the moguls and their cohorts refused to tread. Among them was Myrna Loy who toured Holland and Norway, just a few months before the outbreak of war. She used the opportunity this presented to attack the Nazis and their treatment of the Jews. It infuriated the MGM management, whose representative in Amsterdam warned her against upsetting those nice people in Berlin. When she returned, Arthur Loew, from the Loew organisation, MGM's parent company, sent her an angry note on the same subject. She was not impressed. As she was to write years later: 'This still makes me so mad I could spit. Here I was for the Jews and they're telling me to lay off because there's still money to be made in Germany. Loew and many of the company's executives were Jewish, but they condoned this horror. I know it's incredible, but it happened.' Alas, she was merely confirming a story as well known as Mayer's crying scene.

Where Mayer did appear to show more courage was in his attitude to HUAC and the McCarthyism scare. But it was as much an illusion as the time that Gene Kelly (who would become suspect himself for red-leanings) danced with Jerry the Mouse.

The MGM boss was excused from following Warner into the witness box at the preliminary hearing at the Biltmore Hotel in Los Angeles and then in Washington – because he was afraid of nailing his colours to a mast that he knew was about to blow over; but which way, he couldn't yet be sure. An underling went to see J. Parnell Thomas on Mayer's behalf and got him excused – because he said the mogul's brother Jerry was dangerously ill. He didn't have the courage to go himself, let alone appear as an 'unfriendly' witness. He didn't say that no one was going to intefere with his business and tell him who to employ and who not to, as Sam Goldwyn did. Neither did he at first list names of known Communists and call people he didn't like fellow travellers. Nevertheless, by not going public on the matter, he was managing to accept the blacklist as a fact of life. When he did give evidence, it was in the form of a statement that answered all the needs of the committee: 'I have maintained a relentless vigilance against un-American influences,' said the man who showed that he worshipped America, not merely displaying the loyalty of a citizen. 'If, as has been alleged, Communists have attempted to use the screen for subversive purposes, I am proud of our success in circumventing them,' he said. Then he made the point he wanted people to remember him by. 'It is my earnest hope that this committee will perform a public service by recommending to the Congress legislation establishing national policy regulating employment of Communists in private industry. It is my belief they should be denied the sanctuary of the freedom they seek to destroy.'

He did nothing when the MGM writer Lester Cole, who was one of the Hollywood Ten, was arraigned before the committee and subsequently jailed.

When the Columbia star Larry Parks was ordered to appear before the committee and begged not to be made to name names, Mayer sacked the actor's wife, Betty Garrett, who had an MGM contract and, after her magical performance opposite Frank Sinatra (and along with Gene Kelly, Vera Ellen, Ann Miller and Jules Monshin) in *On the Town*, was being groomed to be a big star. She was instantly placed on the infamous blacklist.

On the other hand, if Mayer needed a member of his staff more than possibly the employee thought he needed him, he used all the charm (by his own definition) that he brought into play to persuade him or her that his love would see that everything turned out all right.

Gene Kelly, for instance, was already established as his iconic musical star. To the red hunters, Gene was a Commie – and was married to a Commie, too. But the star who, by the time HUAC went into a second period of investigation in 1951, had just made *An American in Paris*, was too valuable to be let off the MGM leash. Especially since *Singin' in the Rain* was now on the drawing boards. He wasn't a Communist Party member, but he was known to have left-wing tendencies and his house had been invaded by FBI spies – to discover who attended his open-house parties. His wife, Betsy Blair, on the other hand, *was* about to be blacklisted. She had planned to join the Communist Party, but had been talked out of it by her husband. Mayer worried about this, because he had had her earmarked for a role in a new film, *Kind Lady*. Now he was about to fire her. But then he called Blair into The Office and decided it was time for the charm offensive. The meeting over, he found Gene waiting for her outside. He put his arms around the shoulders of them both and told Kelly: 'She's as American as you and I.'

But, once the film was made, he blacklisted her just the same. She recovered briefly to make *Marty* for United Artists in 1955 and won an Oscar nomination for her trouble, but never worked for MGM again.

At the back of Mayer's mind was the same kind of cowardice that infected the rest of the Hollywood establishment. This was, he decided, not a boat he could afford to rock.

He then compounded the felony by offering Lester Cole not only an amnesty, but also a huge rise in salary and prestige and a total say in what he did at the studio. He would also, Mayer promised, have the help of his favourite producer Jack Cummings, who would always be working with him. All he had to do was say that he was no longer a Communist – the line taken by HUAC itself.

Cole refused. Mayer was apoplectic. He wasn't in tears. This was too important a matter to be left to a crying scene. Instead, he shouted at his recalcitrant writer: 'Get out, you goddamned Commie.' So much for Louis B. Mayer's battle on behalf of his staff.

Jack Cummings was Mayer's nephew, one of those who also rose through MGM's ranks. To his dying day, Cummings had a photograph of Mayer on his desk. He told me: 'I know it's not fashionable to say anything nice about a big man like Louis, but he was a wonderful, kind man. He understood what other producers needed – and if he trusted you, he let you get on with it. There weren't many studio heads who did that.'

Mayer used to call Cummings 'my *macher*', Yiddish for 'top man', which could be taken literally or with a dose of sarcasm, although sarcasm was not part of the mogul's make-up. And he appreciated the nephew's work. 'When we made *Seven Brides for Seven Brothers*,' Cummings told me, 'Louis wanted to know every detail of the story, every costume change, every piece of music. He wasn't easily satisfied, but when he had an idea it was usually a good one, one to be put into practice.'

The director Clarence Brown told the writer Scott Eyman for his book, *The Lion of Hollywood*: 'To me, Louis Mayer was a god. He was a strangely dependent man, we travelled a lot together and if I told him to wait for me while I went to the bathroom or something, he took it very literally.' Brown said that he was sure that people hated Mayer out of 'simple envy'. After all, this was a man who was 'a great filmmaker and a great executive.'

He was also quoted as describing the mogul as 'the second coming of Christ', a man who could do no wrong. The religious antecedents of the two figures are beyond doubt. Further than that, there are not many people who would go that far. Sammy Cahn told me: 'He was kind of a harsh man. I never saw him walk with anyone. When he was with his wife or an associate, they were always a couple of paces behind him.'

The producer George Sidney told me: 'He was a great gambler. He gambled on pictures, he gambled on people. He was one of the most dynamic figures that this business has ever known, that this country has ever known, that the world has ever known. He believed in developing his talents. He took me from the age of 13 to blow out the lamps in the studio, then I made tests for him – we made thousands of tests of unknowns because he believed in developing talent.

'I remember him coming down to the set one day and asking, "Boy, how's it coming?" I said, "It's coming very nicely, I think, but they're blowing my mind, demanding that it be finished before it's ready." He said to me: "Don't tell anyone I told you this and if you do, I'll deny it. But you go right ahead and make your picture. Don't worry about the schedule." '

Eric Johnston, who was the President of the Motion Picture Association of America, no great lover of the moguls in general and Mayer in particular – some would describe it as a peculiar kind of anti-Semitism adopted by gentiles working for Jews – said of L.B.: '[He was] a bombastic egotist. Some people have a capacity for friendship. Mr Mayer's capacity was almost entirely in the field of showmanship.'

Danny Selznick, his grandson, would say of the old man: 'He cried at movies. He cried at Lassie, cried at *The Human Comedy*. He cried at *The Great Caruso*.'

He said that his grandfather was 'the classic Jewish patriarch'. Of course, he extended that patriarchal role beyond his blood children. But his daughter, Irene Mayer Selznick, wrote in her memoirs, *A Private View*, 'My father was not only omnipotent, he was omniscient. In a curious way, I got him mixed up with God. Because of the word "Almighty".' Her dad would have approved of that.

Of course, things have changed since then.

Louis B. Mayer's decisions were not always appreciated, but once having made them, he stuck by them. Stuck by them arrogantly. In fact, you cannot imagine a more arrogant man. He not only knew he was always right, he resented the fact that other people didn't share his sense of infallibility. This was the Pope of Hollywood. His most trusted underlings were his cardinals, who genuflected in his presence and would no more dare speak of him unkindly as, say the Bishop of Naples would dare comment about the pontiff while sitting in the curia.

When Mayer died in 1957, *Variety* commented: 'One does not remember his achievements so much as his monumental pettiness, his savage retaliation, the humiliations he heaped upon old associates.'

It was probably that old insecurity. He had had it when he first went into the movie business. He was never paranoiac, he would say, but always sure that there were people out there ready to get at him.

The Two Great Dancers – Astaire and Kelly

Mayer had been on top for years and his stars were the biggest demonstration of that fact. Stars like Fred Astaire – who actually was not a noticeable fixture at Culver City until *Easter Parade*, although he had begun his movie career at MGM, in a semi-guest spot, with Joan Crawford in *Dancing Lady* in 1933. (His screen test had revealed a man who 'can't act, can't sing, can dance a little'. Fred himself said that he thought he had a face 'like a knife'.)

The archetype Astaire 1930s musicals, his pairings (a term he hated; 'it sounds like a pair of horses,' he told me) with Ginger Rogers in films like *Flying Down to Rio, Shall We Dance, Top Hat* and *Follow the Fleet* were all made for RKO, a studio which, without them, would have long bit the dust which was daily swept up from the shiny black and white floor by its cleaners. Not that Mayer wouldn't have wanted to get hold of those films and their stars for himself. He finally succeeded in 1948, with the first reunion of Rogers and Astaire in ten years. *The Barkleys of Broadway* was also their first film together in Technicolor. It was a just so-so movie, but Astaire as always was perfect and Rodgers more attractive than she had been for a long time. As was said at the time, he gave her class, while she gave him sex appeal. Mayer was smiling all the way to the bank.

In 1950, Astaire was back at MGM with *Three Little Words*, another movie biography of a pair of songwriters, this time Bert Kalmar and Harry Ruby, in which his partner was Red Skelton. Unusual casting, but the film introduced a fun young singer-actress called Debbie Reynolds. In 1951, *Royal Wedding* came and went, a story based on the then not-too-distant wedding of the young woman who was still Princess Elizabeth and her bridegroom, Prince Philip. One good song, the Oscar-nominated 'Too Late Now', and the dance number on the ceiling were the most notable features.

The Belle of New York in 1952 introduced the big Astaire MGM musical. Fred was too old for Louis B. Mayer to claim him as one of his children, but the boss decided he had a near-parental obligation to treat him properly and to nurture him. One of Mayer's favourite Broadway shows had been *The Band Wagon*, in which Astaire co-starred with his sister Adele. He brought in the original songwriters, Howard Dietz and Arthur Schwartz, and Arthur Freed's unit did the rest. Jack Buchanan from the London stage joined Fred and Nanette Fabray (who went on record in my Astaire biography as being the only one who said she positively disliked Twinkletoes) singing 'Triplets'. But the outstanding numbers were 'Dancing in the Dark' and 'That's Entertainment', which not only provided the title for the three compilation movies about the MGM output, but became the only rival for Irving Berlin's 'There's No Business Like Show Business' for the title of national anthem of the theatre. Cyd Charisse was the girl in the film who made people salivate. Astaire had to dance with her and wasn't sure he could – until Mayer convinced him. He looked and he walked around her. 'I was mystified by that,' Ms Charisse told me. 'And then I realised what he was doing. He was making sure I wasn't too tall for him.'

The choreographer on the film, Michael Kidd, told me about the value of Astaire for the studio at that time. 'If you had just come down from Mars and landed at the MGM studio you would have been totally mystified by what went on as we were rehearsing the film. There was Cyd Charisse, whose legs ended up somewhere under her armpits and was simply gorgeous. If you looked at the faces of the technicians you'd see that every eye was on her. And then, after five minutes, you saw those eyes had moved – to Fred. They couldn't take their eyes off him. I think that was what audiences did, too.'

The next musical that Fred made for the studio was big and MGM-ish, enough to make Louis B. Mayer dab his eyes and wipe his glasses. This was *Silk Stockings*, with music by Cole Porter and based on the story of the 1939 film *Ninotchka*, which had starred Greta Garbo.

I once asked Gene Kelly what distinguished him from Fred Astaire. 'Simple,' he said, 'if I put on a top hat and tails I look like a truck driver on his night off.' That was part of the Mayer genius. He couldn't get Fred Astaire when he first wanted him, so he looked for someone else. But he couldn't be a man who was just a carbon copy of the world's most famous male dancer. Kelly was a more athletic performer, a man who could show his muscles when he did his own stunts in *The Pirate*, who found an alternative audience to that of Astaire, which is another reason why Mayer loved him so much. He also had to love him for *Singin' in the Rain*. It is difficult to think of another musical with the appeal of this film in which Gene was joined by Donald O'Connor and Debbie Reynolds. It was a marvellous trio partnership, but this film about the coming of the talkies will forever be regarded as Gene Kelly's picture. His performance of the title number wasn't just great dancing and good singing, it was superb acting. You knew how happy this man was to have discovered that he and Debbie Reynolds could be an item. Louis B. Mayer was happy that he made yet another impact in the musical world.

Ask me what I personally remember about *Singin' In The Rain*, I have no doubt about the answer. It was the film that convinced me, and everybody else sitting in the Odeon Cinema in Luton, that we could dance, too. A good musical is usually one in which you leave a theatre singing the songs – 'Good Mornin'', 'Make 'Em Laugh', 'You Are My Lucky Star' and 'Singing in the Rain' itself – we did all that. But we also danced out of the theatre – in my own case causing a young girl waiting at a bus stop to run for a policeman. She saw me advancing in what I assumed she would consider the true Kelly style. Apparently, she didn't. But then it was a different world in 1952.

Kelly had given warning of the kind of performer he was going to be back when he made *For Me and My Gal.* He didn't stay with MGM. One of his most famous movies, *Cover Girl,* was for Columbia. But he also made *Anchors Aweigh* for Mayer in 1945, the film in which he first looked great wearing a white sailor suit and famously he danced with Jerry the Mouse.

In the war, Kelly had desperately wanted to wear that sailor outfit in anger – to join the Navy, not as part of a publicity campaign for the Allied cause, but doing a real sailor's job. When he was drafted, it was, as he feared, to go round the country looking great in that white uniform. Clark Gable and Robert Taylor joined up and looked wonderful in their uniforms, collars up, smiles on their faces. Gable, who actually served as a gunner on board a bomber, had less reason than Taylor for that smile. His beloved wife, Carole Lombard, was killed when the plane she was taking back to Los Angeles after being part of a Hollywood War bond-issuing drive crashed into the Nevada mountains – later to be the scene of the deaths of the mother of Frank Sinatra and Dean Martin's son.

The war over, *On the Town* did a superb job of showing sailors in peacetime having a day out and looking for girls. Gene Kelly told me: 'It looks quite old fashioned now, but in those days nobody in a film got off of a real ship and went on the town. We were young and silly enough to take the chance.' And what a chance it turned out to be! It could be credited with being the first *real* MGM musical – or, at least, as we came to know it – the first to be shot on location. (*Take Me Out to the Ball Game* in which Gene Kelly *also* joined with Frank Sinatra in 1949, preceded *On the Town.*) Kelly and Sinatra wore the sailor suits again and joined in some great numbers by Leonard Bernstein, although most of the stage show's songs were replaced by numbers by Betty Comden and Adolph Green. 'I can't understand why we were brought in at all,' Ms Comden said to me. 'Lenny's tunes were so great.' But Louis B. Mayer had a conference with Arthur Freed and when Freed said he wanted new music, he got it. 'We were a great little group,' said Kelly 'and we worked very well together.'

An American in Paris had been a total departure from anything that both Kelly and MGM had done. This was essentially a ballet with singing, acting and dialogue. Leslie Caron danced with him to the music of George and Ira Gershwin, which never sounded better on the screen. George's 'An American in Paris' was the theme of the ballet. But there was also 'I've Got Rhythm', 'Stairway to Paradise', 'Embraceable You' and 'Our Love is Here to Stay'. It confirmed that Gene Kelly was now at MGM to stay, even if he did occasionally stray to other studios. The truth was that Mayer – apart from sending him to Europe for a year in 1954 to make *Invitation to the Dance*, but probably mainly to keep him out of the way during the height of the HUAC business – didn't want to lose him.

'The End'

It's Always Fair Weather, just before the *Invitation* film, took an imaginative theme – of three Army buddies who keep a date for a reunion they had agreed on ten years before, and then decide that young men who couldn't live without each other now have nothing in common. Dan Dailey and Michael Kidd, the choreographer, who unusually was on screen in this film, couldn't have been better. *Les Girls* in 1957 was the last of the big MGM Kelly musicals, although he went on to other things at other studios – most notably perhaps directing *Hello Dolly* at Twentieth Century Fox. Unlike Astaire, Kelly certainly was another one of Mayer's children, the group of people who sometimes strayed out of his orbit and whom he had to let go.

The mogul's problem was that he knew, seemingly after everyone else, that the glory years of Louis B. Mayer at MGM couldn't last.

The words 'The End' that were added to his career résumé were the saddest he ever read. Unlike all his competitors, he had never been the majority shareholder of his organisation. While MGM delivered, the Loew organisation, which owned the company, knew that there was no one better to be trusted with their business. But when things began to pale, all the old animosities in his life piled up against him. He and Nicholas Schenck, head of Loews Inc., had always hated each other – dating back to the time when Schenck planned to sell his company to Fox. Mayer, a great believer in the adage that it was better to work with the devil he knew than one he didn't, not only opposed the move, but brought in his friend Herbert Hoover to help with killing off the plan – on the grounds of its being potentially part of a trust. That didn't exactly endear him to the Loews' organisation.

It wasn't easy to get a job at MGM, not the job that you wanted, if Mayer said 'No'. Now he was about to experience a dose of his own medicine. But he got little sympathy for his troubles. The past was catching up with him. Memories were a long time a-dying. The writer-director Joseph Mankiewicz, one of the most talented people in this studio of talented people, told me that he himself could never forget the time when he asked to be allowed to be a producer. Mayer advised him: 'Before you can run, you have to crawl.' Which he took to heart in both its meanings. 'In many ways he was the most dreadful human being who ever lived,' Mankiewicz would say.

One of the breaking points came with the appointment of Dore Schary as his deputy. Mayer was already feeling professionally fragile. Now, although, theoretically, Schary was below him on the MGM totem pole, the much younger man had final decision on almost everything at the studio. 'I have to get his permission to go to the toilet,' Mayer complained.

The man who had been the most important mogul in Hollywood hadn't had any great hits of late. Apart from Elizabeth Taylor, there weren't many new stars in the MGM firmament. The studio hadn't won a major Oscar for a long time and the New York offices were now more and more asking questions.

The presence of Schary only made Mayer feel more insecure than ever before. It was Schary's second incarnation at MGM. He had been with the studio in the 1930s and 1940s as a writer and was then put in charge of 'B' films. Among other brilliant scripts he produced for the company was the archetype MGM product of the era, *Boys Town*, with Mickey Rooney playing a very naughty boy who turns out to be the salt of the earth. Spencer Tracy, playing the Catholic priest, who saved souls via his 'Boys Town' for juvenile delinquents, had one of his formative roles – and won an Oscar. So did Schary. It made him one of the golden boys of the studio, but he left when he was made a producer at RKO, ultimately running the studio.

Now, Mayer realised, the deputy was on the way to running his studio. To his horror, Schary had been enticed back to MGM by Schenck – as much as a threat to Mayer as for his production abilities.

The other breaking point was the issue that had caused so many problems for Warner Bros. – television. The two media came together like an express train hitting the buffers. Mayer hated the new competition because it threatened the old. But he protested that his objections were merely against the poor standard of television programmes – he thought they were amateurish, promoted violence and, sin of sins, didn't do much for the American family. Fighting TV was another Mayer gamble, but one he thought he could win. If he was losing his touch, this was to be a demonstration of the fact.

Schary wanted MGM to be involved in TV. Mayer, again like the Warner brothers, wouldn't allow either a set on studio property and certainly never in a scene shot in an MGM picture. Things reached their head late in 1951. Mayer stormed at Schenck saying, 'Either he [Schary] goes or I go.' To his utter amazement, the Loew's boss told him he would be happy if Mayer cleared out his office – a scene that had been enacted with L.B. himself sitting behind his desk a dozen times. The difference now was that Mayer's tears were real.

It was indeed a difficult time. The big outfits were forced by the anti-trust legislation to divest themselves from their theatre interests and the role of moguls was gradually being diluted. They were much less the powerful emperors they had always believed themselves to be. Schary was going to be much more the solid business CEO of a new era.

In truth, Schenck had for some time been looking for any excuse to get rid of the man who revelled in the perception that people had of him – as the most powerful mogul in Hollywood, almost as a definition of the term. But there were fights. There were lawsuits. Lester Cole, for instance, was suing for unfair dismissal – which was likely to bring the whole HUAC business even more into the open than anyone in the organisation wanted. Others were lining up to claim money from him, cash that they felt he owed. Schenck, for his part, complained that Mayer had been spending too much time away from the studio and too much of that time on his racehorses.

Before he had sold out most of his horse interests in the early 1950s, he had had a stable that became the MGM of the racing world – and he knew enough about horseflesh to see talent in the four-legged animals, and to employ the same quality of advisers to tell him about it, no less than he had always been able to see it in his stars. His daughter, Irene Mayer Selznick, would say that his deepest ambition was to win the Kentucky Derby.

He was jealous of those breeders who did achieve what he considered to be the equivalent of picking up ten Academy Awards for himself. But then he remained till the end of his days jealous of everything with which he was not concerned. As Billy Wilder told me: 'I had just finished making *Sunset Boulevard* for Paramount and there was a series of special previews. One of them was for the industry, for people from other studios, at the big theatre on the Paramount lot. I was walking down from the projection room and there was a big crowd there, all very excited and kissing the hem of our garments. But there was one other little group – made up of Louis B. Mayer and his henchmen. The staff of Napoleon. He was furious. "It is the most disgraceful thing that has been done to Hollywood," he said. "Biting the hand that is feeding you." And he went on and on. He didn't know who I was, but I went up to him and said, "Mr Mayer. My name is Billy Wilder and I directed this picture. Why don't you go and fuck yourself." The people around didn't know what to do. They went into a near faint – that somebody would dare say that to Louis B. Mayer, the mogul of moguls.'

Mayer had tried to sign Dean Martin and Jerry Lewis, but wasn't broken-hearted when Hal Wallis, who produced all their work, wasn't sure if it were a clever move. Mayer had said, 'The guinea [Martin] is OK, but what do I do with the other one?' (It was perhaps the only close-to-racial remark from him on record). He would have signed them but he wanted to approve everything they did – both at Culver City and in clubs and theatres elsewhere.

These were all black marks against him.

Finally, Mayer suffered the indignity of seeing Dore Schary take over his office, The Office, although he was spared the notion of MGM becoming MGS. Schary had no need of that, although he would himself lose the job later on. As for Mayer, he said he was going to make pictures, running a new studio, but it never happened. He said he was going to take over Republic, for long regarded as being at the very bottom of the movie totem pole, but that never happened either. When Nicholas Schenck retired in 1955, Mayer tried to regain control of MGM, but was laughed out of the shareholders meetings. But he did become chairman of Cinerama, a medium he had predicted would have the same effect on motion pictures as had the coming of the talkies. Unfortunately for him, although the system made money, mainly from being used in travelogues, it was virtually eclipsed by CinemaScope.

Soon after leaving MGM, Mayer was showered with awards, the most significant of which was when he received the Screen Producers Guild's Milestone Award. The year before he was fired, he had been given a special Academy Award 'for distinguished service to the motion-picture industry.' He even accepted a prize from the Jewish War Veterans of America, which was nailing his colours to a mast he would have tried to avoid a few years earlier.

He had one great quality, Frank Capra told me. 'He, like all the others, liked to win when he gambled, but he could take it when things didn't work out. He had the ability to survive.' Everything, that is, but the boardroom coup that ended his reign at MGM and then his final illness. On 29 October 1957, Louis B. Mayer died.

At his funeral, Jeanette MacDonald sang 'Ah, Sweet Mystery of Life'. Officially, the cause of death was given as leukaemia. He himself would have said it was a broken heart. A cliche? Sure it was, but then so was his whole life.

5

HARRY COHN

When Harry Cohn died in 1958, the rabbi who was waiting to be invited to conduct the funeral services was asked if he had anything good to say about him. 'Of course,' said Rabbi Edgar Magnin, 'All I need are two words, "He's dead".'

Two thousand people attended his funeral held at a sound stage at Columbia Pictures, of which he had been the iron dictator for three decades or more. 'Just shows you,' said the comedian Red Skelton, 'give the folks what they want and they'll show up for it.' You can't resist going on from that. 'They just wanted to make sure he really died', was banded about at the same solemn ceremony for a man who once proudly said: 'I don't get heart attacks. I give 'em.'

However, some people said nicer things. Danny Kaye made a speech praising Cohn at the ceremony, held on the biggest lot in the studio, which he described as the mogul's 'cathedral'. The three Warner brothers issued a statement saying he was 'one of the great constructive leaders [who] leaves a lasting imprint of creative greatness in his record of accomplishment, extending over the years and through the important pages of motion picture history.'

Kim Novak, who, as we shall see, had her ups and downs with Harry, burst into tears on the set of the Columbia film she was making with Jack Lemmon, *Bell, Book and Candle,* and the tough director John Ford, who swore almost as well as Cohn did, followed her example. (Ford and Cohn were a strange combination, certainly unlikely friends, but the director would say that a 'handshake from Harry was worth more than a contract drawn up by a score of Philadelphia lawyers'.)

They all showed up for the funeral 'performance'.

Actually, people had been showing up for Harry Cohn's pictures for all those 40 years. He was a man a great many people hated but there were others who positively loved him. The songwriter Sammy Cahn put it to me like this: 'When he wanted to be liked he could literally charm the inlays out of your teeth. But he was a real, rough feller. And it pleased him to be that feller.'

Or as Frank Capra went on when we met: 'If you could take his bullying you were there, whether you were good or not. If you could not take his bullying, he would throw you out, even if you were the top writer in the world. A very interesting guy. Dirty, mean, all the bastards that he has been called, they were all true. But this man loved films and loved the people who made films.'

The boss of Columbia Pictures had a lot in common with the other moguls, but there were differences, too. Like the others, he was Jewish. Unlike the others, he had been born in the United States. Like the others, he had always had a love for the movies. Unlike the others, he had started life in show business – for much of the time as a Tin Pan Alley song plugger, working for Irving Berlin's firm of Waterson, Berlin and Snyder. Like the others, he ran a studio as his own private fiefdom.

At least, that is the legend, the one fostered both by Rabbi Magnin and Red Skelton. What is surprising is just how much those who liked him felt loyalty and devotion to him.

Harry was born in New York on 23 July 1891, the son of a mother, Bella, who came from Russia, close to the Polish border, and Joseph, a father who came from Germany and who, as Joan Cohn, Harry's widow, told me before she died, 'was very old school German. His children got it if they did anything wrong.' Apparently, his son Harry inherited that 'quality'. The older man was a tailor who specialised in making uniforms for the New York police force. 'If Harry got into trouble with the police, which he did,' Joan told me, 'his father would ring up one of his contacts and ask them to show him some mercy.'

There were four boys, Max, Jacob (Jack), Harry and Nat and a sister, Anna. The one they all loved most of all was their grandmother, who lived in the same apartment close to Joseph's tailoring shop on 88th St.

'Harry loved to climb into his grandmother's bed – where his father couldn't get him.'

At the age of 14, he went on the stage, singing in a play called *The Fatal Wedding*. The fatal thing for Harry was to discover his love of music.

Harry combined selling songs with playing the piano at nickelodeons. 'He had perfect pitch all his life,' Joan was to tell me.

He worked in an advertising agency and then did a short stint as a streetcar conductor. He loved songs and he loved singers, which is why he became a song plugger. He loved selling, which is why he became a very successful song plugger. It was because he thought that one day the two could be combined, with live music accompanying films, that he first went into the movie business.

King of Columbia

Universal gave Harry a junior job working in their studio as a secretary to its founder mogul, Carl Laemmle.

His brother Jack, meanwhile, worked there as a film editor – an editor who wanted to make movies himself. And that was how he got involved in a conspiracy that would change not just his life, but that of his younger brother, too.

While his boss was busy on the usual kind of arguments that occupied the lives of people in the movie business, he and three fellow employees made a film of their own, called *Traffic in Souls*. Laemmle was at first beside himself at their chutzpah, but was persuaded their film could make money. It made more money than anyone could possibly have imagined. Harry saw it and was intrigued. Cynics could say that the notion of white slavery would prove to be right up his Hollywood street – since he trafficked in souls for the rest of his life.

In 1919, he and Jack, using the money he had made from the movie, decided they could go into business themselves and secured the rights to a series of cartoons, based on characters called the Hall Room Boys, who had featured in a comic strip in the *New York Telegram*. They raised money from a bank to set up a company called the CBC Film Sales Company, the initials of Cohn, Brandt (Joe Brandt, a short-term partner who was nominally president) and Cohn. The corporation was financed at $250. Jack stayed in New York and Harry went to California to make comedies. In 1922, he came up with *More to be Pitied than Scorned*. No one pitied the Cohns. They made a small fortune from the picture.

The name CBC didn't exactly run off the tongue. They weren't helped by the fact that wags were saying that the letters stood for 'Corned Beef and Cabbage'. So the brothers registered a new name – Columbia. Four years later, the two bought a parcel of studio properties, which included nine stages in the area of Hollywood known as Poverty Row, on Sunset Boulevard between Beechwood Drive and Gower Street, using sets borrowed from other studios that had finished with them. But the Cohns had already made money and were paying back the bank loans. They bought an 80-acre ranch, too – a necessity for the many outdoor movies they were going to make.

Harry also found himself a bride by the name of Rose Cromwell. The company grew and the number of employees grew, too. The injunction at Columbia, as in other studios, was Thou Shalt Have Relatives. Harry and Jack gave jobs to cousins, second cousins and seemingly all the in-laws who wanted them. The humorist Robert Benchley once said there were so many Cohns [pronounced 'Cones' in America] that Columbia ought to be known as the Pine Tree Studio. But being called Columbia was enough.

From 1922 on, Harry Cohn was the autocratic monarch of all around him. When he moved out of Poverty Row to new studios on Gower Street itself, his success seemed unstoppable – and at a time when other studios were either going bankrupt or were close to it. The brothers had a new project that should have earned them both a niche in history and an historic amount of money. For two years, they were releasing cartoons about a mouse with big ears drawn by a young man named Walt Disney – who, after seeing his Silly Symphonies being shown with the accompaniment of sound, decided he could go into business on his own. The expletives that Harry Cohn used when he realised that this was the big one that had got away can only be imagined.

Frank Capra would say that Harry's trouble was that he mistook sensitivity for weakness. What there was about Marilyn Monroe that Harry Cohn didn't get isn't on the record. He once gave her a 20-week contract and then let her go without doing anything with it.

A lot of the animosity to Harry Cohn was focused on the way that people saw the King of Columbia and his throne. The other studios looked down on Columbia the way they looked down on Harry Cohn himself. He didn't seem their kind of man at all. So he decided to show them what he was made of – by acting more like a dictator than did any of the others.

Cohn's office, 60ft long and 30ft wide, was modelled on the one he had seen when he met Benito Mussolini. He had been making a documentary in Rome and had been invited to have an audience with the dictator Il Duce.

Mussolini had planned his office so that any underling who came to see him would be so inhibited by the time he got to the dictator's desk, he was a shaking wreck – a wreck who couldn't get away quickly enough. Cohn had precisely the same idea – and demonstrated his debt to Mussolini by having a photograph of him on his own desk, although when America joined World War II, the picture was moved and hung in his private toilet. The actress Barbara Hale described the scene to me as 'the largest stage in the whole world. When I approached his desk, it was the longest walk I ever took.'

As he might have said, but patently didn't, anything that was good enough for the fascist dictator of Italy was good enough for the fascist dictator of Columbia.

Every one of his films, over the years, began with the company's trademark, an angelic woman carrying a sparkling torch. Not quite the Statue of Liberty. That would be taking things too far. He wouldn't copy anything or anyone else. At least, not exactly copy them.

The one thing he didn't imitate was Mussolini's marble floor – because he was frightened of slipping. That was not the way Harry Cohn wanted to be seen – slipping. So he got the studio carpenters to fit a carpet.

The girl with the torch couldn't be confused with Liberty, because he was the only one at Columbia in the business of taking liberties. Liberty was not what he wanted any of his actors, actresses or directors to have.

People who worked for Harry still remembered that desk of his when they had long forgotten the films in which they were involved. Behind it were the serried ranks of Oscars that Columbia had won, which were always subject to debate. The Academy Awards for best movies always went to the producers of those films. But not at Columbia. Harry Cohn believed that since he had paid for the pictures, he was entitled to the rewards – and few producers were brave enough to argue with him.

But the desk itself could inspire fear – for the buttons that were installed underneath it. With a click of a finger on one of those, he could monitor what was going on in any one of the sound stages. That was intimidating enough. But Harry extended the power of the button.

Secretly, he would get his electricians to bug his stars' dressing rooms – which was even more illegal than purloining the Oscars.

He did it for a mixture of motives, a combination of paranoia and prurience. He was always afraid of spies, either from the dreaded New York office – which controlled finances and was now run totally by his brother Jack for whom he had little affection and much animosity – or from executives or other employees whom he was convinced were ganging up on him. He was also resentful of love affairs between actors and actresses and didn't see why he should not be allowed to share the action. Which is why he ordered bugs in the dressing room of one of his favourite stars, Glenn Ford, whom he believed was romantically involved with Rita Hayworth.

Ford told me: 'He was convinced we were having a very steamy affair on his premises, which we actually weren't. But the day came when the electrician told me he had been ordered to bug my dressing room. It was in the brass chandelier over my desk. He also had a microphone planted in Rita's dressing room, but it didn't work. The one in my room did. That didn't worry Harry because he knew that we would pop into each other's room, so he would be satisfied. The fact was that Rita and I gave him all that he wanted. Harry was having a fit, he listened while he believed we were making love. So we made it worth his while, complete with all the sound effects. If I told you what we were saying, it would have been censorable. It was pretty obvious we weren't talking about the time of the day. But Harry couldn't let on that he had heard all this. It would have been admitting he had ordered the bugging. I can tell you, I don't think he slept for a week. I think it was the only time I outsmarted him. He must have got tired of listening and ordered that the microphone be taken out. He didn't know I had already unscrewed it.'

Despite it all, Glenn told me he loved Rita – and so, in fact, did Cohn. The fact that Harry loved Rita was demonstrated by the movies he gave her and the leading men who were signed up. It wasn't just anyone who would be allowed to play opposite Fred Astaire, but Rita did twice – in *You Were Never Lovelier*, in which Fred sang 'Dearly Beloved' to her and 'You'll Never Get Rich', which contained probably the only Cole Porter score without a single hit. But Harry Cohn knew that in Mr Twinkletoes and Rita Hayworth, he had a winning team. And so did Astaire – who had greatly admired her father Eduardo Cansino. He, of course, was not subjected to the boss's paranoia or his prurience. You didn't spy on Fred Astaire.

The desk and its buttons were not the only Harry Cohn weapons. He also had a baseball bat.

Glenn Ford remembered for me: 'It was about three-feet long and was signed by Babe Ruth. It was Harry's most prized possession. He used to walk around the lot, slapping his thigh with it like a riding crop. He'd point it at people if they were sitting down and ask why they weren't working or just "Why is he sitting down?" It was the most frightening thing – you know, like Mengele at Auschwitz, pointing at who would live and who would die.'

Certainly, the course of true devotion between producer and star didn't always run smooth. 'One day,' recalled Ford, 'he made the mistake of calling my wife. The Columbia soundstages were very close to each other – sometimes they adjoined each other. When you weren't working, you'd visit another set, have a talk or a cup of coffee with, say, Humphrey Bogart. Two or three ladies one time would come and visit the set. That didn't bother me. But Harry saw this and rang my wife and said: "You know your husband is up to no good." She asked what it was all about and he said, "I don't know, but there's this certain lady who's been coming around every day and it's been going on for a long time now."

'I went home that night. I got home early, at about three o'clock. My wife said "What's this with you and this young lady?"

'I said, "What?" In a Rembrandt of understatement I got annoyed. I got into my car and, breaking all speed limits, drove at about sixty miles an hour down Sunset Boulevard and I drove up to Columbia and parked in the restricted parking lot. You were supposed to be let in by the policeman. I didn't care about that. I walked up to the second floor to Harry's office, kicked the door in and I went to his desk about a mile away from the door. I looked around and saw what he had on his desk. I saw a baseball bat. It was legendary in the studio, Harry and that baseball bat. I reached over to the desk. I took the bat and beat it, wambo, crack, on to the floor. It ended up in three pieces. I said, "Next time you call my wife, Harry, you know where this is going to wind up." He looked at me and said, "I think you mean it."

'I said, "You bet I mean it" and walked out. He said, "Just a minute. You'll never work in the studio again. You are out of the business." I said, "Fine" and walked to the door and he said, "And give me that piece of bat you've got in your hands." So I took the piece of bat and put it on his desk. Two days later, I figured, I'm through with Columbia. I've got my reservations back to New York. I had a call saying "Mr Cohn wants to see you." I went to his office and the bat had been put together again by the props department, beautifully put together, varnished. You'd never know it had been broken. I reached out to pick up the bat and Harry said, "Please don't. Please, Glenn, don't." I said, "All right, Harry." And he said, "You start a new film next week."

'I said, "I thought I was finished." He said, "Well, don't take any notice of that. Sometimes I say things when I get annoyed."' The film was *Texas*, with William Holden and Claire Trevor. 'I cancelled the ticket and I was there for fourteen years.'

After the incident, Ford told me he and Harry 'got on fine'. He used to take me to baseball games, football games.' That was when to him, Mr Cohn became Harry. 'I had always called him Mr Cohn and he had always called me Glenn.'

They had a good relationship thanks to those trips. 'He always picked me up in his limousine. We sat in the back. It was like there were two Harry Cohns. The one I had fought with and this Harry Cohn which I didn't, up to then, know about.'

He was always walking with underlings. One of these was the studio manager, Jack Fier. Orson Welles said of him, 'There is nothing to fear but Fier himself.' To which Fier responded: 'All's well that ends Welles.' As Glenn Ford told me: 'Fier and all the others would laugh when Harry laughed and scowl when Harry scowled.'

But there was value in his power and the apparent bullying, a lot of his employees thought.

His ever loyal PA, Evelyn Lane, said. 'He taught Mrs Cohn manners. He taught me manners.' But he didn't always display them himself. 'He came on the set one day when I was talking to a camera operator, called Andy. Harry rarely came down on the set, so nobody in the crews knew him. He called out to me: "When you get through holding that labourer's hand, I want to talk to you."'

Every one of his stars, at one time or another, was made to believe that he was a labourer toiling in one of Harry Cohn's vineyards. Glenn Ford told me about the time that he noticed paint had peeled from around the handle of the door in Cohn's office. 'I said to him, "Harry you know why that is? The paint has been worn by the sweat on the hands of the people you summon as they leave the office." I said that should be part of the coat of arms of Columbia Pictures. He then shouted to his secretary, "Donna, I don't ever want that door painted," and I don't think it was painted till after the day he died.'

People were truly scared of Cohn, said Ford. 'I can think of a lot of actors who were frightened of him. The trouble was they were trying to outsmart him – and you don't outsmart a giant. I think a lot of writers were scared if they weren't properly prepared. If you're going to play chess with a champion, you have to know how to play chess.'

Cohn struck it rich with Gene Kelly in *Cover Girl*. The 1944 movie in which Kelly sang 'Long Ago and Far Away' to Rita Hayworth (with Nan Wynne providing her voice) was one of his biggest hits. It resulted in a celebrated court case with the director Charles Vidor suing to cancel his Columbia contract and collect $75,000. Cohn said that the film had exceeded its $1,200,000 budget by $60,000 and alleged that Vidor had treated Gene Kelly 'horribly'. Vidor, for his part, said that Cohn had insulted his former wife, Evelyn Keyes, and had tried to break up their marriage. Worse still, Cohn had told her that the director 'had had affairs with every woman on the lot – all at my address.' Meanwhile, the judge Ben Harrison was passed a 900-page dossier that included a mass of 'dirty words' that Cohn had used against Vidor. Cohn's former secretary Mildred Scherme told the court that her boss didn't tolerate the director. He used to order her, 'Give him a drink and throw him out.'

The director's attorney Hubert Morrow said that if the judge sided with Cohn he would be showing that he approved of Cohn's language. No, said the judge, both Vidor and Cohn were really actors, and refused to take the allegations seriously.

So Vidor didn't 'outsmart' him. But, long ago and far away, Glenn Ford's guile was used on one of the very few times that anyone did do that. 'Everyone was on the defensive,' Evelyn Lane told me. 'He was a great expert in reverse psychology. He was a spitballer – a man who would seemingly get out of line, to get information.' And how! Joan Cohn told me that her husband's favourite saying was, 'When an actor wants something, you can spit in his eye and he'll say it's raining.'

He learnt that if his business was going to work, he had to trust people. Like Fred Briskin, whose father Irving Briskin was a vice-president of Columbia. They and their wives – Harry's first wife Rose and Briskin's wife Ida – had all come from the same part of the New York Lower East Side.

Irving Briskin told Cohn he wanted to make a Western. 'OK,' said Cohn, 'but I'll only pay you when it's finished.' They used to call that sort of thing a 'negative pick up job'. The film cost $25,000 – money that Irving Briskin borrowed from the Bank of America. 'My father gave off an air of confidence,' Briskin told me. It was something he plainly needed. 'The film was terrible. So bad that Harry refused to pay for it. So they made another deal – my father would make another film and if it was good, he'd pay for both. He did – and got a six-picture deal. As a result, my father became a vice-president and they became friends. They travelled together. Harry was a very good man. If people want dirt from me, they've come to the wrong person.'

So there was honesty in Harry Cohn. Others thought that *Traffic in Souls* could have been Harry's motto – not least towards his own brother Jack. But Jack Cohn tried to stand no nonsense. (He was a man of strange moods, Joan Cohn would tell me. 'He was hail-fellow-well-met. I never knew if he approved of me.')

'A Very Tough Man'

Like all the moguls, Harry had a succession of rows with writers, whom basically he admired, although he took note of all the times when they came in and then left for home. His problem was that he couldn't spell. To one employee, he said: 'The name of this company is Columbia. That's C-o-l-o-m-b-i-a.' 'Sorry, Mr Cohn,' said the man, 'you ought to learn that it's spelt C-o-l-*u*-m-b-i-a.' He learned not to argue – when he picked up his final pay cheque that is.

On one of his tours of the studio complex, Harry found the writers' section uncannily quiet. 'Why aren't you working?' he demanded of them. 'I pay you to write.' At which point there was a crescendo of typewriters banging away. 'Liars!' he screamed.

Harry could be a liar most of the time. At least, that was what many of the writers felt. He loved making sport of them as of almost all of his employees. He once asked a writer to submit 20 pages of script. The man did and was then called into Harry's office. After the humiliation of taking the mile-long journey to the mogul's desk, Cohn looked at him with those steely blue eyes and declared: 'It's the worst piece of junk I've ever read.' In fact, reported Frank Capra in his own memoirs, Cohn had not read the script at all. The writer protested that he thought it was 'pretty good'. 'All right,' said Cohn, 'come back later.'

Harry Cohn was involved in everything concerning his films – and sometimes those of other people. Sidney Luft, sometime husband of Judy Garland, the father of Lorna Luft and stepfather of Liza Minnelli, produced the last really important Garland movie, *A Star is Born*, which was made by Warner Bros.

'Harry was a very tough man, very hard,' Luft told me. 'Unlike other studio heads, he didn't like lending his actors or anyone to other studios or borrowing them.' *It Happened One Night* was obviously an exception. So was *A Star is Born*. 'Judy wanted Jean Louis, who was under contract to Columbia, to design her clothes. We already had a young woman designer, but Judy didn't like what she did and we let her go. Harry, to my surprise, allowed Jean Louis to go to Warner Bros. – but under one condition: he insisted on seeing the rushes. Jack Warner was happy to let him do that. Actually, they got on very well together, despite what you have heard about rivalries between the studio heads. Harry Cohn got on well with Goldwyn, too. But not Louis Mayer. He was a different matter entirely, running a factory.'

Evelyn Lane denies that. 'He loved Mayer. His desk was an exact copy of Mayer's [it must have been some other desk]. As a matter of fact, after the war, he and Mayer and the Warner brothers went to Europe together at the request of the US Government to have a look round and see if they could make pictures which would boost the people who had suffered in the war.' They sailed on the Queen Mary, which was rather more luxurious than most of the places they saw in Europe, such as Dachau, Belsen and Auschwitz.

'Harry was no cry baby,' his widow Joan told me, 'but he almost cried when he saw those horrific camps. When he came back to New York, it was when Ann Warner and I met for the first time, waiting for them. When they came back, we opened a magnum of champagne. It was [later that night!] when my son Harry was conceived.' Soon after that trip, he brought a cousin who had survived the Holocaust out of Poland and then to America. 'He never forgot his heritage.' Even though he came close to becoming a Catholic. In New York, Joan said, he felt more of a Jew than he did in Hollywood. She joined him there after he had attended his brother Jack's funeral and they went round Harry's old stamping grounds. 'He showed me the old building he was born in.'

Harry Cohn needed to feel part of something, but mainly he needed to be on top. He dictated not just his films, but everything about the way his business operated.

That Mussolini desk of Cohn's was typical of the care that he took about his office – a place that had a projection room and even his own dentist's surgery, as well as the regulation barbershop, adjoining his private washroom.

The French-born designer Jean Louis had been taken over to Columbia just as he was completing his contract term with the New York couturier, Hetty Carnegie. 'She complained, but really didn't have a case against Cohn, but she sued him. To everyone's surprise, Harry fought the case. It was a matter of publicity, I think. I liked Harry. He had the most marvellous, beautiful blue eyes.'

Harry knew that. His widow, Joan admitted to me: 'He used to try to frighten people with his eyes.' Including her. 'I said to him, "Don't do that to me." Once he said to me: "I have given you everything. I have given you your career." I said, "What career? I had a career in New York, but not at Columbia."' Her clever career move was to marry Harry. In her life as at the studio, he was the man who controlled everything.

'He put the signature on everything before it happened, on gowns, on hairdressers, on everything,' as Joan said.

Publicity was always in his mind as it was in the minds of most people in the movie industry. But sometimes he definitely wanted to keep arguments quiet. Kim Novak had her rows with Cohn – and would have provided the news media with a swathe of stories had he wanted that to happen.

He was furious with one of his favourite directors, Dick Quine for having an affair with Kim. 'How many times have I told you that I don't want people who are working for me getting involved with ladies who work here?' he screamed at Quine.

'I said, "This is how it is. It's a very important relationship and that's how it's going to be."

'You know what his reply was? "Get out of my office". He had given in.'

It wasn't the only affair involving the ice-blonde beauty that worried Cohn. He was much more concerned when he discovered, on the plane on the way back from Las Vegas, that she was sleeping with Sammy Davis Jr. The eruptions from his seat, the screams of the word '*schwartzer*', a very impolite Yiddish word for 'black', could be heard all over the aircraft. He got himself so distraught that he had a heart attack in mid air – after saying that he wouldn't object so much if it were Harry Belafonte she was having her affair with. But Davis was too black, too ugly and . . . too Jewish. For once his dictum about giving the attacks and not suffering them himself was proved wrong.

The affair with Davis didn't last long – apparently no thanks to Harry Cohn. 'She took Sammy to meet her family. But it didn't make them love each other more. After that, Harry called Kim a dumb Pollak,' Joan Cohn recalled for me.

He was delighted when Davis and Novak broke up, needless to say. 'He didn't want to hurt either of them, but he thought it would be very bad for his investment for her to marry a black man,' Joan said. 'He was only thinking of a property.' Which was precisely why Harry Cohn wasn't exactly regarded as the nicest man in Hollywood. 'Anyway,' his wife added, 'he couldn't stand dumb broads.'

As she said: 'Harry worked very hard with Kim because she was so great on the screen. It was like *Pygmalion*. She was being groomed for something she wanted and she didn't know how to get it.'

There were other problems. 'The trouble was,' Jean Louis told me, 'that Kim, who had a wonderful body, refused to wear a bra.' That came to the surface when she was making *Picnic* in the 1950s. 'I told Harry that and he absolutely insisted. Either she wore a bra or she was out of the film. "I've got a good body," she said. "And I never wear a bra." I told her that she could wear what she liked at any other time. Nobody minded if she walked through the lot without a bra, but when she was on camera, she had to wear one.' She did.

That was a comparatively mild end to an argument and Kim Novak still made *Picnic*. The director of the film, Joshua Logan, later recalled: 'I must say it was a very pleasurable experience. Harry Cohn was a rough man. He shouted and screamed and used rough language. But I eventually had respect for him. Very much so.'

He allowed Logan to treat his stars as he believed they should be treated and this included Novak. As Joan Cohn told me: 'Josh had to punch her to make her cry. Josh said, "I can make most people act, but this is difficult."'

The only doubt in Logan's mind was where that film was going to be shot. He said he wanted to film it in Kansas. He thought the flat planes of the state would be just right. 'You can film it any fucking place you like,' Cohn replied. 'So long as it makes a million dollars for Columbia.'

Novak went on, too, to make *Pal Joey*, opposite Frank Sinatra. It was based on the Broadway show which introduced Gene Kelly to the theatre-going public. But Harry Cohn didn't want him. In the midst of the HUAC affair, he was frightened there was too much mud out there all too ready to stick.

The idea was that Billy Wilder would write the screenplay. He had his own ideas and was ensconced in a room at Columbia to get the project going. 'I wanted Marlon Brando for the main part,' Wilder told me. 'He couldn't sing or dance, but Joey was a drummer and Marlon was a pretty good drummer.'

Wilder was in the studio for eight days, during which time, he had lunch with Harry twice. 'After eight days, I had a message that Harry had changed his mind. He didn't want to do it with me. So I packed up my typewriter and went home. Two days later, I had a bill for two lunches I had eaten at Columbia – $4. That was the end of my dealings with Harry Cohn.'

Cohn seemed to worry a lot less about his writers and their writing than he did about the clothes his actresses wore. He talked about Novak and her bra for years after the film had gone back into the Columbia vaults.

He always decreed that none of the dresses that Jean Louis made should be too low cut. 'He insisted that there should be no cleavage visible,' the designer told me. 'It wasn't that he didn't like seeing a woman's breasts himself – he plainly did; there was plenty of evidence that he did. But he thought it would be difficult to sell a film in those days if a woman showed too much.'

As Evelyn Lane put it: 'He always thought that what you didn't see was the most sexy. That's why he approved of what the Hays Office was doing.'

Judy Holliday could be pretty sexy, too, with a bust that excited Harry Cohn more than her face or the rest of her figure (he called her 'that fat Jewish broad'). She also had an astonishing sense of humour. Cohn decided she was such a strong asset that he persuaded HUAC to avoid calling her to its hearings – even though he knew she had Communist sympathies. But business was business and so was Judy Holliday. When he bought the Garson Kanin story *Born Yesterday*, he concluded she was the only one to star in it opposite Broderick Crawford. The film was a huge success and lines for it were quoted everywhere that the cognoscenti gathered – particularly the one in which she says: 'Do me a favour will you? Drop dead!'

There were not a few Columbia stars who felt much the same way about Harry. Jack Lemmon was decidedly not among them, although it took time for Harry to realise what he had in the bright, highly articulate actor. He didn't like the actor's name, so he decided to change it. He came up with 'Lennon' instead of 'Lemmon', which he thought would make Columbia the laughing stock of Hollywood. (It was before the Beatles.). 'It sounds like Lenin,' Jack Lemmon told me he told Cohn. 'It'll make me seem to be a Commie,' 'No,' said Harry. 'That's Leyneen. I know. I looked it up.'

Harry retired muttering – after he realised he had lost the battle of the names in the drinks session he was having with Lemmon at the Beverly Hills Hotel's Polo Room. It was so dark in there that the actor found he was discussing the deal he was making for a seven-year contract with Columbia to a total stranger; Cohn was at an adjoining table.

Harry and the Casting Couch

When Harry and Lemmon did get together, it was one of the best decisions he made. Lemmon did exceedingly well with him, not least with another Judy Holliday movie, *It Should Happen to You.*

Harry wondered about that title. Did it sound too sexy? He was persuaded it was just sexy enough to attract the customers. Actually, there were more sexy ways of pleasing Harry Cohn. For among his, shall we say credits, was another that has never appeared in a *Who Was Who* entry. Harry Cohn invented the casting couch. It was about him that the famous joke arose: 'So you want a part in pictures?' If the answer was 'yes' – and it nearly always was – he got what he wanted. If he was particularly pleased, he would then say, 'Now, do you want to try for the Academy Award?'

The writer Melville Shavelson came across that phenomenon – as a spectator, of course. 'Harry Cohn was Atillah the Hun in a double-breasted suit,' he told me. 'He used to call a meeting in his office and when we arrived, his secretary would inform us that Harry was having another meeting. We'd be kept waiting for an hour or an hour and a half. Then when we eventually did get into the office, there was no one else there. After Harry's funeral, we figured it out. Behind his desk, behind all those Oscars, was a secret door with a secret stairway to the dressing room of his current leading lady.'

By leading lady, he did not necessarily mean the one starring in his latest film. He had a different production entirely in mind. Sometimes, the two did go hand in hand – just as did Harry and the lady in question.

Evelyn Keyes was his star on *The Jolson Story*. 'Harry got into his head that he wanted to marry me,' she told me. 'He was already married, but he was going to push that wife aside to make way for me. Well, I was having a pretty good time at that period, and whoever I was out with, it would be noted in the gossip columns. And when it was, the front desk would say, "Miss Keyes, before you go on the set, Mr Cohn wants to speak to you." "Oh, so you're at it again?" he demanded. "Did you let him f*** you?" I would never have an affair – if you know what I mean – with anyone I wasn't interested in myself. And Harry was not my type at all. Mind you, I'd have been frightfully rich today if he had been one who I *was* interested in.'

Within that limitation, he was, nevertheless, able to make Evelyn Keyes a big star with *The Jolson Story*. It turned out to be one of his biggest successes.

This was a film with a mystery behind it. The mystery was this: who wrote it? The screen credits said it was Stephen Longstreet. In recent years, it has emerged that Longstreet's name was there on the instructions of Cohn. Longstreet actually wrote very little of the film. The first drafts and the outline for the picture were written by John Howard Lawson, whom Harry knew was a Communist. He saw trouble on the way and ordered the man's name off the credits. (Lawson, who was later jailed as one of the Hollywood Ten, was said by his son to have asked to be omitted from the credits – because he was against the idea of blackface, in which Larry Parks, who played Jolson, was seen. That's highly unlikely. Blackface was barely an issue in 1946). Most of the final writing was done by another Columbia executive, Sidney Buchman. It was one of the biggest hits of 1946 – a pretty good year for movies with Goldwyn's *The Best Years of Our Lives* and Cohn's own *Gilda* among them – and certainly the biggest grossing musical.

The Jolson Story

Al Jolson had been the biggest star in America, but as the war years approached, his star was definitely waning. Harry may well have stopped the film from turning into a flop. He was always involved in audience research. He would go to previews of all his movies – wearing dark glasses, in case he was mobbed. Columbia, under Harry's supervision, had pioneered the idea of the Gallup organisation attaching electronic sensors to preview audience's wrists. Almost everything on the film had a highly positive response. But one five-minute number, the Yiddish song 'Cantor for the Sabbath' was given a thumbs down. Harry ordered it out. Sixty years later, a copy of the scene, rescued from the cutting room floor, was bought by the International Al Jolson Society, whose members think it was one of the great losses in film history.

Although Jolson had excited thousands of GIs when he became the first entertainer to perform to the troops in World War II, he was no longer the World's Greatest Entertainer, the title he had immodestly – but not totally inaccurately – awarded himself. So the columnist Sidney Skolsky still needed to peddle around the various studios the idea of a movie biography of the man he told me he considered the 'king'. As we have seen, Warner Bros. turned him down – to his amazement. But he knew that Harry Cohn was as much a devotee of Jolson as he was himself – and the studio head became hooked on the idea. It started out as a low-budget production to be called *Minstrel Man*. By the time it was ready for shooting, Harry Cohn had decided to spend $2 million on the production – a huge amount for the time – and to film it in Technicolor, which was by no means a usual thing to do, even for a musical, and call it . . . *The Jolson Story*. It took six months to film,

Cohn had been a fan of Jolson ever since his early days in Tin Pan Alley. That was one of the reasons for agreeing to make the picture, but also there was also another factor. He loved the idea of the man who had been his idol now actually working for him. Jolson had taken a job at Columbia the year before – supposedly as a producer. But he hadn't produced anything. In fact, he said, 'The only time the phone rang was when someone wanted a plumber.'

He desperately wanted to star in the picture himself but Cohn convinced him that a man who was then 60 years old would have great difficulty persuading audiences at the beginning of the movie that he was just 20. Then he said he wanted James Cagney to play him, but neither Cagney nor Warner Bros. were keen on that. Finally, Cohn informed him that the part was to be played by Larry Parks, then only a little-known bit player. Evelyn Keyes played his wife (Mrs Joan Cohn wasn't keen on that. 'Everyone knows you're not pretty,' she told the star one night over dinner at the Cohn mansion). Both Evelyn, who was meant to be Ruby Keeler in all but name (Keeler wouldn't allow her name to be used) and Parks would be recognised as big stars as a result of the film. But it was Jolson who really scored. He may not play himself, but he would sing. Of course. He was placated by the money he was paid for doing so – said to have been $25,000 – but more because it had the potential to bring him back into the limelight.

While the film was being shot, Jolson was rushed into hospital. There was the fear that this was a recurrence of the illness which had ended his troop entertaining in the last year of the war and which led to his having a lung removed. Cohn went to see him in hospital. With his usual, kind, considerate solicitous, warm feelings for everyone, he looked at the singer and demanded: 'Hey, yer gonna die on me?' Virginia Schiff, one of Cohn's secretaries, remembered the day for me. 'He also said to Mr Jolson, "Are you gonna be all right?" and Jolson just sat up in bed and sang his heart out. When Cohn left, he lay back and collapsed.' But he didn't die for another four years.

When Al recovered, Cohn ordered a whole batch of new songs to be recorded – while the going was good. Word leaked out that he was on better form, with a better, deeper voice, than ever. People from all over Hollywood found reason to come on to the Columbia lot to see Jolson perform old numbers like 'Rock-a-bye Your Baby with a Dixie Melody' and 'Swanee' and a completely new/old song (Al had suggested to the musical adviser Sol Chaplin new arrangements for an old tune called 'Waves of the Blue Danube'. Chaplin wrote the arrangement, provided lyrics and 'The Anniversary Song' was the biggest hit of the year. (They supposedly shared the royalties, only Jolson's were three times bigger than Chaplin's).

The film was sensational – in more than just the sales it brought. Parks was sensational, too. He mimed Jolson's voice (singing the tunes himself but with Jolson's voice played so loud that his own voice was drowned out) more brilliantly than anyone had ever lip-syncked before. As one critic wrote at the time, 'You could even see the fur on his tongue.'

It was indeed a good year for Columbia. Twenty-five years after its birth, the company that had been financed for $250 was now worth $25 million. Suddenly, Al Jolson was top of the pops, beating Bing Crosby and Frank Sinatra to the head of the hit parade, week after week. The film was so successful that a sequel was made three years later, called, *Jolson Sings Again*, the credits for which this time confirmed that it was written by Sidney Buchman.

Evelyn Keyes wasn't in that film. The woman playing his second wife was Barbara Hale, who liked Cohn. 'I thought he was quite charming, which put me off a little – because I expected him to be very gruff. We met more of necessity than anything. He would have to approve wardrobe. He wanted to be sure that you were going to do what he wanted. Then he would overwhelm you with charm.' But she was never subject to the casting couch. 'No. That's why I didn't walk past his office too often. When I heard about the casting couch, I was terrified – because of his reputation and his very presence.'

When Jolson died in 1950, he was recognised as America's favourite entertainer. All down to Harry Cohn, who, it has to be said, adored Jolson – although there are those who doubt it.

'That was not true,' Dick Quine told me. 'They didn't get on at all. He was furious with Jolson for singing at my wedding, I remember.' But they made it up.

Joni Tapps, who became a Columbia vice-president – his job was to be in charge of music sales as well as being a senior producer – and had been brought into Columbia to supervise *The Jolson Story*, told me, 'When Al died, Harry heard the news and burst into tears. He was inconsolable.' His competitors, who always tended to smirk and look down on Columbia, stopped doing that.

Joni Tapps, however, spent his whole time at Columbia being scared of his mentor, who claimed that he really liked him. When he made *The Eddie Duchin Story* with Tyrone Power playing the popular pianist, he told Cohn that the recordings were wonderful. 'Good,' said Cohn. 'By the way, whatya doing tonight?' He said he had a date with a beautiful girl and told him the name of the restaurant where they would be – and the phone number of his date. A terrible mistake. At midnight, Cohn rang him. 'He said, "You told me the music was wonderful, Knucklehead [his favourite term for the producer]. Well, it isn't. It stinks. Come straight over." So I had to abandon the idea of getting laid.' He got to the studio and Cohn was waiting for him, smirking beneath his apparent anger.

'I said to him, "I said it was wonderful. It really is." Then Harry put the record on the turntable and looked at me triumphantly. Of course, it stank. He was playing a 33.3 rpm record at 45 rpm. He knew what he had done. He was just jealous of me having a date with a beautiful girl.'

Tapps should have known his boss's favourite parting line to errant employees: 'Gower Street is paved with the bones of executive producers. Get the hell out of here.'

He had his uses for Harry. One of them was to provide accommodation when he needed it most. Cohn would tell his wife he was going off to a football game and she would make him sandwiches – which he then ate at Tapps' apartment in the company of the chosen mistress of the day. Joan Cohn would always say she knew nothing about such things.

As for Larry Parks, his career shuddered to a halt with HUAC and McCarthyism. He admitted to the committee that he had been a member of the Communist Party, but for days refused to name the names of others who had been members with him. He pleaded with the committee not to make him 'crawl in the mud'. But days later, crawl he did – reading a list of the names of people who were known Communists, which had been submitted to him. He was damned because he did what he did, just as he would have been had he kept totally quiet. Cohn was one of the cowardly moguls who caved in and refused to renew Parks' contract.

Larry's wife Betty Garrett was surprisingly generous when I spoke to her about that era. At the time of the Washington hearings, she said she had sat, nine months pregnant, in front of a television set with tears pouring down her face. On the screen, she watched her husband being crucified. 'Larry had a grudging admiration for Harry. He could be really crude and quite a monster. Yet they had got on quite well. When he made *The Jolson Story* and *Jolson Sings Again*, Harry could not do enough for him. He even offered to get Larry girls. He kept saying, "What can I do for you, kid?" As far as Harry Cohn was concerned, that amounted to the same thing.

'They had fights. There were rows over his contract – which resulted in a lawsuit between *Jolson* pictures.

'In order to get Larry to do the first picture they wanted him to sign a new seven-year contract. He already had done four years, so that meant he would be tied to Cohn for 11 years,' Betty continued. 'He balked at that because seven years was slavery enough. Harry told him, "If you don't sign this, you won't only not get *The Jolson Story*, I'll ruin your career."'

And he went on to prove it by ordering Parks to wardrobe to be given a cap to wear as a taxi driver in a bit part in a *Boston Blackie* 'B' movie.

'Larry said, "OK" very brightly, tried on the cap – and finally gave way and signed the new contract. He was paid $750 a week for *The Jolson Story*. The rise he got for the new contract was negligible. Yet Larry and Harry had a wonderful relationship. I always felt that Larry admired him as he admired all people who had a lot of energy.

'Harry went back to work, running his studio. And, to be fair, he gave me my first job after all the problems with the blacklist were seemingly over.'

Actually, before she came to Hollywood, Cohn had 'courted' her, Betty said. She was starring in the Broadway show, *Call Me Mister*. 'He invited me for a private dinner in his hotel suite. I had already signed a contract with MGM, but nobody knew. He said I should come to Columbia and make a test. He said it would be so nice to have me and Larry working at the same studios. I mentioned that Larry had been to a party with Evelyn Keyes. He said, "Oh, he was at her house? You see how important I think it is for the husband and wife to be at the same studio." '

The Brothers Cohn

If Jack and Harry Warner hated each other, it was nothing compared with the relationship between Jack and Harry Cohn (could there be something sinister in Hollywood brothers being called Jack and Harry?). They positively detested the ground under which they hoped each other would soon be buried.

'Jack would occasionally come to Hollywood and bawl out his brother, with a great deal of curses and expletives,' said Evelyn Lane.

Once, Jack had the temerity to say: 'You know, you should make some Biblical pictures,' the director Dick Quine recalled. 'Cecil B. DeMille is making millions out of the films he makes at Paramount.' Now, Harry would never say yes to anything that Jack suggested. But he thought about it and then said to Jack, "You don't know anything about the Bible. I bet you don't know the Lord's Prayer [which is not such a ridiculous thought for a not-so-nice Jewish boy like Harry Cohn, but Jack took the plunge]." Jack said, "Here's $50. I bet you don't know it." They both put down their money. And Jack said, "I can tell you the Lord's Prayer . . . 'Now I lay me down to sleep'." And Harry said, "OK, you win. I didn't think you knew it. Here's my 50 bucks." '

Religion was always something of a problem with Cohn. His children were brought up as Catholics. As Evelyn Lane told me: 'He was so proud when his son served Mass and he asked me to come along to see it.' He had shown that pride, according to Ms Lane, when he witnessed them being baptised, too.

Joan Cohn wanted him to convert to Catholicism, but he had always resisted that. 'I think he was a better Catholic than his wife,' recalled Jean Louis. He contributed to Catholic charities and, when he was seriously ill, the nuns at a mission he supported prayed for him. 'Nuns always loved him,' his wife told me. 'He was once flying to New York first class and saw there were nuns sitting in coach, which meant that they didn't get any breakfast. Harry took out some money and told the stewardess to give them some breakfast, but not to tell them. She did tell, though.'

It is doubtful if he had done that had he seen a group of Jewish religious students. He made a point of going to work at the studio on the holiest day of the Jewish year, Yom Kippur, although it was said he refused to take phone calls on that day. When one of his directors told him he was leaving early on the day before the Fast so that he could take his father to a service, the man was laughed out of the office. Harry couldn't believe that any adult would still do that.

It was no more than Joan Cohn would have expected. She had got to know what he thought about Judaism – a journey her family had never taken. As she told me: 'I never knew a Jew till I went to New York as a model. But both my husbands [she later married Laurence Harvey] were Jews. Jews make great husbands. But Harry, who did have a bar mitzvah, always said he never cared.'

He did, though, make a Biblical film or two. He was handed the script of one film and erupted. 'Look here,' he said, 'you've got a guy here saying, "Yes, siree." This isn't a goddamned Western.' To which, the hapless writer replied: 'What he is saying is "Yes, sire", "Sire" means "Your majesty".' 'OK,' Harry agreed. The wonder was that he didn't expect his employees thereafter to call him 'Sire'.

His brother wouldn't have enjoyed that. Jack was the one man whose opinion Harry never wanted to ask. 'He was a delightful, sweet man, but with nothing like the graciousness of Harry,' said Joan Cohn. Yet so many people preferred him to his brother. 'Harry,' added Joan, 'was hated simply because he ran the company so well.'

Of course, the rows between Harry and his brother Jack were legion. Dick Quine, one of his favourite directors and sometime actor told me: 'Everything that was decided at the conferences in Hollywood, he had to sell to New York on the phone next day. And believe me that wasn't easy. The two brothers would fight over everything.'

Jack Cohn's grandson, Bruce Curtis, told me that he always believed that Harry was 'very good for the family. He was a wonderful person. My father died when I was twelve and that was when I first saw him – at my father's funeral. Every time I saw him, he'd give me $20 and a kiss on the cheek.'

Bruce's mother was responsible, he said, for getting Harry and Jack together after one of their most celebrated rows. 'They talked business. My grandfather had a big farm in Westchester, New York. He was always on the phone. I was always told he was talking to Uncle Harry [which was more than you might think when you consider the reputation they had]. My grandmother Jeanette always blamed Harry. She said he always made my grandfather's life a misery. Harry was always the ogre. My grandmother said it was Harry who caused my grandfather to die. Yet Harry took her to the opening of *The Bridge on the River Kwai*, which was his last public appearance. Jack Cohn was a kind of weak man.'

That was one night the family won't forget. Harry also took his then 13-year-old son John to see it. John told me. 'He went to New York to see it because he had had a fight with Sam Spiegel over it. But he was ill and wouldn't go to hospital. He said to me, "Dony [the name he and his mother called him], I've just seen the greatest film ever." He asked me which I preferred, *Pal Joey* or *Bridge on the River Kwai*. I told him, *Bridge on the River Kwai*. He just said "OK".'

John said that he and his brother had a good relationship with their father. When important people came to the house to discuss business, he would be allowed to come down to meet them. 'Then he'd say, "Show's over" and I'd have to go upstairs.' Once he was walking home from school, John recalled, and Kim Novak drove up beside him. '"Want a ride?" she asked. 'I just froze.'

A lot of distinguished guests came to the Cohn home and were seen by 'Dony', his brother Harry Jr (originally named Harrison) and adopted sister Catherine. The one who impressed Joan Cohn most was Chaim Weizmann, who would become the first President of Israel. 'He was shrouded in a light. I knew nothing about this man, but found out about his work. He was the most Christ-like figure I ever met' – which might have made the great man smile. 'I felt privileged that I could be on a level with this man and I had no right to be there, on his level. I had met popes, kings, queens and cardinals, but none impressed me more than this man.'

Love Him or Loathe Him

Whenever there was a big star making a film, a row between them and Harry was fairly certainly guaranteed. Rosalind Russell, who was known as one of the more dignified female stars, had got Harry into a fight he didn't see coming. Cohn had authorised a new wardrobe for Ms Russell costing $22,000. Jean Louis told me: 'She said that she might like to wear some of her own clothes. I told her it would not be necessary because I had designed dresses for her that were just right, made of beautiful silks and furs. She knew, however, that if she did wear anything of her own, she would be paid extra for doing so. Harry asked me afterwards how many of her own dresses she had worn. "None," I said. "Oh," said Russell, "throughout the filming I was wearing my wedding ring. You have to pay me for that." I had drawn up her costume contract and Harry went mad. "You, you, you!" he kept saying' – and then he changed the last word. 'You, you Jew!' shouted the Jewish mogul to the very non-Jewish designer.

Jean Louis was expected to make clothes for others in the film business. 'Louis B. Mayer's daughter Edie Goetz asked Harry if he minded if I made her some dresses. He said I could with pleasure. I made about twenty dresses for her – as I did for Mrs Cohn, who had a wonderful body to dress. I also used to make Harry's own clothes.' He made a wedding dress for the actress Kathryn Grant when she married Bing Crosby. It was Harry's wedding present.

As far as Jean Louis was concerned, Harry Cohn demonstrated a kindness not always recognised by others in his employ. 'I was working on a picture when I had a telegram from France telling me my mother was dying. Harry insisted that I go straight to her and made all the arrangements for me. "You can have ten lovers," he said, "but you will only ever have one mother".'

Harry wasn't always as lucky as he would have liked his staff to believe. He could be thwarted in business, which was not a pleasant sight to witness. He wanted Groucho Marx to work for him. But Groucho refused. 'My father didn't like Cohn at all,' said his son, the writer Arthur Marx. The Marx son was working at Columbia at the time, writing a script for one of the famous *Blondie* pictures, which were highly popular but not exactly an example of high art. 'Harry Cohn discovered I was Groucho's son and ordered that I be fired.'

Maybe that was all a question of taste. His personal 'executive assistant' Evelyn Lane, who had first gone to Columbia as a budding actress, told me: 'His taste was always impeccable. I think there was a time when Columbia had more Oscars than any other studio. Every foot of film that was shot in his studio had to go on to his private projector. He cut every film himself.'

He also met every important visitor himself – after getting Evelyn Lane to vet them first. 'If there was a banker coming in, I had to romance him a little bit,' she said. 'I mean, to see that he had proper accommodation, proper dinner arrangements; if a dinner was to be arranged for him I had to do it. Then, there was Rita Hayworth, whom he adored. Harry made sure that I was with her when she had to be photographed. I had to sweet-talk her into coming to the studio sometimes when she didn't want to leave her home.

'If any of them had a beef, I had to deal with it.'

The woman who also did that was Lillian Burns, wife of the director-producer, George Sidney. 'She would sit in on studio conferences.'

But Evelyn always believed she herself was the one with a special relationship with her boss. 'Towards the end of his life I used to drive him to the airport; I handled everything for him. But he knew what he wanted. He was always fastidious. I've never known anybody who was so clean,' she said. 'His underwear – he never wore an undershirt; just shorts – was made in England, his shoes were made in England.'

He was particularly fastidious as far as women were concerned, says Evelyn Lane. 'He wanted every woman to be treated like a lady.'

But then there was that casting couch. 'He'd go to Vegas every weekend,' said Ms Lane, 'and bring chorus girls back with him – to test them, he'd say. He'd test them in another way when he was there and then bring some of them back with him. No, he was no saint.'

This was a man who loved the law. 'But he wasn't a frustrated lawyer,' Evelyn Lane told me. 'He wasn't a frustrated anything. Yet when he heard that there was an interesting court case – like at the time when the Rosenbergs were put on trial – he sent for the transcripts.'

He always wanted to be informed – and for people to know just how informed he was. It was part of his power complex. 'You go to dinner with Harry,' Glenn Ford recalled, 'and he had three telephones on the table beside him. I know that two of them didn't work, but there were others who didn't know that. It was part of Cohn's intimidation process.'

Ruthless

The image of Cohn as a ruthless dictator is more frequently corrected by people who knew him than I could have imagined. As Evelyn Lane told me: 'He had one love. He loved talent. Anyone who ever knew him loved him. The trouble is damned few people really knew him. I knew things about Harry Cohn that his own wife didn't know. I knew the man who was very possessive of his people, his contract people, everyone. I was walking up the stairs one day when I came across him. He said, "Come up to my office." As we were going up the steps, he accidentally shoved a stenographer who tripped. He apologised and said to me: "Find out if that girl was hurt." It would have worried him terribly if she had been.'

He was also proud of the things he had which no one else did. 'He always wanted the first of everything – the first colour television (one was given to him by RCA) and the very first car phone. When he heard about the phone, he got very excited,' Evelyn Lane told me. 'When did they invent that?' he asked. He knew they had invented television and he shared the views of his competitor moguls on the then little box in the corner.

'He hated TV all the way', said Joan Cohn 'because it interfered with the thrill of making films.'

He was conscious of the future. 'About a year before he died, he said to me, "I've got to get someone to run my studio when I'm gone".' But he didn't. There was a boardroom battle that failed to immediately resolve the situation.

Maybe one of the reasons was they simply couldn't find anyone like Harry to replace him, that despite everything, despite the ready insults, Harry Cohn was indeed unique. When B.P. Schulberg joined Columbia after losing his job as production head at Paramount, Cohn shouted at him at a crowded board meeting: 'Hello, B.P., how does it feel to have a wife who knows more about the film business than you do?' Schulberg's wife was a leading agent.

He wasn't rude to everybody who dined with him or crossed the threshold of his 'Mussolini' office. Frank Sinatra, for one, had to be treated with kid gloves.

He was an asset that Cohn didn't want to let go. It wasn't always that way, however. Sinatra's career had been seriously on the skids. He had, as we have seen, been fired by Louis B. Mayer. He had lost his contract with Columbia Records (no relation to Columbia Pictures) and it was fair to say that in this pre-rock 'n' roll era, his singing style no longer had young girls screaming for more. He had appeared at the Copacabana nightclub in New York one night when he couldn't sing a note – nothing came out of his mouth when he tried. But he had heard that Harry Cohn was about to make a movie of James Jones's novel, *From Here to Eternity*, which Jack Cohn had bought for $82,000. Harry regarded this as the epitome of stupidity, although he was to change his mind.

Sinatra was convinced there was a part in the movie for him – not just any part, but that of the skinny Italian soldier, Magio, who dies following a fight with the cruel sergeant they called Fatso, to be played by Ernest Borgnine. The trouble was Harry didn't need Sinatra for the part – and didn't want him. He already had Elie Wallach earmarked for the role. Sinatra, who had been in Africa with his fiancée Ava Gardner, flew back to the States, begging for a chance to test for the part. Harry Cohn said no. 'It was a humiliating experience for him,' Daniel Taradash, the writer of the screenplay, told me. 'Harry Cohn was determined to say no.' At which point, Ava Gardner entered the picture, surprising since she and Sinatra were constantly having rows and their on-off engagement was more off than on. Also on hand was Cohn's wife Joan. She told me: 'Ava came to me and begged me to get Harry to give Frank a screen test. Eventually, he agreed.'

Sinatra paid all the necessary expenses and did the test without payment. Harry Cohn was vaguely interested. 'But there was no chance of Sinatra getting the role,' said Dan Taradash. 'He wanted Wallach. In fact, he had Wallach.' But then he didn't. The actor decided he would rather accept the offer of a part in a straight play and so left a vacancy for Magio. And, as it turned out, for Frank Sinatra. Sinatra took the role and won an Oscar for best-supporting actor into the bargain (there were also six other Academy Awards – among them, Best Picture for Taradash, for the director Fred Zinnemann and for others involved in the film). It launched Frank Sinatra on to a brand new career and on to the status he held until his death. Wallach's play died without trace, but *From Here to Eternity* triumphed in 1953. It did something that no other film ever did – record business at the Radio City Music Hall in New York in the height of a Manhattan summer before air-conditioning had been installed there.

Taradash gives most of the credit to Harry Cohn. 'Cohn was a man of instinct,' he told me. 'He was wrong some of the time, but most of the time, he wasn't. He said, "I'm going to give you something." Quite a gift that, writing a big, big hit. He also gave Montgomery Clift something. Clift played Pru, the bugler in the movie. He said "We have to see Pru play the bugle before he plays Taps." I thought that was a thoroughly bad idea. But Harry Cohn was insistent on it and it was a great scene. So he was right.'

Fred Zinnemann thought he was right, too. 'My main impression of him,' he told me, 'was of a man who was desperately anxious to find someone who would say no to him. Then he would test it and if the man really meant it, it led to a very fruitful relationship. On the other hand, if he found people were frightened or tried to please him, he was very rude and very coarse if he wanted to be.'

Glenn Ford told me that the thing that mostly brought fights between Cohn and his staff was incompetence. 'I have seen him reduce people to nothing in his office because the man had made dreadful mistakes. I know Harry was supposed to have used bad language. When he thought he had to do so, he did. He never did to me.'

But he did to the veteran director Rouben Mamoulian, who directed *Golden Boy*, perhaps the best-ever boxing picture, for Columbia. He told me, 'Here was a man who told you he didn't want to be liked, who told you he was ruthless, cruel and only wanted you to do what he wanted to do. Well, there it was. I thought inside his heart there had to be something very good. He said no. There wasn't.' That was quite an admission. He was talking about the character in the film but he could have been describing himself.

Mamoulian initially thought that when he was first called to the Cohn office the Columbia boss wanted to do *Porgy and Bess*, which, as we have seen, had been turned down by every other studio. 'I went to see Harry and he was there with his brother Jack and various other people. I said, "Harry, it's wonderful that you want to do the film." He said, "What film?" I said, "*Porgy and Bess*". He said, "I don't want to do *Porgy and Bess*." I told him that my agent Charlie Feldman had told me that he wanted to do it. "I said that to Charlie," he told me, "because I wanted to speak to you." He had brought me there under false pretences and I was very angry. He said he had other scripts he wanted me to read. I was furious.

'He then went into his store room and came out with a big box of Havana cigars.' He also gave Mamoulian three scripts. A week later, the director told Cohn that he didn't like any of them. He offered to send the cigars back, but he had already smoked five of them. 'He took a long time to answer – and then said, "Oh keep it." Then came *Golden Boy* and he was wonderful. He didn't complain about anything.'

What Harry Cohn did complain about was that Mamoulian had used the word 'please' when talking to Cohn's secretary. 'You don't say "please" to a secretary,' he admonished him. And then demonstrated the fact – by shouting at the hapless girl, 'Here – come over here. OK, get out.' He said to Mamoulian, "That's how you handle a secretary."

But how do you handle a mogul like Harry Cohn? Stanley Kramer, reputedly Cohn's favourite director, put it to me like this: 'Harry Cohn was emblematic of the whole generation. And not all bad. The imagery that he radiated at this time of the Hollywood tycoon was so true with him. He, like the others, represented The Movies.'

Kramer directed *The Caine Mutiny* for Cohn. There were never any mutinies at Columbia. It was no easier to form an uprising against him than it was for one against Adolf Hitler – or Benito Mussolini. Those who worked for him would appreciate the comparison. Like the actor Cornel

Wilde, to whom Harry Cohn could sometimes be very nice. Sometimes. As he told me: 'He could be extremely charming, solicitous, a good humour. Strangely, there were times when he seemed a very ugly man. At others, he was very attractive. Strong, fine, beautiful eyes. Many a star fell into that trap of his. He would woo them; he said that they could have everything that a star would like to have. They would sign long-term contracts with him – and then discover what he was like when the courtship was over. But sometimes, he would try to overcome that by doing something nice. But what a son of a bitch!

'He would do the dirtiest, nastiest things to people. Sometimes, he was in the right mood. He would look directly at you and there was communication. But when he was in another mood, when he was Mr Hyde, all that changed. His eyes looked mean. His whole expression was ugly, venomous. He could fly into terrible rages. He humiliated people who wouldn't fight back.'

Wilde made *A Song to Remember*, the story of the composer Chopin, for Columbia. As far as he was concerned it was a film to remember, although a lot of other people would have chosen to forget it. 'I fought back at Harry whenever I had need to. By and large, we got on fine.'

Nina Foch, an attractive actress on the screen from the 1940s into the 1980s, worked for Columbia, including being considered for a role in *A Song to Remember*. But Cohn fired her after she took a part in a New York play. 'My agent was furious and I fired my agent. But it turned out to be the best thing I could do.' Harry actually said to her, she told me: 'It's a shame you're not pretty because you can act.' But a New York journalist disagreed with Cohn about her not being pretty. He wrote that she was 'beautiful and feminine'. She said she wanted to say: 'Go boil your head, you pig.' But she was under contract – until Cohn decided she had broken it. Eventually, she said, she grew to respect him. But it was from afar.

Fortunately, there were sufficient stars who realised that their careers were sometimes better protected by not fighting back. In the 1930s, Harry Cohn and Columbia had what could have been considered a golden era. In 1934, they had announced that Grace Moore would star in *Interlude*. She was Harry's contribution to the culture of America, but instead of *Interlude*, she made *One Night of Love*. It was more to his liking. He was fed up with what he called 'arty drek' (Yiddish for garbage – or worse). Three years later, the studio publicised the fact that it would be making 62 features the following year, as well as 126 shorts (under its *Screen*

Snapshots documentary series), and four serials. Meanwhile, Harry had paid the almost unheard of sum of $200,000 for the rights of the Pulitzer Prize-winning novel, *You Can't Take it with You,* which was made into a film with James Stewart, Lionel Barrymore and Jean Arthur.

Frank Capra had been with the company longer than anyone else, but Cohn constantly called him 'Dago'. The epithet stuck even when Capra brought him not just *It Happened One Night*, but the Gary Cooper double, *Mr Smith Goes to Washington* and *Mr Deeds Goes to Town* in 1936 and *Lost Horizon.*

Capra told me: 'I described the book of *Lost Horizon* to him – he would never read a book himself – but in a few words I explained it to him and he went for it. He had great confidence and trust in me. He never said "No" to any film that I wanted to make. The budget for that year was $4 million. Of that, $2 million was for *Lost Horizon.* And with that other $2 million, they were going to make twenty films. If that movie failed, he was through. We got into a car the evening that we did the deal. It was raining. I was driving and I thought the windshield wipers were saying, "big flop, big flop, big flop." But it wasn't. He had faith. And this is where I could trust his true character. Was he going to say, "I told you so"? He said, "I'll still give you that seven-year contract".'

The star Joan Fontaine would say: 'He was a very rough zircon.' Calling him a rough diamond was going too far. 'He was a kind of gangster. I remember seeing him at [the nightclub] El Morocco. I was in a telephone booth and he thrust the door open and said, "Get out of here right away. Let's do a deal here and now. I don't want to talk to your agent. So many thousands for a three-picture deal, take it or leave it." I left it, of course. I wasn't going to do that. I think I said I would want script approval. He said, "Not on your life. You'll do what I tell yer to do."'

Sammy Cahn always said that he was closer to Harry Cohn than any of the other studio heads. 'I knew him better than any of the other moguls, because I got as close to him as anyone could get. I was almost like a son. We used to spend sometimes fifteen hours a day together. I lived at the Sunset Towers [hotel] and Harry would come barrelling down Sunset Boulevard at about 9.30 or ten o'clock, with a briefcase that was bulging. I'm not sure that this briefcase was ever opened. I am sure it was a prop.'

To the writer Melville Shavelson this was another of those moguls who 'flew by the seat of his pants'. 'He set up a meeting for my partner Jack Rose and me with some other writers of the film we were about to work on. We had lunch in his private office and Harry Cohn said he went to see a movie last night. It was about the Civil War. I asked what it was about. He said, "I don't know. I turned my chair this way, I turned my chair that way. I just couldn't take it. It'll never be a hit. I didn't wiggle my ass once." One of the other writers said to him, "Mr Cohn, what makes you think you have an ass which can monitor for America"?'

But then he always had ways of monitoring his world. 'He built a fortress around himself,' was how his widow Joan Cohn described it to me. Louella Parsons would describe him as 'an implacable enemy but one of the kindest and best men in the world.'

Not if you hadn't yet established yourself he wasn't. He often needed to be persuaded to hire people whom he, on principle, would decide were not right. It took hours of persuasion some time. Jean Arthur, who became a staple of the comedies of the 1930s, was one of those he wasn't sure about. 'She's got a great voice,' said an executive. 'Yeh, but look at her face. Half angel, half horse.' Fortunately, the angel side won.

Apparently, he and the former Joan Perry never had that sort of doubt about each other – if you can excuse the numerous girlfriends in his life; and indeed if you excluded their first meeting at a New York house party.

'He asked me,' Joan recalled, '"What are you drinking?" I said, "Lemonade, sir." He said, "How would you like to go to Hollywood?" I said, "I don't think so, sir."

'I told him that I had several engagements in New York. He said, "You can always break them. You don't seem to realise this is business." He asked me what I made in a week, I didn't tell him. He said, "I'll give you $150 to $200 a week."'

She did go – and tested for a part in *Golden Boy*, appearing in a scene with William Holden, posing for pictures with Rita Hayworth.

Holden asked her for a date. People at the studio warned him off. 'They said, "Hey, don't you know, she's the boss's girl? Lay off."'

He knew what was good for him – and laid off. The word ran round Columbia that Mr Cohn had a new girl.' And, he told her, a new star.

Harry's Girl

'Actually, I had never been an actress,' Joan told me. Nor had she had the name Joan Perry before. She was Betty Miller until he ordered it changed. Part of her contract was that he could change her name to whatever he wanted it to be. 'I was a starlet.' A starlet whom Harry wooed with a picture, captioned with a series of letters – 'B.A.G.G.A.I.W.T.T.M.Y.A.S.'

She knew what the letters meant: 'Be a good girl and I will try to make you a star.' She told me: 'I had no idea he had picked me out. I was furious that Rita [Hayworth] was getting all the attention. She was a wonderful dancer and he was grooming her.'

But, before long, he had other plans for Joan. Because of that, he ordered that there should be no stills of the two women together. 'He then said, "I'm going to make a star of her, Rita – and marry you." I said, "But you are already married." He replied, "Not for long".'

He saw in her a young, sexy woman. To her, he was 'extraordinarily handsome'. Other women felt the same. To her face, they said how lucky she was. Behind her back? 'All women are bitches,' she told me. 'My dear, I know.'

Once the marriage before a judge had been agreed, she introduced Harry to her family. 'He was the first Jew my father had ever met (my mother was dead by then), but they got on well. They were both interested in sports. It certainly never bothered me that he was much older than I was. I always had a father fixation. Harry was a gutsy man. I only survived because he survived.'

The day they were married by a Judge Percourer on 30 July 1941, Harry, displaying a desire for domesticity no one had previously noted, stopped off at a grocery shop for some fruit. While in the shop, the man behind the counter told him, 'I see that Joan Perry got married today.' 'Oh yes,' said Harry, 'who did she marry?' 'Oh,' said the man, 'some jerk named Harry Cohn.'

Rouben Mamoulian might have said that about him, except that the word 'jerk' would not have been part of the erudite Mr Mamoulian's vocabulary.

'When I first went to an interview with him for *Golden Boy*, his conversation was full of four-letter words. I said to him, "Harry, stop using the goddamn [that word was all right, apparently] four-letter words. I don't like to hear those words all the time." But what are you going to do with a guy like that? But then he said, "Is it my fault if I use literary language?"'

In truth, he admired what he would have called literary people. Despite what Frank Capra said, Cohn was well read. But his command of the language and its literature was somewhat limited. Reviewing a script, the writer told him that he thought it would be a good idea if the main character had a speech that he could deliver as if it were a kind of Hamlet's soliloquy. Cohn said he didn't want that and used his own literary knowledge to demonstrate the fact. 'No,' he said, 'it should be like "To be or not to be".'

Harry could use that 'literary language' at any time of the day or night, especially when he sat at the huge Queen Anne table in the family dining room in the mansion on Crescent Drive, Beverly Hills, and entertained celebrities and Columbia executives who had to regard a dinner invitation as a summons that couldn't be ignored – and at which they were expected to know every line of every script on which they were working. They were also expected to accept Harry's practical jokes – like wiring their chairs to low-voltage batteries. Cohn was never happier than when he could press a button under the table (not unlike the one he kept under his desk at the studio) and watch his guests squirm but say nothing as he administered an electric shock.

The language on these occasions was as bad as the food was good, which was very good indeed. He had the unfortunate habit of talking about leading men and women, not as that, but as 'p***ks' and 'c**ts'. If his children heard that language, which they sometimes did, he had an answer to people who queried the behaviour: 'They ought to learn about these things.'

But some things they really ought not to have heard. Like the time he said to the star, Margaret Sullavan: 'I understand you're great in the hay.' She stormed out of the room in disgust, but just as she opened the door, she said: 'Yes I am.' At another meeting, he shouted at a well-known actor, 'Say who do you think your wife is fucking these days?'

Cohn's wife liked to deny that sort of thing happened. 'There was never any profanity in our house, which he had given me as a present.' So no need of four-letter words. However, there were girls who were known to use literary language themselves when they were invited on to Cohn's yacht. One was the actress Gloria Henry who told me about the time she accepted an invitation. 'He said "I'll have someone come and pick you up Friday afternoon and you'll fly over to Castlina." There were just the two of us on the way to the airport. We were taken to a seaplane, then we were taken to his small yacht, with one cabin at the back that slept two, and a living room and a dining room. I said that this was not what I expected. The only other person there was Harry. I didn't know what to do. I was very naive. I really didn't know what to do. I felt like an idiot. I was stupid. I was there with this very powerful man. I could only hope that someone else was coming.

'We went into the living room. Harry was served drinks. He must have thought I was very liberal. I remember him saying, "You mustn't think this is immoral." It must have been wonderful to have that power. We were talking seriously. We played gin. He kept pouring more brandy. I thought he couldn't take advantage of someone who was drunk. He took me to the back of the boat and I threw up. It wasn't very romantic. Then I remember he called Walter Kane, the man who brought me to the boat. He was shouting, "What are you doing sending this girl to me? Get your ass over here." Then he told me I had got off pretty lightly, which I suppose I had. He asked me, "Are you turning me down?" I said, "Yes," and he got pretty mad. He said, "You might get somewhere in this studio one day, but it will be over my dead body." '

She had been about to test for a film called *Return to October*. She never got the part. 'I've often wondered if I would have got it had I agreed to sleep with him.'

Other people were invited on to the yacht – actually, a small former Coast Guard boat – for purely business reasons. One couple were the studio's musical director Morris Stoloff and his wife Elsa. 'We would go to his house for dinner, too,' she told me. 'He had lots and lots of flings, but he was a good husband, too. There was a soft side to him. But there was nothing in between. You either liked him or loathed him.' She was one who, on balance, liked him – and so did her husband; he brought three Academy Awards to the studio, which meant that he was always in Harry's good books.

Lester W. Roth, a California judge, had been one of Harry's legal team. 'He made important contracts, but sometimes, and very frequently, he had misconceived an actor's ability and would look for ways of getting rid of him or her. One was with a very important actress. She had a pretty watertight contract. So we decided the only way to get rid of her was to offer her a small, degrading part. But she took it.

'On the whole,' said Judge Roth, 'he was a fine human being. I had very few encounters with Harry that weren't pleasant. But not always. I was sitting in his office one occasion. There was a preview that night. And his secretary came in. He said to her, "No use taking you there. It's a comedy and you'll laugh straight away. No use asking your opinion." '

Glenn Ford agreed with that. He had first met Cohn in 1938, when he was Tallulah Bankhead's stage manager. 'They asked me to come out and make a test and then put me under contract. I was with him for 14 years.'

He told me: 'I had heard all those stories about Harry Cohn and the terrible things said about him. But he was indulgent. He even allowed me to have in my contract that I never had to wear make-up. Yet he was very possessive of his actors. He called them "my children" [which appears to be something of an infectious disease among the moguls] and said, "I'm going to take care of you" – which he did. That required that you did what he told you to do and didn't argue with him. That's why I ended up making over two hundred films for him. Sometimes, we made a new film every week; sometimes two at the same time.'

And Harry knew everything about every one of them – except *Gilda*, one of the most important movies to come out of the Columbia studio. The 1946 film noir about a South American gambler who rekindles his love for an old flame, to coin one of those clichés for which there is no adequate substitute, showed Rita Hayworth at her most devastatingly beautiful. Glenn Ford was her lover and as he said to me, it was hugely significant in both their lives. 'We loved each other very much, but what Harry really knew about that is a matter for doubt.'

Harry found out less about *Gilda* because no one – not the stars, not even the writer Marion Parsonett – knew how it was going to end.

But then, as we have seen, he set about finding out about his stars – by bugging their dressing rooms.

Harry's word was his bond, says Ford. 'I never signed anything. He would say, "Do you agree?" I'd say, "Yes, I agree" and we shook hands. He never went back on his word. The one thing you never did with Harry was try to lie to him. You always told the truth, because he was way ahead of you.'

One of the first things ever they had agreed on was changing his name. 'I was Gwyllyn Ford; Gwyllyn was a Welsh name. Harry said I had to change it because it wouldn't look good on a marquee.' They thought about alternatives. 'What's the name of the street that we're on?' he asked. Ford told him what he knew already. He told him it was Gower Street. He said: 'I always wanted a son whom I'd call John. I'm going to call you John Gower.' Ford had no doubts about his answer: '"Harry," I said, "you've just lost me again. I'm on the way back to New York. I'm proud of the name Ford. We founded the first paper mill in Canada."'

The town of Glenford in Quebec was his father's birthplace. He added the final 'n' and offered his choice to the boss who said, 'I like that.' The name was changed legally. (Cohn also changed the name of his favourite studio designer Jean Louis Berthant to Jean Louis. He said he couldn't pronounce the designer's original last name.)

'Harry became my friend,' Ford told me. 'He was a good friend, a loyal friend. I was never once put on a suspension. If I didn't like a film, he'd say, "If you don't like it, convince me." The mogul's choice wasn't always right. He cast Ford as Don Jose in a Columbia version of *Carmen*. 'It was terrible – can you imagine me as Don Jose?' said Ford. 'But it was worth the price of admission to see Rita, who was beautiful. Rita, Bill Holden and I were his three children.'

And Harry thought it was worth that, too. 'When I complained to him about the film, he said: "Would you like to see the grosses?"'

The grosses of one man everyone knew as Henry were not so large, but Harry Cohn thought them important. He had heard that Henry Martin, a black servant in the days when Harry was married to his first wife Rose, was on hard times. So he set him up with a stall on the Columbia lot, in which he sold candies and snacks and did shoe shining on the side. He was the first black man to operate a food concession at any major studio. Cohn lent him the money to set up in business. It really was a loan. Henry paid him back. Harry's will stipulated that Henry would get the money back – but, by the time he did, there was a lot more of it, because Harry had invested the original sum.

Virginia Schiff, a long time studio secretary, remembered a daily ceremony at Columbia: 'When Harry arrived every morning, he would sweep by the studio and Henry and the policeman would wait over the road – Henry would step into the driver's seat, while Barney, the policeman, the guard at the gates to the studio, would walk him across the road, while Henry parked the car.

'He was frightened someone would take a potshot at him,' Virginia added. Which was fairly typical of his paranoia or was just plain fright – the reason why he insisted that he and Joan had to take separate planes when they went anywhere.

Harry had a new Lincoln car every year, but loved to drive a Thunderbird. If his chauffeur drove him to the office fast, he would tell him, 'Just because *I* drove it fast doesn't mean to say you can drive it that way home.'

When Henry had an accident that required the amputation of the best part of a finger, Harry paid for his treatment at the Cedars of Sinai Hospital, the most prestigious in Los Angeles. 'He stood at the end of my bed,' Virginia Schiff recalled Henry saying, 'and told me not to hurry to get well, because he had plenty of money for his treatment.' And she added: 'He paid for Henry to have a private room, but the poor man felt too lonely there, so he moved into a room with three other people. The night before the operation, Harry called to see all the doctors who were treating him, asking that he have all the best attention. He said, "If you can avoid the operation, I would like you to do so. I don't want the tip of his finger cut off if it can be avoided."' That was another side of Harry Cohn, dictator of Columbia Pictures. 'He didn't want anyone to know about this. He said it would ruin his reputation.' A reputation for stinginess among other things. Which is why he went round the studio at night, turning out all the lights – which seems to be endemic among the moguls – and why when he caught one of the film editors shaving in work time, he fired him.

That was a part of the human side of Harry Cohn's life. New Year's Eve was celebrated at home with guests like Artur Rubenstein and Jose Itburbi playing. 'You had to be on time for dinner,' Joan Cohn told me. 'He would say, "I do not keep my chef waiting."' Much less formal was the annual Christmas party in his office. Freddie Briskin told me: 'He had a props man called Charlie Grinucci, one of the originals in the studio, and Harry allowed him to sit at his desk. Grinucci would sit there, just writing out slips firing various executives. Harry loved it.'

It was indeed a night for the reversal of roles. Harry acted as the studio janitor. His wife Joan told me: 'It was the only night that he ever came home a little tipsy. Vernon Mason, his diagnostician, prevented him from drinking.' But not from womanising. As we have seen, Joan denied knowledge of his other women. She was much happier talking about his golf or the tennis he played with the former Wimbledon champion, Alice Marble, at the Beverly Hills Hotel.

The last time that Glenn Ford saw Cohn was when Harry sent for him at the end of his 14-year contract. 'Somehow, he looked a lot smaller. His beard had gone white. He had become so much smaller behind that big desk. He wasn't the same man. I went over to Harry and shook his hand. There were tears in his eyes. The only time I ever saw him cry. It wasn't like Louis Mayer. He said to me, "You know why I like you Glenn? It's because you were never afraid of me."' Ford kissed him on the cheek and told him, "Harry, I was never afraid of you because I have such respect for you. As a man and as a picture maker."

He worried about what would happen after he died – what would happen to *him*, that is. Rouben Mamoulian told me that he often talked to him about life after death. '"I am a great believer in that. After all, what are we here for?" Harry said to me. "I want you to prove it."'

A number of people talk about his trying to earn a place in heaven –

because he always thought the cards were stacked against him. 'I don't want people to like me,' he said 'because I know that I'm a son of a bitch.'

A son of a bitch who insisted that some people called him 'Harry'. Virginia Schiff told me: 'He wouldn't answer his sons unless they called him "Harry", too. He didn't want to be "Dad".'

'There was something about him that was very childish,' said Mamoulian. 'I told him that there was good in him.' To which he uttered one of his usual more colourful obscenities. 'Harry Cohn was a bastard,' the director added. 'You were never surprised if Harry Cohn lied, because you expected it. You would have been surprised if he told the truth. But he never claimed to be anything else. He was a bastard. So what are you going to do about it?'

But business had always been good. In 1953, Harry was reported as topping the list of company executives' salaries – with monthly earnings of $207,800. It was the year that Harry announced that he was going to start shooting his films, four ways – in 3D, 2D and wide screen in both media simultaneously.

The following year, Harry supervised three major films, *The Caine Mutiny*, *On the Waterfront*, which was to become an all-time classic cementing Marlon Brando's status as the most highly regarded male star in Tinseltown – and famed for the line 'I could have been a contender' – and *The Long Grey Line*. The 'trades' – *Daily Variety* and *The Hollywood Reporter* – noted that *From Here to Eternity* was 'still going strong.' Unfortunately, Harry himself no longer was.

Only Joan knew that he had cancer, a growth on his neck that he could hide. But he got more and more sick at times and was taken ill while staying on holiday at the Arizona Biltmore Hotel in Phoenix. He had had another heart attack. 'There was no doctor,' Joan Cohn told me. 'There was a highly qualified nurse who got a doctor and he was put in an oxygen tent before being taken to hospital.' He died in the ambulance. He was 66. 'He had just made me promise to organise a proper funeral for him,' said Joan. And that turned out to be a mystery worthy of a new Columbia film.

Two days before his death on 25 February 1958, he told his son John, 'I'm tired, Dony. I think I'm going to sell out. The fun has gone.' Actually, he once did agree to sell the business – but changed his mind and then refused to sign the papers. As Joan told me: 'A friend said, "If he sells out, he'll be dead." So I talked him out of it.'

Yet, as Louella Parsons noted, he had a foreboding of his death and had called a meeting for the day that he died – to discuss the appointment of a possible successor.

Rabbi Magnin was actually not there at that star-studded funeral service held on the biggest stage at Columbia before interment at Forest Lawn. A priest was. It wasn't a religious ceremony, refuting suggestions that his widow Joan tried to convert him on his deathbed. Officially converted, that is. But there were religious elements –Catholic elements. At Joan's request, a priest sprinkled holy water over the grave at the famous Forest Lawn cemetery. This was the post mortem baptism that it was claimed he had had. 'I didn't see any reason not to do that,' she told me. 'It wasn't a profanity. His last words,' she continued, 'were "Jesus Christ, help me".' The priest came to the house to pray. 'Not a single rabbi did that,' said Joan. 'A man stood shivering in the mortuary in case a rabbi came to pay his respects, but there were only nuns and my friend, the monsigneur, who said, "I can only pay respects to my wonderful friend in my own way as a priest and say the Sorrowful for him."' The priest who sprinkled the holy water on the grave, Monsigneur Patrick Concannon, was her escort to the funeral. 'Harry always asked our children, "Pray for me" and they did.' And promptly took their mother's 'stage' name Perry. 'I thought they might not like to have the name Cohn one day,' she told me. Was it perhaps too Jewish?

There were prayers, too, ironically, from a lot of Columbia employees. Not all kindly. But others were.

As Glenn Ford said: 'Nothing was the same after Harry died. He was a giant.'

6

ADOLPH ZUKOR AND JESSE L. LASKY

Adolph Zukor and Jesse Lasky were very much among the founding fathers of Hollywood. Both were there at the very beginning. But their careers, seriously influencing the way Tinseltown operated, were much shorter. Yet they were there in the background for virtually the whole of their adult lives. And they were appreciated.

'Lasky was a darling. Zukor was a lovely man.' Thus spoke Rouben Mamoulian, one of the really great Hollywood directors – a term not to be lightly thrown around. Nor was his comment about these two very different Hollywood founding fathers.

They were both moguls, but with distinct differences. One – Zukor – was a little man who had once been a boxer. But he was a big triumphant success in the mode of the other men we have discussed already in this study. The other – Lasky – got himself into serious financial problems and eventually lost control of the studio in which he and Zukor had invested everything, their money – and their love.

Love? It could be nothing less. In fact, you could almost say that the two men were married to each other; in a purely platonic way of course.

They were the men who founded Paramount, a studio whose logo at the beginning of every one of their movies featured the crest of a snow-capped mountain with a belt of cloud near its summit. They were the

Paramount Chiefs. But, unlike either the gentlemen in Africa in loin cloths and with bones in their noses – the cliché characters who were featured in a stack of Paramount pictures, not least the Bing Crosby-Bob Hope 'Road' movies – or their fellow studio bosses, they were their own men who operated in their own way.

Not just Hope and Crosby, but Mary Pickford, Gloria Swanson and Gary Cooper as well as a few hundred other men and women with household names could claim Mr Zukor and Mr Lasky as the men who gave them their start in the business.

In so many ways, they were unlike the other Hollywood moguls, not least in that they were each married to just one woman, and apparently happily – Zukor to Lottie Kaufman, to whom he gave two dozen red roses every birthday, but who predeceased him by almost 30 years, and Jesse Lasky to Bessie Gainnes, said to have come from prosperous Boston Jewish society.

Certainly, there are few of the vituperative stories that marked the careers of the other moguls. But occasionally, there were things said that neither man would have liked to read in a newspaper or in his career résumé – like the time when Lasky's daughter called Zukor a 'killer' (not literally, of course) in sharp contrast to her father's easy-going manner.

Certainly, Zukor could be cynical. When he went back to his native Hungary to visit his parents' graves, for instance, he said that no one could imagine how many relatives he suddenly discovered he had. But that didn't mean he wasn't generous to them – real relatives or not. He decided to give charitable donations to those whom he considered worthy. The way to do this was to hold a session in a local hall, where he heard the stories of the supplicants – sitting behind a curtain, so that no one could beguile him by their appearance. Or otherwise.

There are, naturally enough, the jokes – all true, all verified by a score of witnesses – that I have instituted in this volume.

My favourite has to be when Zukor celebrated his 100th birthday, then as now, a unique Hollywood event. All the big names in Tinseltown were there to honour him that evening in 1973. One by one, they came to pay him court as the little man, much smaller in physical stature than his competitors even during his personally most productive period, looked up, smiled indulgently and occasionally seemed a little perplexed. One of those who came up to him was the comedian Jack Benny, then a mere 79. Zukor looked into his eyes and said, 'Oh, you still alive?'

Benny would die the following year. Zukor had another two years to go.

It was a time of the great comics. Bob Hope was at the celebrations, too. He was chosen to supervise the big event of the centenary commemorations – showing Zukor around the Paramount studio that he had himself created. Melville Shavelson was there, too. 'I heard their conversation, a little stilted, more Hope than Zukor. But then the old man spoke: "Bob," he said, "I saw your last picture. It was too long. I saw your last television show. It was too long. But don't worry. Life is too long." '

'Actually,' said another Hollywood wit, the writer Hal Kanter, 'although he was celebrating his hundredth birthday, people said he was really one hundred and ten. He just took off his usual ten per cent distribution charge.'

As with all good stories, there are variations of the tale. One involves Zukor's known gift for philanthropy. Once a month, there would be a charity event at New York's Astor Hotel at which an award (paid for by Zukor himself) would be given to a Paramount employee. Jerome Pickman, the now 93-year-old former head of marketing at Paramount, told me: 'Each time, someone had to escort him from the office to the hotel. One day, it was my turn. A big man stood over him and said, "I'm Jakowitz from Des Moines." "You're Jakowitz?" Zukor asked him, surprised. "You're not dead yet?"'

Zukor had had quite a life, not just long but also eventful and productive. He had been born in the Hungarian town of Risce to a poor ('a new pair of shoes was an event,' he recalled), religious family who hoped he would one day become a rabbi. At 15, he left the country still ruled by the mutton-chopped Franz Josef, who in addition to being Emperor of Austria was also King of Hungary.

Leaving for America was in the conventional mogul rags-to-riches mould. So was the fact that he found a menial job – sweeping floors. And, when his English got better, he earned $10 from a Chinese pastry cook, who paid him to write 50 slogans for his fortune cookies (20 years later, Zukor, by then a successful mogul, had a visit from the same cook, asking if he could give him more; he agreed to do so – but the price had gone up to $10.50.) As was traditional for a mogul, he then went into a trade as different from what would soon be known as the Hollywood movie business as could be imagined. Or . . . on consideration . . . was it? It might not have seemed that glamorous at that time, but being the head of a fur business gave him an opportunity to meet some of the most glamorous women in America. It was a highly successful furrier's business in Chicago, owned by Morris Kohn, another Hungarian, who before long made him a partner. He also cemented another partnership for the young man. He introduced him to his niece Lottie Kaufman. Soon afterwards, in 1897, Lottie and Adolph were married.

Maybe it was the marriage, perhaps his ambition would have driven him anyway, but he was inspired to go into something a lot more exciting. Show business. He started by going into partnership with a man called William Brady, who ran a few theatres – one of them was made to resemble a train carriage. They stayed solvent for only a short time, mainly from showing *The Great Train Robbery*. But he *had* gone from the garment trade right into show business.

Sounds familiar? If it does sound very much like the Samuel Goldwyn story – substituting Zukor's furs for Goldwyn's gloves – that is only coincidental. Having said that, it was –indirectly – through Goldwyn that Zukor and his sometime partner Jesse L. Lasky got together.

As we have seen, Lasky was Sam's brother-in-law, which, as we have also seen, was not necessarily a recipe for either happiness or success. Lasky, unlike his future partners, was American-born – in San Francisco in 1880, which made him the oldest of the Hollywood founding fathers. Like the others, he was born with an entrepreneurial gene in his make-up. To say nothing of a love of entertainment.

Entertainment and music. Stories about him playing in vaudeville give the instant impression of a casual performer who didn't know very much about either his instrument or the music he played. In fact, Jesse was a musician who could have made a career, not just with a leading orchestra, but also as a soloist. However, that wouldn't have satisfied him. He needed all the fun and excitement that the vaudeville audiences could give him. At least, that is what he said. But he had had other adventures before going on the stage with his sister Blanche, both playing the cornet.

Jesse had tried his hand as a newspaper reporter – not enough fun there – and had even gone prospecting for gold in Alaska – no gold, just a lot of snow there. He had been a band leader playing in Hawaii. But it was after these explorations into what he hoped would be a fun and prosperous future, that the entrepreneur came to a conclusion that would influence everything he did: his real expertise (even more than his gift with playing the cornet) was on the business side. Yes, he wanted to stay in vaudeville – but there was more money to be made as an impresario. So that was what he became – and stayed until Sam Goldwyn, then still

Goldfish, came into the picture and they established themselves as the unquestioned creators of Hollywood.

Adolph Zukor was lurking in the background when Goldfish and Lasky sent Cecil B. DeMille's party off to Flagstaff and approved their rental of the barn in Hollywood. But just lurking. He had other things to occupy his time by then.

The fur king had taken a strange sideways turn: he switched to running a penny arcade amusement centre, complete with peep-show machines. He called the enterprise Automatic Vaudeville. It was a mixture of two important words for the period – 'automatic', which spelt modern; 'vaudeville', which was where everyone went. But, hardly surprisingly, that was never going to be enough. As with so many of the founding fathers, he needed partners. And, as in those other stories, the partners would shape what he did thereafter, no matter for how short a time they were together.

Marcus Loew

It was in the penny arcade that Zukor got to know Marcus Loew, who was starting his cinema business. They decided to form a partnership. The man who soon became treasurer of Loews Inc., which not only ran the movie-house business, but came to own MGM, was already bitten by the motion picture bug – and quickly infected his partner, Adolph, who by then had invested a few thousand dollars in his bank account.

It was money that Zukor decided he could use productively in films, too – by taking on the American distribution of the Sarah Bernhardt French film, *Les Amours de la Reine Elisabeth*. The year was 1912 and the American public had never seen an historical drama before. Most of them had never even heard of Mme Bernhardt either. But for those who had, it was an excitement to tell their children about. To the others, who put down a few cents to see the movie Zukor called, more simply, *Queen Elizabeth*, it was a fascinating experience.

For Zukor, it was a fortune maker. He made so much money, in fact, that he decided to go one better than distributing other people's films – one better, too, than Marcus Loew who was content with *showing* other people's films – by making his own. These would be pictures in the *Queen Elizabeth* mould: dramas that would impress audiences to a live play. Famous Players, he called his outfit – with the subtitle that became better known than the main name, 'Famous Plays With Famous Players'.

Some of those famous plays were pretty terrible to watch – but people didn't know that at the time. They were told they were going to see filmed versions of classic plays and didn't expect to get more than what that seemed to imply. Indeed, they were delighted to see complete plays filmed, so they believed, just for them. There was no need to 'open them out', as the motion picture industry subsequently discovered they could do.

Zukor's success wasn't confined to the classics. He early on realised the power of sex in the cinema – and the value of a pretty girl before the cameras. That was how Mary Pickford came into his orbit, a Zukor discovery whom he was clever enough to publicise as 'America's Sweetheart', even though his later head of production, Benjamin P. Schulberg always took credit for one of those nomenclatures that entered Hollywood history.

He also made what he falsely liked to claim was America's first feature film – ignoring a little thing called *The Squaw Man*, with which he would always wish he had been associated. But *The Prisoner of Zenda* starring James K. Hackett in the movie that would be made four times more, was a huge hit. It always would be that – most notably in 1937 with Ronald Colman in the dual role of Rudolf Rassendyll and King Rudolf of Streslau (or Ruritania, as it was in the original version, a fictional place name that came to stand for any mythical central European country where the leading citizens wore white uniforms with gold epaulettes – when not in hunting gear, that is – the women, long flowing dresses and diamond tiaras, and always with a sprinkling of peasants who knew their place and when to doff their caps). There was also a 1984 TV mini series, which would have been no more predictable for Adolph Zukor than was the difference the original production would make to the film industry.

Famous Players was the talk of the fledgling industry – which was how Jesse L. Lasky came to suggest a merger with his own Jesse Lasky Feature Play Company.

Goldfish wasn't sold on the idea, but he was placated by the accountants' estimates that there was a fortune to be made by pooling their resources. There was a further sweetener. As we have seen, Sam would be chairman of the board. As we have also seen, it couldn't last. He and Zukor hated each other, but then Sam would have hated anyone who wanted to call himself a partner. His continuing dislike for Jesse Lasky had more to do with the fact that they were in business together than that they were brothers-in-law, which was a difficult enough situation for him to swallow at the best of times.

Lasky and Zukor had no such problems when their joint company, the Famous Players-Lasky Corporation, was finally incorporated in 1916, although until 1917 it still operated under the name of the Lasky company. In the years from *The Squaw Man* onwards, it had produced 148 movies – several of them, including *The Girl of the Golden West* in 1917, directed by Cecil B. De Mille. Zukor was the president, Lasky was his deputy.

They were doing so well at the outset that they were able to take in a smaller film operation called . . . Paramount.

Paramount

It started because the two partners resented the expense to which they had to go to have their films distributed. The practice, until 1915, had been for films to be distributed in America state by state. Then a group of individual producers clubbed together to take over a national distribution. That was the original Paramount.

The only way, Lasky and Zukor agreed – it was actually Zukor's idea – that they could avoid the prices the group were charging was to take that company over themselves. It would, in time, reduce their annual budget – the most expensive item of which was the weekly $10,000 they were paying Mary Pickford.

Before long, Lasky changed the name of Famous Players to Paramount Pictures. It was a good move. They had a name that could roll off any tongue that was in the business of rolling – and in the 1920s, they were already the talk of the town and that town was Hollywood, helped with the appointment of B.P. Schulberg as head of production. Zukor himself had followed *The Prisoner of Zenda* with another movie in a similar mould, the first movie version of *The Count of Monte Cristo* and then with *Tess of the D'Urbervilles.*

De Mille stayed with Paramount until he was ready to head his own production firm in 1925. Both Zukor and Lasky – whom De Mille called his 'brother', another indication of how different these men were from those who ran the other studios – were sorry to see him go. But they survived – for a time.

De Mille, despite his affection for the two men, knew their weaknesses, particularly Zukor's capriciousness. He was a fine man, said the director, but sometimes he 'would put his two fists together and, slowly separating them, say to me, "Cecil, I can break you . . . like that."' So, not a man to mess with.

Not in the way his employees behaved either. He established his own version of a charm school on the Paramount lot – with the principal task of teaching budding actors and actresses what he called 'decorum'. The way some stars behaved, that was no bad thing.

In 1922, the company stunned American womanhood with *The Sheik*, the archetypal Rudolph Valentino movie, and followed that the following year with *The Covered Wagon*, one of the most famous Westerns of the age.

When the talkies arrived, Lasky persuaded his partner (against his inclinations) to give Maurice Chevalier a contract. Zukor had been reluctant to sign the French music hall star because virtually every other Hollywood studio had been approached to give him work and all had turned him down. Sound films had turned America into as much an isolationist society where entertainment was concerned as it was in international politics. Everything had to be all-American. But Lasky saw it as a great opportunity.

Warner Bros. had Jolson. Chevalier was of the same generation with what the Frenchman once told me was 'the same kind of punch'. Lasky, caring more for the star than Paramount's financial situation, gave him $1,500 a week. Zukor heard Chevalier on his arrival in America – and realised that his partner had probably not made a dreadful mistake. It was a fact proved by films like *The Playboy of Paris* and *Love Me Tonight*.

They were films that showed the good things in life – which Lasky believed in for himself all the time. Certainly, he enjoyed them rather more than did the staid Mr Zukor. One day, Zukor knocked on the door of the hotel room where his vice-president was staying. It was about 6am and Lasky was just in the process of taking his suit off and getting into bed after a night on the tiles. He realised that the other man wasn't likely to be impressed. So he had to persuade his partner that he had the business' interests more in mind than anything else. 'Oh,' he said, 'I'm just getting ready for work.' 'That's what I like to see,' said Zukor, 'my friend and vice-president starting work nice and early.'

Seemingly, they had little in common – the little ex-Hungarian, who had once been a boxer, and took life very seriously (especially where their studio was concerned) and the taller, older American who wore little pince-nez spectacles and believed that money was there to be spent. He had a home on Le Brea Avenue, in the heart of the best part of Hollywood. Its swimming pool and tennis courts were among the first to be installed in a private home in the town. Zukor looked for no such luxuries. As he once said: 'We eat three meals a day. We have better than normal comforts. I have no great desire for yachts, for getting into the social areas where we don't particularly fit in.'

Jesse Lasky Jr, a film writer, told me that his father had once bought a Stutz Bearcat car – one of the most luxurious sports vehicles of the age – and bet the ace producer Mack Sennett $5,000 that he could drive from coast to coast in three weeks. He won the bet, but the car was wrecked by the stress of the journey. That would not have worried him for long. 'My father,' he said, 'usually owned three Rolls-Royces at the same time.'

Lasky made it clear right from the beginning that he was not going to allow the film business to interfere with his millionaire lifestyle. As Jesse Jr wrote in his memoir, *Whatever Happened to Hollywood?*: 'Dad fancied himself as an intrepid explorer and, happily, had the wealth to indulge his whim. He would search the map of America for some wild mountain range or little known wilderness, then plan his expedition like an invasion.'

He was the one who was full of outlandish ideas for films, too – some of which, without Zukor's stewardship and holding Lasky back, would have wrecked the company, too. It took a degree of chutzpah to believe that making two silent film starring Enrico Caruso would be a good idea. It wasn't a good idea. He had more luck with the diva Geraldine Farrar who made a silent version of *Carmen*. She turned out to be a good actress who could manage well without singing.

There was one film that Lasky decided needed sound effects – *Wings*, a love story, starring the young Gary Cooper, Richard Arlen and the number-one pin up of the age, the 'It' girl, Clara Bow, which was set around the lives of two World War I fighter pilots. It was a time when the idea of flight was beginning to be taken seriously by American audiences. Focusing on the role of airplanes in the Great War was a perfect way of cashing in on this enthusiasm. The Great War itself was a ready-made story.

Great War, nothing, This was going to be the Great Movie. Indeed, it should have been Lasky's Great Triumph. It was a big hit, but although it did extraordinarily good box-office business, the real hit in the picture never happened. The film was going to have the most spectacular battle scene ever filmed. The US Army were lending a whole armoured division. In San Antonio, Texas, carpenters had created a model village – which was going to be blown to oblivion at a signal from a tower over the set. The signal came and the tanks rolled and the battle commenced. The explosions, fired by the latest electronic techniques, happened on cue. The only problem was that the signal didn't come from the director, William Wellman, but from a bored young lady, reputed to be the daughter of San Antonio's Mayor, who climbed to the top of the tower and called out to friends down below who couldn't hear her – so she took off her silk scarf and waved it. Battle was joined, not just by the troops down below, but by Mr Wellman, who not only wasn't ready to film the exploit, he hadn't yet told the cameramen to get to work, and so not a single frame of the most elaborate – and expensive – battle scene ever to be filmed was recorded. The picture did well, even without the battle. Or at least the one Wellman had planned. Whether the mayor's daughter survived the onslaught isn't on record, but chances are she did. It was not something she was known to speak much about.

What Clara Bow and her two male stars thought about it all isn't on record either – especially since both Zukor and Lasky ordered not a word to be published about the disaster. With the stars they had, they really didn't need much else to talk about. Stars were what counted in their corner of Hollywood – not least, personalities like Gloria Swanson, whom Paramount were paying the unheard of sum of an annual $1 million – for films such as *Her Gilded Cage* and *Male and Female* – and were willing to pay even more, except she decided to go it alone and form her own company. It should be noted that she was never to be listed among the Hollywood moguls and would have done well to stay with Lasky and Zukor. Except of course, that she was well advised by her lover, Joseph Kennedy, father of the future US President, who had his own Hollywood company, a small outfit called RKO.

Marlene Dietrich also had a great deal to thank Paramount for. She had made *The Blue Angel* in Germany, in two versions – one in German, the other in English – directed by Paramount's Josef von Sternberg on loan to the Berlin company, UFA.

Sternberg (allegedly Mr Joe Stern, who had been born in Brooklyn) wired Lasky that she was the sensation of the age and that he ought to bring her over to Hollywood and sign her. Jesse did just that – without even seeing a still photograph of the star.

When she did come to California, Lasky threw a typical Hollywood party for her. She turned up – shock, shock – wearing trousers. Even more startling, she came with two men on her arms – one was her husband, Rudolph Sieber, the other her Svengali, Josef von Sternberg, supposedly her lover.

If that was shocking in itself, it was nothing compared with the impact of her first Paramount movie, *Morocco*, in which she not only wore trousers, but a man's suit, smoked through her trademark cigarette holder – and kissed another woman on the lips. Her reputation as an alleged lesbian was established, true or not.

Dietrich was to make nine Paramount films between 1930 and 1936, including some of her most famous, like *Shanghai Express, Blonde Venus* and *The Devil is a Woman.* Soon afterwards, she moved to Universal, run by Carl Laemmle, and made the definitive Dietrich movie, *Destry Rides Again* there. But it was Paramount that introduced her to America and so created one of the town's legendary stars. The run was broken when David O. Selznick chose her for his archetype Hollywood vehicle, *The Garden of Allah.*

The fact that it was Jesse Lasky who was so hands-on didn't worry Adolph Zukor one little bit – and so long as his deputy brought in the dollars with sufficient noughts on the sales figures, he was happy. Particularly when there were films like Dietrich's or the 1931 hit *Dr Jekyll and Mr Hyde,* starring Fredric March and directed by the man who liked both his bosses so much, Rouben Mamoulian.

Paramount operated from both Hollywood and New York, just like the other studios. Lasky was in charge on the West Coast, Zukor was in the East. He didn't interfere much with the way his films were made, he was interested mainly in contracts and what in a future generation would be known as 'the bottom line'.

Unlike the other studio bosses, however, Zukor decided that New York was a good place to actually *make* movies, not just a centre from which to sell them.

He personally took charge of building what was at the time hailed as the most up-to-date studio in America – at Astoria in Queens. It contained the biggest sound stage in the industry – which is still in use, nearly 90 years since he first put up the complex. His idea was that Paramount would benefit from the ease with which both actors and technicians could get to work without having to travel far from their New York area homes.

'In 1920, Zukor and Lasky opened it,' Hal Rosenbluth, head of what is now the Kaufman Astoria Studios, told me, 'in order to capture the biggest talent in the world, who were working on Broadway. There were crews here in this city and we were able to train more. In the Second World War, technicians like cinematographers were trained here in the army and then went on to work in Hollywood.'

Undoubtedly, Zukor's great talent, from running his fur company onwards, was as a shrewd businessman. Astoria was an example of how the businessman put his skills into operation. Hal Rosenbluth added: 'He built this facility for $2.5 million, an extraordinary amount of money for 1920 – but still cheaper than in other places. It became *the* place to work in those days. When you worked here, you were playing Yankee Stadium. It was such a clever move on Zukor's part.' He put the eminent producer Walter Wanger in charge of the enterprise, but it was all Zukor's idea and he made the final decisions.

It was where, of course, the film industry had been born and worked out better than any other previous attempt at recreating Hollywood on the East Coast.

Before Zukor built Astoria, there had been a studio in New Jersey, but, said Rosenbluth, 'that was before the George Washington Bridge was built and Zukor didn't want to go there. So he built at Queens.'

It was an example of what was already established as a Zukor quality – his prescience. As Rosenbluth put it: 'He saw the talkies coming' – and this was going to be a great place to film them at a time when everyone in the business thought that the best actors were on Broadway. 'He was a huge influence – until the inmates took over the asylum.'

There were those, however, who thought that Adolph Zukor belonged in the asylum himself. He had an office at the Astoria studios, but nobody ever saw him there – because he had his own private staircase leading to it.

Nevertheless, if he were a ghostly presence at Astoria, he was obvious elsewhere in what had become the Paramount empire. Until legislation split them up, like the other major studios, they owned a stack of theatres to show their films. The 91 year-old A.C. Lyles used to go to his local Paramount cinema and was overwhelmed by the experience. 'Once a week, I wrote to Mr Zukor asking for a job. Eventually, he gave me one, working in the theatre – and then brought me to Hollywood as an office boy.' More than 70 years later, he was still working for his old company, producing TV films. 'He was an extremely loyal man,' Lyles told me, recalling his old boss.

And so was Jesse L. Lasky, said by *Variety* in 1927, to be worth $20 million, which made him, by their reckoning, the eighth most-wealthy man in show business. Zukor probably had as much money, but no one, apart from his bank manager, knew exactly how much it was that he had. And he didn't spend it the way that Lasky did. The Paramount vice-president had bought his own canyon in the Malibu Hills, on which he was going to create the finest hacienda in America. He had also built his own private pier leading on to the Pacific.

The Great Depression affected Paramount and its two main personalities more than it did the people running the other studios. Lasky was himself broke. He owned $1.5 million of company stock. He was forced to sell it for $35,000.

The company plainly had got into equally serious financial difficulties and both Zukor and Lasky were victims of a boardroom coup – Lasky was fired and became an independent producer, while for a time Zukor was exiled to a small Paramount office in South America. B.P. Schulberg lost his job too – one suggestion was that Zukor was incensed at his production chief having an affair with the actress Sylvia Sidney – and eventually inserted an advertisement in *Daily Variety*, asking for work.

Later, Zukor was 'kicked upstairs' to become president of the company – but was more active than many of his colleagues and employees anticipated.

Barney Balaban, another important figure in the Hollywood hierarchy, took over as president in 1936 and Zukor was made chairman of the board – in the hope that he would leave the business of running Paramount to others. It didn't happen. In fact, he was always given credit for his role in the Paramount story. Which was why, as late as 1949, he was given a special Oscar for his contributions to the film industry.

Balaban was Zukor's choice to take the job. He ran the Balaban and Katz vaudeville circuit and before that he worked in a cold-storage plant – in the days before refrigeration. He was the oldest of five sons and a sister. It was his mother who had first advised him to go into the movie business. 'She had gone to a movie and left after five minutes,' Jerome Pickman told me: 'She then told Barney that movies were a good business to get into.' "Ma," he said, "how can you say that? You were only in there for five minutes." She answered: "Any business in which people pay before they go in and then don't get their money back has to be a good business."' That was the sort of thinking that made the men who made Hollywood.

Zukor used to tell the Mrs Balaban story himself – and that's why he made sure that Barney took over his main job. The 'old man', however, stayed with his fingers (all of them) on the Paramount pulse. He still went in regularly to the New York Paramount offices. Jerome Pickman saw him often. 'I loved the old man,' said the retired executive, 'he was the man who was still known to the top brass in the company as "the boss", but was "Mr Zukor" to everybody else.'

His 100th birthday didn't make any difference to what he considered to be his work. In extreme old age, Zukor would still attend board meetings. 'The only trouble,' Pickman told me, 'was that he would always, without fail, fall asleep. He'd wake up and say, "What's going on here?" So everything we had discussed had to be reprised for him.'

In his private office, he was king. As Pickman told me: 'He'd sit on a high chair with his feet dangling. He took out a big Cuban cigar and started sermonising.'

That happened the day that he saw Pickman in the lobby of the Paramount building, looking forlorn. 'What's the matter?' he asked. Pickman told him that business wasn't as good as he had hoped it would be.

'I remember him telling me in what became one of those sermonising sessions, "Jerry, this is show business and show business is like a wheel and like a wheel it goes round and round. You've got to hang on. It'll come round again." I always use that as my philosophy.'

Meanwhile, Jesse Lasky continued to make films for studios that had previously been competitors, not just Warner Bros. but Fox and RKO, too. Some of those films became important products of their age. So did Warners' *Rhapsody in Blue* and *The Miracle of the Bells,* the movie in which Frank Sinatra donned a dog collar and tried – not altogether successfully – to convince audiences that he was a priest. Lasky released that under his own name, the real mark of a successful independent. But it was no indicator of what was to come.

He tried again to set up his own major company with his old partner's previous best-known asset, Mary Pickford, as a partner. But the Pickford-Lasky Corporation was a dismal failure and both partners lost money.

At one time, he contemplated suicide – by swimming from his California home beach, as his son Jesse Lasky Jr put it, 'in the direction of Japan.'

He was always hoping to produce new movies. After a lot of negotiations, he finally persuaded Louis B. Mayer to let him make *The Great Caruso* for MGM. Perhaps he wanted to exorcise the ghost of the real Caruso in those two silent films. Mayer had said no, but finally relented, although Lasky's position was as a producer 'in association' with Joseph Pasternak. He did it for $500 a week, with no other rights. That was a humiliation, especially since the Mario Lanza film was a huge success.

In 1952, Lasky's frequently profligate past caught up with him and he was sued by the Internal Revenue service for unpaid taxes. It was a tough moment for the veteran who enjoyed being the dapper man about Hollywood. He eventually persuaded his old company, Paramount, to let him make a film for them. But it wasn't to be. He died in 1958 – in an ambulance, after collapsing with a heart attack at the Beverly Hilton Hotel. He had been giving a lecture there – about the film business.

The trouble with Jesse was that, while his erstwhile partner was still in the business, still on the notepaper as the chairman of Paramount and still going to meetings – before the days when he fell asleep during the deliberations – little was now a reality for him. The man who for years had had more fun from his business than any of the other moguls, had done his share of suffering. The past, for him, had become a dream. A unique kind of Hollywood dream. Zukor lived for another 18 years, probably still dreaming himself, at those board meetings.

7

THE GIANTS

They are all long gone now, but as Irving Berlin almost wrote, their melody lingers on – although there are those who might say it was more a case of the 'malady' lingering on, the disease they created of dominant power, nepotism and total control. When they went, the old original Hollywood went with them. And so did the entertainment habits of generations.

The old studio system died along with the contracts they manipulated so successfully – for themselves. And when it did, the cinema-going public realised what it had lost – not just the moguls themselves, but also the overworked stars who cared about the movies they made. And most importantly, cared about the people who saw them.

They respected their audiences. Stars were glamorous in those days. Women wore fine clothes even when they weren't attending Oscar ceremonies. Men wore jackets with matching trousers and never went without a shave. That was how the people who paid to see their movies wanted their idols to be. Cinema customers had no reason to think those stars were any different in real life from the figures they saw up there, magnified a hundred or more times, on the big screen.

It was the moguls who put them there – and when they left, either willingly or by force, naturally or at the whim of a board of directors who didn't know a sprocket from a close-up, we were all the poorer.

Hollywood has regained its position in our lives, partly through television – the hated television of the era when the moguls were in power – and from films which are once again filling theatres all over the world;

cinemas which the studio bosses could never have envisaged, big buildings with big screens, sometimes six of them in the same theatre.

But the business itself couldn't be more different. Sam Goldwyn, the Warners, Louis B. Mayer, Harry Cohn and Zukor and Lasky as well as Carl Laemmle of Universal and Fox, founder of the eponymous studio, unlike the global bosses of today who are now in charge of the old logos, understood as well as loved films. Shortly before his death, Billy Wilder told me: 'Things were very different in those days. They had guts. They threw you dirty curves. But you were not dealing with an unknown enemy. Studio heads could say "no", but they could also say "yes" and "yes" meant "yes". Today "yes" means "maybe".'

Julius Epstein echoed that sentiment when he called them 'robber barons,' but, he admitted, 'You always knew where you were with them. You got decisions, sometimes instant decisions – and when you make films, that's what you need. Decisions.'

The best comment of all about Once Upon a Time on the West Coast came from Melville Shavelson: 'There used to be giants in this town. Now all we have are the Dodgers.'

INDEX